Open Skies

# OPEN SKIES

## Transparency, Confidence-Building, and the End of the Cold War

Peter Jones

Stanford Security Studies

An Imprint of Stanford University Press
Stanford, California

Stanford University Press
Stanford, California



Printed and bound by CPI Group (UK) Ltd, Croydon, CR0 4YY

Library of Congress Cataloging-in-Publication Data

Jones, Peter L. (Peter Leslie), author
Open skies : transparency, confidence-building, and the end of the Cold War / Peter Jones.
pages cm. — (Stanford security studies)
Includes bibliographical references and index.
ISBN 978-0-8047-9098-7 (cloth : alk. paper)
1. Treaty on Open Skies (1992)—History. 2. Arms control—Verification. 3. Airspace (International law). 4. Confidence and security building measures (International relations). I. Title.

KZ5885.2.J66 2014
341.7'33—dc23 2014010065

ISBN 978-0-8047-9231-8 (electronic)

Typeset at Stanford University Press in 10/14 Minion

To the Honorable George P. Shultz

Statesman, Scholar, Mentor

## CONTENTS


| | | |
|---|---|---|
| | Preface | ix |
| | Foreword by Sidney D. Drell | xv |
| | Introduction | 1 |
| 1 | From the First Open Skies Initiative to the Stockholm Conference | 9 |
| 2 | Open Skies Reborn | 18 |
| 3 | The Issues Explored | 36 |
| 4 | The Ottawa and Budapest Conferences | 59 |
| 5 | Interim Negotiations | 92 |
| 6 | The First Vienna Round | 112 |
| 7 | End-Game | 128 |
| 8 | Into Force and Into the Future | 148 |
| | Conclusion | 165 |
| | Notes | 175 |
| | Bibliography | 216 |
| | Index | 231 |

# PREFACE

Since 2011, I have had the privilege of being an Annenberg Distinguished Visiting Fellow at the Hoover Institution at Stanford University. Although I was brought on to do work on conflict resolution and Track Two diplomacy, I have been able to take advantage of my periods in residence in this wonderful environment to take part in many discussions and workshops on a wide variety of subjects.

In March of 2012, a small workshop was held at Hoover about the Open Skies Treaty. The purpose was to review the Open Skies regime, and, more important, to explore how it might be expanded to keep pace with international developments in the two decades since it was signed. A particular catalyst of the discussion was a paper written by Sidney Drell and Chris Stubbs, which argued that Open Skies should be updated, to allow it to play a greater role in the verification of deep cuts, and the eventual elimination of nuclear weapons and other Weapons of Mass Destruction (WMD).[1]

The workshop was my first reacquaintance with Open Skies in over a decade. I gave a presentation on the negotiation of the treaty, and another on the application of Open Skies in different regional contexts. Mostly I listened to those who were working on the implementation of the treaty. I learned a great deal from the discussions, but also noted that few of these people understood the issues that had confronted the negotiators of the treaty. This took the form of frustrations expressed over what were seen as needless limitations and complications that the original drafters of the treaty had mysteriously placed on its own evolution.

I found myself drawn back to Open Skies in the wake of this workshop. The subject had been a focus of my life, both professionally and academically, from 1989 to 1995. In 1989 I was hired to work in an organization called the Verification Research Unit within the Arms Control and Disarmament Division at Canada's Department of External Affairs, as it then was called. I walked in at just the moment Open Skies arose on the agenda and was assigned to work on it. This completely unplanned development was to become a significant focus of the first period of my service with External Affairs, from the earliest work to develop the idea in early 1989 until the signing of the treaty in March of 1992. I attended all three Open Skies conferences as a member of the Canadian delegation, and was responsible for coordinating much of the day-to-day work within the Canadian bureaucracy to develop policy toward the idea. I also wrote a number of scholarly papers and articles on the subject in the early 1990s. Following that I had little involvement with Open Skies until the workshop at Hoover in March of 2012.

Although my remit at Hoover was not Open Skies, I wondered in the wake of the workshop if there might be the makings of a book that would explain how the treaty came to be. As this work has gone on, I have come to the view that the basic purpose of this book is multifaceted. First, I want to present the history of the development of the treaty—the first really comprehensive, book-length treatment of it—and explain why the treaty is structured as it is. My hope is that those who follow the world of arms control and confidence-building will find this book a useful addition to their field. Second, I want to explore how Open Skies affected, and was affected by, the extraordinary times of its negotiation, during which the Cold War ended and the Soviet Union collapsed. As readers will discover, it was a difficult negotiation that did not hit its stride until some of the key delegations, which had been mired in Cold War thinking, transformed their view of what Open Skies should be, to catch up to the developments between 1989 and 1992. But it should be made clear that this is not a book about the end of the Cold War as such; it is about the Open Skies negotiations and their times. I leave it to historians of those years to draw the connections between the Open Skies talks and the debates that take place over the wider themes of the era. I hope this book will provide them some useful insights into one aspect of that crucial period. Third, I hope that a detailed history of this negotiation will contribute to the understanding of how actual negotiations work in practice as seen from the inside. Finally, I want to share my thoughts and insights into the role that cooperative aerial monitoring can play in helping to transform other difficult relationships around the world. I thus conclude the book with some thoughts concerning how the Open Skies experience may inform other attempts to use cooperative aerial monitoring to build trust.

Upon commencing this project I had a naive view that it would take a few months. It took more than a year. My earlier work, on which much of this book is based, had to be extensively rewritten to take into account much scholarship that has been written since 1995, and also the release of many documents since then. More broadly, the tumultuous years during which Open Skies was negotiated are now better understood and documented. Finally, in order to make the story as complete as possible, I had to write about the development of the regime since the treaty was signed in 1992, and also develop some thoughts into where it may be going in future.

Writing a book is a solitary experience in many ways, but also a collaborative one. In my case, I was extremely fortunate in that many of my former colleagues in the negotiation agreed to read this book in draft and share their recollections and insights with me. Ralph Lysyshyn and John Noble, my bosses during the Open Skies negotiation, and heads of the Canadian delegation to the different Open Skies conferences, were very helpful. Commander (then Lieutenant Commander) F. W. (Ted) Parkinson was on the staff of the Arms Control Section in Canada's Defence Department during the Vienna conferences and attended most of these sessions. He too read the book in draft, contributed his insights, and has allowed me to cite him.

I have also benefited from the insights of international colleagues. Ambassador (ret.) John Hawes led the U.S. delegation to the Open Skies conferences in Ottawa, Budapest, and Vienna and was a key figure in the negotiations. Alex Garroch (RAF, ret.) was a sensor expert on the UK delegation at the Budapest and Vienna conferences and was also much involved in the work that was done to develop the compromises over the technical issues. Alex was also deeply involved in the early days of the implementation of the treaty, before leaving the RAF. Marton Krasznai was the deputy head of the Hungarian delegation to the Ottawa and Budapest rounds and the head of delegation to the Vienna round of the Open Skies negotiations. His reminiscences and insights have been invaluable, particularly in providing insights into what was happening within the Warsaw Pact. All three of these individuals have generously read the book and made many comments and suggestions. Finally, a number of diplomats who took part in the negotiation agreed to read the book and provide insights but requested anonymity, as they are still active in diplomacy around European security issues.

Many others have read the book and shared their insights. Ambassador (ret.) Jim Goodby was not involved in the Open Skies talks, but those must be about the only major arms control or confidence-building negotiations of the Cold War period that he missed. Jim read the book from the point of view of a scholar and practitioner of East-West arms control generally, and offered many helpful insights as to how the events of the Open Skies negotiation relate to the broader history of such negotiations. Diana Marvin is a senior official in the U.S. State Department who has been responsible for U.S. Open Skies implementation and policy for many years. She warmly encouraged this book and provided a wealth of insights into where Open Skies has gone since it was signed—and also proved herself to be a formidable proofreader! Professor Hartwig Spitzer of the University of Hamburg is one of the world's foremost experts on the implementation of Open Skies, having written on it extensively and having served as a sensor expert on the German delegation to many meetings relating to the implementation of the treaty. He too provided many thoughts and insights upon reading the draft of the book.

Others who have played a significant role in the work that went into this book include Professor Philip Sabin of the War Studies Department at King's College, London, who was a source of enormous help and encouragement in the years of writing. Professor Lawrence Freedman (now Sir Lawrence) and Dr. Patricia Lewis were also most helpful during this period.

Ronald Cleminson was head of the Verification Research Unit when I first joined External and was very generous to a young colleague with his wisdom and vast experience of verification and monitoring matters.

Former secretary of state George P. Shultz was instrumental in my coming to the Hoover Institution and has been extremely supportive of my work ever since. It was at his urging that the Open Skies workshop was held at Hoover in 2012, as part of the work he has done with his colleagues Henry Kissinger, William Perry, and Sam Nunn to explore how the world could be rid of the horror of nuclear weapons. More generally, I have been extremely fortunate to receive Secretary Shultz's wisdom and experience of diplomacy and statecraft, insights that have informed the way I approached this book.

I am particularly grateful to Sid Drell for agreeing to write the Foreword to this book. A giant in the arms control world for many decades, Sid has devoted his considerable abilities in the last few years to the cause of a nuclear weapons–free world. In that context, he has led work to explore the possible application of the Open Skies regime to the verification of the kinds of agreements that will be required to achieve such a world. His work points the way to exciting new directions for Open Skies in particular and cooperative aerial monitoring in general.

All of these people have helped in many ways to make the book what it is. But it goes without saying that I am solely responsible for any failings it may contain.

At Stanford Press, I wish to thank Geoffrey Burn, James Holt, John Feneron, Martin Hanft, Mary Mortensen, Rob Ehle, Christie Cochrell, and Mike Sagara for their unfailing assistance and constant encouragement.

Finally, and most personally, I want to thank my wife, Karin. Our two children, Emma and William, are, for me, by far the most important results of my long involvement with Open Skies.

# FOREWORD BY SIDNEY D. DRELL

The Open Skies Treaty is one of the better-kept secrets of the world of international arms control and confidence-building. Not many are aware of the fact that the United States can fly an unarmed military reconnaissance airplane anywhere over Russia and thirty-two other treaty signatory nations with only twenty-four hours' notice of the intended flight plan. Similarly, the Russian Federation has a reciprocal right to conduct aerial photography flights over the United States and other treaty members. More than a thousand of these reconnaissance flights have been flown over Europe, Russia, Canada, and the United States since the Open Skies Treaty was negotiated. All missions are jointly manned by personnel of both nations—the observed and the observer—and the information gained by the agreed upon and equal sensors is shared with any treaty signatory nation who asks for it. The treaty stipulates the maximum ground resolution of the images obtained by the cameras. At visible wavelengths this is roughly comparable to that obtained by commercial satellites. It also allows for thermal infrared sensors for nighttime viewing, and coherent synthetic aperture radar viewing for all-weather activity monitoring and detecting militarily significant changes in deployments of conventional forces.

President Eisenhower first proposed cooperative aerial monitoring overflights to the Soviet Union in 1955 during the height of the Cold War as a means of building confidence and reducing the dangers of surprise or unintended conflict. Immediately and forcefully rejected by the Soviet Union when first proposed, Open Skies lay dormant until the waning days of the Cold War and the negotiation of the Conventional Forces in Europe (CFE) Treaty limiting the deployments of conventional military forces in Europe.

At that point, in 1989, the considerable value of cooperative aerial monitoring as a confidence-building measure that would test the Soviet Union's commitment to openness and transparency was appreciated by President George H. W. Bush. He was strongly supported and encouraged by Canadian prime minister Brian Mulroney, who also urged expansion of the idea beyond the United States and the Soviet Union to include all the nations in the NATO and Warsaw Pact communities. It was also appreciated by the then Soviet general secretary Mikhail Gorbachev. This led to an intense negotiation period starting in 1989 and culminating in a treaty signed in 1992 that finally entered into force in 2002, following its ratification by the Duma of the Russian Federation.

It is natural to ask why there would be great interest in Open Skies. It has been operating quietly for the past eleven years, pretty much in the shadow of more sophisticated national technical means of monitoring activities potentially threatening to our national security. Unlike 1955, when President Eisenhower first proposed it, there now exist globe-circling reconnaissance satellites of very high sophistication and broad capabilities providing much information of what countries are doing with their military forces, and in particular with their strategic nuclear weapons. And so one asks, What does Open Skies contribute? The basic answer is that aircraft can cover targets in ways that satellites cannot, taking into account local weather patterns, and they are available to all nations, not just the few that can presently support satellite programs. Perhaps most important, Open Skies flights are *cooperative*; unlike satellites, they require the consent and active cooperation of the state being overflown. There is thus an important political benefit in terms of encouraging a much greater degree of openness and transparency in relations between states, which contributes to confidence. That said, the technical capabilities of the sensors presently included on Open Skies aircraft are quite limited. Unless the sensors evolve to include more advanced technologies and higher resolution, there is a danger that Open Skies will become less and less relevant. But with vision and leadership, the Open Skies Treaty could evolve to provide substantial long-term benefits in many fields. These include the adaptation of the present regime to help meet the challenge of the verification of future agreements to greatly limit the number of nuclear weapons in the world and other WMD, key U.S. foreign policy objectives. Open Skies provides for short-notice *unrestricted* territorial access for aircraft, which—if agreement could be reached to equip them with more modern technology for obtaining higher-resolution images, and also with atmospheric collection options that sample and collect particulates (data that simply cannot be detected from satellites)—could play a huge role in future efforts to verify steep reductions in WMD.

Expanding the number of signatory nations beyond the current thirty-four in the Organization for Security and Co-operation in Europe, or creating similar regimes in other regions, will lay an important foundation for the technical verification challenge ahead. Cooperative Aerial Monitoring (CAM) has an ongoing role in the future, for both confidence-building and data collection. Particularly in conjunction with other treaty verification elements, CAM can provide information that is difficult to obtain any other way. Cooperative Aerial Monitoring can be expanded to include verification of compliance with a number of issues currently under discussion, such as a cut-off on the production of nuclear fuel for military systems and the accounting for all nuclear weapons–grade material in the world, which is now part of an ongoing agenda involving many countries and will be strengthened by having an ability to collect atmospheric samples. An expanded regime of cooperative aerial monitoring can also help to verify agreements banning chemical and biological weapons. Furthermore, at the political level, the ability for cooperative sharing of information, which is now entering into a more active phase, will benefit greatly by building on an expanded Open Skies as an existing model. It is a gateway to a world with greater reliance on cooperative means to raise confidence in controlling possible arms races, avoid conflict, and, one day perhaps, get rid of all nuclear weapons. There are also possible uses for cooperative aerial monitoring beyond those associated with arms control and military confidence-building. The health of our environment is a matter of increasing concern and urgency. Future agreements on environmental matters may require some form of cooperative monitoring, and the lessons of Open Skies, and perhaps even the regime itself, will be very relevant here.

It is fortunate that Dr. Peter Jones, an astute and highly experienced Canadian political scientist and former arms control negotiator, has written a book that lays out for us the unique complications of negotiating a multilateral cooperative treaty to meet and prepare for new challenges. This is an enduring and successful example of transparency and cooperative confidence-building and provides an important framework for broader verification measures, which are likely to become more comprehensive as we move to a future with fewer and fewer arms. Peter Jones was deeply involved in the negotiations of the Open Skies Treaty from the very beginning, for six years from 1989 to 1995, and has subsequently been involved in exploratory discussions to develop the idea of cooperative aerial monitoring and other confidence-building measures in other troubled regions of the world. This book is a powerful font of valuable information on how the Open Skies negotiations ultimately succeeded. For anyone interested in how Open Skies was negotiated, but also more broadly, in how a complex international negotiation actually works, this is an outstanding account and analysis of how this treaty was brought to realization. I found this book a very informative read; important for guidance as one looks ahead to a world with more cooperative monitoring, and a valuable record of what it takes to succeed in negotiations of this type that, it can be hoped, will be pursued in the future.

Sidney D. Drell
Stanford University

Open Skies

# Introduction

Why a book about the negotiation of the Open Skies Treaty? The treaty is functioning well. It has been the cause of no great dramas—at least none that have garnered any public attention. Moreover, many believe that the advent of widely available commercial satellite imagery has rendered Open Skies obsolete. These last perceptions are not correct. Open Skies has shown itself to be far more than a Cold War agreement, and, with leadership and vision, it is capable of considerable further evolution. Open Skies, or cooperative aerial monitoring more generally, has the potential to be at the forefront of attempts to build confidence in many regions of the world and to verify other agreements, both disarmament and environmental, into the future. Moreover, the manner in which it was negotiated, and the obstacles, both technical and political that had to be overcome, hold considerable lessons for those who would embark upon the negotiation of any ambitious Confidence-building Measure (CBM) in many different contexts in today's world. There is much to be learned from the Open Skies experience on many different levels.

Beyond that, the advent of commercially available satellite imagery, though it has changed the world considerably, does not invalidate Open Skies. Cooperative aerial monitoring has unique advantages of both a political and a technical nature. Aircraft can linger over an area, or visit it repeatedly over a short period of time and from different angles and altitudes. Aircraft can adjust their flight paths and altitudes to compensate for changes in the weather. The extraordinary expense of building, launching, and maintaining satellites is such that images and other data returned by aircraft compare very favorably in cost terms. Aircraft can be outfitted with sensors that are not available to satellites, such as sensitive air sampling devices (not yet permitted on Open Skies aircraft but which could be added, if agreed). Finally, for those countries that do not have so-called National Technical Means (NTM), or spy satellites, aircraft are the only way they have of independently acquiring overhead imagery from platforms they control.[1]

These are significant benefits to aerial observations. For the United States, and other countries that maintain NTM, Open Skies still has benefits. In addition to those listed above (meaning that, even for countries with NTM, there are still benefits from overflights), there are three additional benefits to Open Skies that matter considerably. First, even though the U.S. has other means of acquiring overhead imagery (and though Open Skies flights still have unique benefits), it is often in America's interest that countries in vulnerable areas should also have the means to acquire data that can put their minds at ease in a tense situation. For many years, as overhead imagery became more widely available, many were concerned that the "democratization" of this unique data would somehow equate to a loss for the United States. This does not have to be the case.

Second, in cases in which the U.S. wishes it to be known that something is happening, but does not wish to expose the capabilities of its reconnaissance satellites, imagery from an overflight can be released. Finally, Open Skies, and cooperative aerial monitoring generally, is different from NTM in that the acquisition of the imagery is *cooperative*. A country cannot prevent a satellite from flying overhead. But that same country must not only acquiesce to an overflight; it also must actively cooperate to make that flight possible. This is the essential quality of Open Skies that was so attractive to President Eisenhower when he first proposed it in 1955. The aspect of mutual reassurance—the act of saying, "We are not preparing to attack you, and you may come and see for yourself"—was key to the deeper objective of the regime in the wider sense of building confidence between adversaries.

This book recounts and analyzes the history of Open Skies from the first time it was proposed by Eisenhower in 1955, through its relaunch by President George H. W. Bush in 1989, through the subsequent negotiation of the treaty, and up to the present day. It concludes with some thoughts as to how the Open Skies idea may be further developed in other contexts and for other purposes. As with both the 1955 and the 1989 iterations, this will require high-level political vision—but the potential rewards are great.

The bulk of the book focuses on the negotiation of the treaty as the Cold War was coming to an end. It is a fascinating story, and a case study in how the politicians were ahead of their bureaucrats and their diplomats on both sides of the Iron Curtain. For it was the political leaders who saw the value of Open Skies and who pushed their bureaucratic structures, still mired in the negotiating traditions of the Cold War, to go beyond their comfort levels and come up with an agreement that broke out of the traps they had lived with for half a century.

Chapter 1 briefly recounts the considerations that led President Eisenhower to first propose Open Skies, and those that led the Soviets to reject it. As those who would work on the later iteration of Open Skies in 1989 would discover, the factors that led Eisenhower to propose the idea were quite similar in many respects to those that motivated Bush many years later; it was a simple, easily understood idea that would test whether a new Soviet regime (one apparently committed to better relations) was really prepared to make fundamental changes in long-held positions. As such, it was a win-win proposition for the United States: if the Soviets accepted it, the U.S. would gain access to new sources of information; if they said no, the United States would score a valuable propaganda victory. Of course, in the days before high-altitude reconnaissance flights and reconnaissance satellites there were some very practical benefits for the U.S. Over the years, the question of aerial monitoring arose again in different contexts but was always turned down by the Soviets. In the 1980s the Soviets displayed slightly less resistance to aerial monitoring of specific locations as part of a wider package of other Confidence-building Measures under negotiation in Europe. But nothing they agreed to in that context could reasonably have led anyone to imagine that a full-blown Open Skies regime might one day be possible.

Chapter 2 recounts the process whereby Open Skies came to be launched again in 1989. As before, it was a "top-down" initiative, launched by a small group of officials and publicly endorsed by the president with little bureaucratic support. As before, one of the key objectives was to test a Soviet leader's apparent commitment to mutual coexistence and openness. But there was a key difference: the 1989 proposal was launched as a multilateral one to include all of the countries of the North Atlantic Treaty Organization (NATO) and the Warsaw Pact. Key to this new aspect had been the high-level intervention with President Bush of Canadian prime minister Brian Mulroney. Arguing that the benefits of Open Skies, both political and military, would best be realized on a multilateral basis, Mulroney exerted significant influence over the decision to relaunch Open Skies and to do it multilaterally. Canada would go on to play a significant role in getting the negotiation underway and keeping it alive during the tough times. In this Canada would be joined by a country on the other side, Hungary, that also saw the benefits of the idea.

Once again, however, Open Skies had been launched as a top-down, political initiative with little support in the bureaucracy in the United States; it had no champions at the working level. Instead, most of the key players who would have to come together to put some flesh on Bush's idea saw Open Skies as potentially interfering with other priorities and were either indifferent or hostile. Although they could not openly oppose a presidential initiative, many within the U.S. national security bureaucracy would have been happy to see Open Skies quietly die. The Soviet bureaucracy, meanwhile, was deeply suspicious and would also have been quite content to see the idea go away. It was against these pressures that the activities of Canada and Hungary in keeping the idea alive and forcing the pace would play the greatest role over time.

Even though much of the U.S. bureaucracy was initially lukewarm toward Open Skies, the president had proposed the idea and it had to be developed. Chapter 3 thus explores the issues that arose when the NATO countries began to develop a concrete position. Lacking firm guidance from the political level on the basic objectives of the exercise, this process soon degenerated into a squabble over the details. Many in the United States sought to develop a regime that would maximize the intelligence-collection aspects of the treaty. They sought also to develop the regime firmly within the East-West paradigm that had dominated security negotiations for several decades. It was during this period that the first signs of push-back arose. The Canadians began to wonder if the emerging concept of the regime was not too adversarial. The French began to argue that the regime should not be structured in a way that accentuated the East-West dynamic, which they believed to be faltering, but that it should permit easy accession by the neutral countries of Europe. Most of these discussions went on within NATO. The few opportunities for interaction with the Soviets during this period revealed a cautious but noncommittal approach. There was no opportunity for any kind of "prenegotiation" of the sort that often precedes a major international negotiation.

When the two sides came together for the first conference, they found that their basic positions—indeed, their basic conceptions of the treaty itself—were very far apart. Chapter 4 covers the first two rounds of the talks in Ottawa and Budapest, where the U.S. and Soviet delegations dug in and took the attitude that it was up to the other side to make compromises. This may have reflected a view on the part of powerful elements of their delegations that it was the best way to ensure that the treaty would not be realized.

What was also discovered during the Ottawa and Budapest rounds, however, was the degree to which the solidarity of the Warsaw Pact had disintegrated. The non-Soviet members of the Warsaw Pact soon joined their Hungarian colleagues and openly sided with the Western delegations in calling for a much more intrusive and open regime than the Soviets were prepared to accept. What the Eastern Europeans did insist on, as part of a formula that came to be known within the negotiation as the "Grand Compromise," was that the regime be equal—that whatever capabilities the NATO allies would enjoy in terms of sensors and data-processing should be equally available to all participants. This was to be a foundation of the eventual treaty, and it had the effect of moderating the more extreme aspects of the U.S. insistence that each country be able to use whatever sensors it wanted, with very few restrictions. While the Eastern Europeans were challenging the position of "their" superpower, some of the NATO countries began to do the same with the United States. Although Canada was the only NATO country to break ranks formally on the issue during this phase of the negotiations, others privately signaled growing frustration. For the European allies, Open Skies was not the priority at this time; the treaty to limit conventional forces in Europe (the so-called CFE Treaty) was. But the moment would come for Open Skies as the CFE Treaty encountered its own difficulties later on.

It was also during the Ottawa and Budapest rounds that the issue of whether and how to incorporate the neutral countries of Europe began to be faced. There was a growing recognition that the alliance-to-alliance structure of the negotiation was becoming increasingly anachronistic, but the negotiation was not ready to tackle the issue directly. The search began, however, for a way to permit an ever-increasing level of participation for the neutral countries in the discussions. This raised two issues. First, France became increasingly convinced that the Open Skies regime should be developed within the context of the Conference on Security and Cooperation in Europe (the CSCE—later to become the Organization for Security and Cooperation in Europe – the OSCE). The United States resisted this approach, as it did not want to have a CSCE measure applied to the territory of the U.S. Second, the dispute between Greece and Turkey over whether and how Cyprus would be allowed to join the regime, though it had nothing to do with Open Skies as such, would go on to become one of the most long-standing and frustrating issues dealt with by the negotiation.

With the failure of the Budapest round an interim period began, covered in Chapter 5. The key development of this phase was that the politicians took control of the negotiation again and established, for the first time, the parameters of the regime they sought—a moderately intrusive, cooperative CBM. In meetings between presidents Bush and Gorbachev, and then between Secretary of State Baker and Foreign Minister Schevardnadze, it became clear that these leaders saw Open Skies in different terms than had their officials to that point. The leaders were able to work out a formula for compromise, based on the "Grand Compromise" advocated by the smaller countries in Ottawa and Budapest, and instructed their officials to get on with it. For the first time, Open Skies had a clear set of goals, endorsed at the highest levels, that could be translated into practical regime requirements. This was, without doubt, the turning point.

Wider events during this period also moved in favor of Open Skies. The CFE talks hit a serious snag as the Soviets moved a large amount of conventional equipment out of the CFE zone of application, and thus beyond the monitoring and verification provisions of the CFE Treaty. Suddenly, for the European allies, who had always relegated Open Skies to second place in importance behind the CFE talks, Open Skies became extremely important as their only means to monitor Russian conventional military equipment beyond the Ural Mountains. Moreover, the negotiations to create an aerial verification component of the CFE Treaty had failed, so there was no wide-area aerial aspect to the CFE verification system even within the zone of application of the treaty. It was the European allies, and particularly the Germans, who picked up Open Skies at this point and began pushing hard for a treaty. Politically, this period featured the coup attempt in the Soviet Union that would ultimately lead to breakup of that country. The coup also discredited many of those in Moscow that had opposed Open Skies.

The Open Skies talks thus resumed in Vienna in the autumn of 1991. There were two rounds of talks: the autumn of 1991 and the winter and spring of 1992. These rounds are the subject of Chapters 6 and 7. It was during this period that certain countries emerged to take control of the discussion and push it along. Although the United States and the Soviet Union (and later Russia) were key to the eventual success of the regime, it was countries such as Germany, France, and Britain that did much of the heavy lifting in Vienna, with Canada, Hungary, and others assisting. Also during this period, as they began to look seriously at how the regime would work in practice, it became ever more clear that the adversarial approach first advocated by the NATO countries—an approach that sought short-notice overflights for intelligence-gathering purposes—would not have worked; that such flights require a cooperative approach. Also during this period the ever-increasing pace of change in Europe necessitated a new approach to the question of how the neutral countries would be admitted to the regime—but the issue of Cyprus held back formal compromise. It was thus necessary to devise an ever more complex set of temporary fixes to allow the neutrals to participate in the discussions.

The Open Skies Treaty was signed on March 24, 1992. But it was not complete. A number of key provisions had been deferred. Thus began a lengthy period of ratification, implementation, and entry into force. This is covered in Chapter 8. Ironically, it was actually during this period, *after* the treaty was signed, that the overflight regime was finally worked out in detail as those who would operate the flights got their hands around the regime and designed practical ways to fulfill its objectives. Political issues, such as the Cyprus question, continued to bedevil the process. A formula was found, however, to permit the neutral countries to join the regime, except for Cyprus. Chapter 8 also contains thoughts on how the Open Skies idea might be applied in other contexts and for other purposes. Since the beginning of the talks the issues of extending the regime to other parts of the world, and also permitting the use of Open Skies flights for environmental and crisis monitoring, have been envisaged; there are provisions in the treaty itself for these purposes. For various reasons, which are explored, none of this has yet happened. In the last few years, some authors have also proposed that Open Skies could be useful in verifying deep cuts in nuclear and other Weapons of Mass Destruction (WMD). Again, this would require an evolution in the Open Skies regime, and this chapter explores what such an evolution would look like and how it might happen.

The Conclusion of the book reflects back on the Open Skies experience to date and offers some lessons and observations to those who would consider expanding the present regime or applying the idea of cooperative aerial monitoring in other contexts. It is my firm hope that this will happen. I continue to believe that the Open Skies idea has much to contribute to stability, verification, and confidence in many parts of the world. As with the process that led to the treaty in the first place, however, high-level political vision and leadership will be required.

# 1 From the First Open Skies Initiative to the Stockholm Conference

May 1989 was not the first time the idea of an Open Skies regime was put forward. President Dwight D. Eisenhower proposed such a regime in Geneva in July of 1955 at the Four Power (U.S., USSR, UK, and France) Summit. The considerations that prompted the first initiative bear resemblance to those of the 1989 version. In both cases a small group of presidential advisors were instrumental in imposing a "top-down" initiative on an unwilling U.S. bureaucracy. In both cases the adoption of the initiative had a great deal to do with the political needs of the moment, and particularly a desire to publicly test the leadership of the USSR.

Indeed, historians—particularly those who have studied the 1955 Open Skies initiative with the benefit of access to declassified archives—are divided as to Eisenhower's motives. Some believe it represented a real desire to propose a measure that would have benefited both sides and reduced tensions and fear of surprise attack. Others regard it as having been a somewhat cynical ploy that was never intended to be accepted, but rather to expose the Soviet penchant for extreme secrecy and contrast it unfavorably with a U.S. willingness to "take risks for peace." In the latter connection, it will be recalled that desultory nuclear disarmament discussions were underway at this time, and there was a perception in many quarters that the United States was not prepared to entertain serious proposals for disarmament. In fact, we now know that there was a raging debate within the U.S. government over whether it would be possible to pursue serious negotiations on disarmament with the Soviets, who were widely perceived to be far ahead in conventional weaponry, and also fundamentally untrustworthy. Moreover, given that Eisenhower had decided to rely on the threat of massive nuclear retaliation for Soviet transgressions, even conventional ones, there were suspicions that the U.S. was simply not interested in seriously pursuing nuclear disarmament.[1]

The idea for Open Skies arose during a meeting of a small group of analysts working for presidential advisor Nelson Rockefeller. Rockefeller, whose mandate was to "find ways to exploit Soviet vulnerabilities on information, ideology and international issues,"[2] had brought the group together in advance of the upcoming Geneva Summit. His charge to the group was to come up with initiatives that might be used by the president at the summit to demonstrate U.S. willingness to consider real arms control, and to test the Soviets' willingness to do the same. This group met at the Quantico Marine base in Virginia between June 5 and 10, 1955.[3]

The Quantico panel was aware of the superiority enjoyed by the United States in most areas of the military competition, and especially in the nuclear sphere. Nevertheless, the extreme secrecy of the Soviet state made it difficult for U.S. planners to get a firm grip on the extent of Soviet military capability. There were also concerns that misperceptions might lead to an inadvertent escalation during a crisis. It will be remembered that surveillance satellites had not yet been deployed, and U.S. U2 reconnaissance flights did not yet exist.

The idea of cooperative aerial inspections was suggested by Max Millikan of the Center for International Studies at the Massachusetts Institute of Technology (MIT), who had heard it discussed at a seminar in Cambridge, Massachusetts.[4] The Quantico panel was impressed by the idea. They particularly liked the fact that it would test the Soviets' willingness to accept the kind of intrusive measures necessary for the verification of the disarmament proposals then under discussion. Open Skies was thus seen as a win-win: if the Soviets accepted it, the United States would gain access to vast areas it could not presently monitor; if the Soviets rejected it, a dramatic and easily understood public relations point would have been scored by a U.S. that would be seen as being prepared to accept intrusive inspections for peace against a USSR that was not.[5] Accordingly, the group included a recommendation for some type of intrusive aerial inspection regime in their report to Rockefeller on June 10, 1955.[6]

Rockefeller presented the idea to the president in early July.[7] Eisenhower was attracted to it, but his secretary of state, John Foster Dulles, was leery. Although he had some reservations about the proposal itself, Dulles's main concern was that the president not be stampeded into making proposals for the sake of the moment that the United States might come to regret at a later date. It should also be said that an intense rivalry existed between Rockefeller and Dulles, with the latter being especially jealous of his prerogative as the main presidential advisor on foreign policy matters.[8] Also involved in this discussion was presidential disarmament advisor Harold Stassen, who saw Open Skies as a way to shift U.S. nuclear disarmament proposals from an "all or nothing" approach to one in which specific issues—such as the inspection regime that would be necessary for disarmament—could be tackled one by one. In this, Stassen was also opposed by Dulles, who did not believe that the Soviets were interested in real disarmament and could not be trusted. Dulles was concerned that Soviet disarmament proposals were a propaganda ploy designed to undermine U.S. public support for continued development of nuclear weapons and to split the Western alliance, and he believed that the United States should avoid discussion of them.[9]

When Eisenhower left for Geneva, then, Open Skies was not on his list of matters to be raised. Instead, Dulles had won, and the president went to Geneva prepared to listen to whatever the Soviets might offer. It had, after all, been their idea to hold the summit in the first place. Indeed, both Eisenhower and Dulles had been leery of the whole summit idea, fearing that little of substance would be accomplished and that the Soviets might score a propaganda victory at the West's expense. But they recognized that their allies, France and the UK, were keen on the summit for their own internal political reasons and that world opinion was also receptive to the idea.[10] Eisenhower therefore agreed to Dulles's advice on Open Skies but asked Rockefeller to have members of his staff familiar with the plan in Geneva, in case he changed his mind.[11]

As the summit unfolded, Eisenhower became uneasy at the fact that little of substance was being proposed by either side. The U.S. news media was becoming somewhat restive, and the president wanted to make a statement of "drama and substance."[12] Rockefeller once again raised the idea of Open Skies during an evening meeting in the president's quarters. This time the president was prepared to accept the idea and overruled Dulles.

The next day, July 18, 1955, Eisenhower made a statement intended to lay the ground for Open Skies. In it the president spoke of the dangers of surprise attack in the nuclear age:

> Perhaps, therefore, we should consider whether the problem of the limitation of armament may not best be approached by seeking—as a first step—dependable ways to supervise and inspect military establishments, so that there can be no frightful surprises, whether by sudden attack or by secret violation of agreed restrictions.[13]

This statement was treated as little more than a part of a wide-ranging opening statement. Eisenhower did, however, take the opportunity of a meeting with Soviet defense minister Zhukov on July 20 (the two had collaborated closely during the war and were personal acquaintances) to test Zhukov's possible reaction to the idea of inspections. Eisenhower asked Zhukov what he might think of the idea of an inspection system "of large installations, such as airfields, long-range bombers and guided missile factories that could not be hidden." Zhukov indicated acceptance in principle: "[W]hile its detail should be studied, he [Zhukov] was, in principle, in full agreement with the President's remarks." Zhukov went on to say that he understood that the purpose of the inspections would be to provide a guarantee against surprise attack.[14]

It is unclear if Zhukov fully understood what Eisenhower was proposing in this discussion. Zhukov may have believed that Eisenhower was raising some variant of an idea that the USSR had itself proposed on May 10, 1955, for a far-reaching agreement to prohibit nuclear weapons and reduce conventional arms. The May 10 proposal included as its verification system the idea of a set of ground inspections at fixed points, such as ports, major road and rail arteries, airports, and so on.[15] The May 10 Soviet proposal had been rejected by the United States as insufficient, an attempt to divide the allies and an attempt to capitalize on the Soviet conventional military superiority, but perhaps Zhukov felt that Eisenhower wanted to explore a part of it further.

The next day, on the morning of July 21, 1955, Eisenhower delivered the Open Skies proposal. After stating that "[no] sound and reliable agreement can be made unless it is completely covered by an inspection and reporting system, adequate to support every portion of the agreement," Eisenhower stated:

> I should address myself principally to the delegates from the Soviet Union, because our two great countries admittedly possess new and terrible weapons in quantities which do give rise in other parts of the world, or reciprocally, to fears and dangers of surprise attack. I propose, therefore, that we take a practical step, that we begin an arrangement, very quickly, as between ourselves—immediately. These steps would include: to give each other a complete blueprint of our military establishments, from beginning to end, from one end of our countries to the other; lay out the establishments and provide blueprints to each other. Next, to provide within our countries facilities for aerial photography to the other country—we to provide you the facilities within our country, ample facilities for aerial reconnaissance, where you make all the pictures you choose and take them to your country to study, you to provide exactly the same facilities for us . . . . Likewise we will make more easily attainable a

> comprehensive and effective system of disarmament, because what I propose, I assure you, would be but a beginning.[16]

The effect of Eisenhower's proposal was considerable. The leaders of France and the UK immediately offered to support the plan (the UK's prime minister had been briefed by Eisenhower that morning). The Soviet delegation expressed interest, but more cautiously. Nevertheless, as he recorded in his memoirs, Eisenhower had some hope when the meeting ended:

> For a time it appeared that the intransigent Soviet refusal to permit any useful inspection system in the USSR might be effectively shaken. The proposal, Bulganin declared, seemed to have real merit, and the Soviets would give it complete and sympathetic study at once. The tone of his talk seemed as encouraging as his words.[17]

Once the microphones were switched off, however, the Soviets lost no time in expressing their true feelings over the idea. That same day Khrushchev informed the president that he did not agree with Bulganin's public statements:

> From that moment until the final adjournment of the conference, I wasted no more time probing Mr. Bulganin; I devoted myself exclusively to an attempt to persuade Mr. Khrushchev on the merit of the Open Skies plan, but to no avail. He said the idea was nothing more than a bald espionage plot against the USSR, and to this line of argument he stubbornly adhered.[18]

The reasons for Soviet suspicion of the first Open Skies proposal would prove quite similar to their initial suspicions of the 1989 proposal. Certain segments of the Soviet military were concerned that the United States would use unfettered overflights to gain information that could improve their targeting of the USSR. As one analyst later noted:

> [In] 1955 the United States possessed all the necessary weapons for a counterforce nuclear attack against the Soviet Union. The major obstacle to confidence that such an attack could be carried out without a massive Soviet counter-attack was the lack of accurate and complete targeting data. The US Strategic Air Command was faced with a rapidly expanding target list . . . . In this context, the Open Skies plan can be seen as a military intelligence measure of the highest importance, one which would strengthen the weakest link in the US nuclear war-fighting plans.[19]

Moreover, as Vladislav Zubok, a Russian scholar of the period, notes, "Essentially, this proposal [Open Skies] . . . was a last minute attempt of the US experts in psychological warfare to top evident Soviet propagandist achievements with one spectacular initiative." Zubok continues:

> The Soviet reaction to Open Skies at the Geneva Conference was . . . justified by the existing rules of the Cold War; the US would have gained from aerial intelligence much more than the Soviet Union, and, besides, at that time the effectiveness of the Soviet "deterrent" still relied predominantly on the preservation of uncertainty and ignorance in the US about the true size of the Soviet strategic arsenal (in reality it was almost nonexistent, with the exception of a few "Myasischev" bombers that could make one-way flights to the United States but could not return).[20]

Although the Soviets had killed the idea, it received a generally positive reception from the Western press.[21] For this reason, the Soviets could not appear unwilling to discuss it. Over the next few years, fitful talks were conducted. Various proposals were put forward to implement Open Skies in stages in different geographical locations.[22] As in 1989, Canada became interested in the idea. Ottawa would later propose a trial Open Skies regime in the Arctic that the Soviets would quickly reject. Other allies, most notably France and Germany, would be suspicious of various other plans for regional applications of aerial inspections in different zones of Europe, which they saw as potentially weakening the alliance or otherwise creating tendencies that could have encouraged the German public toward neutrality.[23]

Interestingly, ideas surfaced in the Open Skies talks of this period that would arise thirty-five years later. The Soviets, for example, argued that any flight conducted over their territory, or the territory of their allies, would have to be on a host-country supplied aircraft. They also asked that they be entitled to overfly U.S. bases in third countries.[24] Many years later, a Soviet diplomat, who had spent several years as ambassador to Washington, wrote that Open Skies had been discussed at a presidium meeting after the Geneva Conference. Khrushchev insisted that Eisenhower had been bluffing and took the view "that no one in the US Congress would agree to allow Soviet planes to fly over, say, the Capitol in Washington." This raises the intriguing possibility that Khrushchev, who was known for an impetuous streak, might have been tempted to agree to Open Skies in the expectation that the United States would then publicly walk back from it. However we shall never know, because the Politburo "would not even hear of letting American planes fly over Soviet territory and rejected Khrushchev's tactic."[25]

Despite the discussions on the idea of applying Open Skies in different geographic zones, which went on for some years, the United States decided after Geneva that it would not prove acceptable to Moscow. Accordingly, Washington went ahead with a program designed to fill its knowledge gaps by unilateral means. The U2 high-altitude reconnaissance plane was under development at the time Eisenhower went to Geneva in 1955.[26] It was succeeded by more advanced reconnaissance aircraft and by surveillance satellites. Interestingly, Open Skies would intersect with the U2 one more time. At the Paris Summit in May of 1960, Eisenhower wanted to make one last attempt to get Soviet agreement to some version of an Open Skies regime. But the summit exploded before he could do so when Khrushchev made public the fact that the USSR had shot down Francis Gary Powers's U2 shortly before the summit and demanded an apology. Eisenhower refused, and the summit collapsed.[27]

In a sense, however, the Open Skies proposal lived up to one of the aims of the Quantico panel; it tested the Soviets' willingness to accept intrusive inspections, and they were found wanting in a very public way. Over the succeeding years, Western politicians would point to the Soviet refusal to accept Open Skies as proof of the sinister, totalitarian character of the Soviet government. Although some of this rhetoric might have been, as the Canadian foreign minister would later say, "forced, but nevertheless justified,"[28] it was effective in pointing out the differences between the USSR and the West in a dramatic way that the public would readily understand. As one Soviet officer would later say:

> We believed for a long time that everything—or virtually everything relating to the military sphere—should be shrouded in an impenetrable veil of secrecy and the thicker this veil of secrecy, the more secure we supposedly are. But it transpired that excessive secrecy did not enhance but weakened our security since the opposing side could believe—and often did—that we were hatching most perfidious plans in secret and preparing most unpredictable actions.[29]

With the development of reconnaissance aircraft, and later satellites, the apparent need for an Open Skies regime seemed to disappear. The fact that these means of surveillance were not cooperative; that each superpower was able to monitor the other not as a positive act of cooperation but rather as the result of technologies that could not be stopped, was not seen at the time as being particularly important.[30] So long as the data they returned was sufficient to allow for a measure of knowledge of the military preparedness of the other side, and, later, for arms control verification, the result was judged to be the same.

Furthermore, the fact that only two countries had access to these technologies, though an irritant to others, was not seen as a danger to peace in Europe. The bipolar alliance structure of Europe served to promote stability, and the two countries that needed access to satellite data could share it if they chose to. To many there did not seem to be any reason to reconsider the Open Skies proposal as the years went by.

A significant evolution of views concerning aerial inspections for confidence-building took place in the talks on European Confidence-building in Stockholm between 1984 and 1986. The Western nations proposed that overflights be permitted to monitor the agreed limitations on large-scale military maneuvers that were the focus of these discussions. As the U.S. delegation to the talks stated, overflights of the exercise area would "be the optimum method of checking compliance."[31] The Soviets adamantly opposed the idea, displaying many of the same concerns they had in the earlier Open Skies discussions.[32]

Shortly before the Stockholm agreement was to be signed, however, they demonstrated a sudden change of view. The exact cause is not known, but the arrival of Gorbachev in the senior ranks of the Soviet leadership and the ongoing debate in Moscow over the future path of relations with the West may have played a role. Much as would be the case with the Open Skies negotiations a few years later, however, a Soviet willingness in principle and at the political level to accept aerial inspections was one thing; the actual negotiations over how this would be done was quite another, particularly as the Soviet military exercised an important role in developing the actual provisions of the agreement.

In developments that would be familiar to Open Skies negotiators, the Soviets refused to accept the North Atlantic Treaty Organization (NATO) proposal that the country performing the inspection bring its own aircraft. The Soviets insisted that the country being inspected have the right to provide the aircraft if it wished to. In an effort to break the impasse the countries of the neutral and nonaligned group in Europe proposed that their aircraft be used by both sides, but the Soviets refused again. Their concern was that a foreign aircraft "could be equipped with the appropriate intelligence gear that can check not only the actions of the troops in this region, but also be capable of reconnoitering any installation that is not the object of monitoring. This would be unlawful intelligence activity and a violation of a state's sovereignty."[33]

Eventually, it was agreed in the Stockholm Document that the aircraft "for inspection will be chosen by mutual agreement between the inspecting and receiving states."[34] Further protections against use of flights for gathering information outside the scope of the Stockholm Document included provisions that the receiving state's representatives on the aircraft would have final say on where it might go, and would have access at all times to all charts and other navigation documents used to plot the aircraft's position. Moreover, the flights were limited to human observers with binoculars—no sensors were permitted.[35]

When Open Skies was proposed again by President Bush, relatively few aerial inspections had been carried out under the Stockholm Document. However, even with the restrictions the Soviets placed on the Stockholm aerial inspections regime, a Rubicon had been crossed in terms of Soviet willingness to receive aerial inspections. Added to this were the on-site inspection provisions of the Intermediate Nuclear Forces Treaty of 1987, which were also a significant evolution in Soviet views on intrusive verification.

By the late 1980s the stage was thus set for a reconsideration of Open Skies. All that was required were the right circumstances and someone to give it a push.

# 2 Open Skies Reborn

With Khrushchev's rejection of Open Skies, the idea was stillborn. By 1989, however, the changes wrought by Mikhail Gorbachev in the Soviet approach to international affairs and military secrecy had created an environment conducive to a re-examination of Open Skies. In particular, Soviet agreement to on-site inspections in the context of the Stockholm Agreement of 1986 and the Intermediate-range Nuclear Forces Treaty (INF) of 1987 had reversed a longstanding Soviet taboo on intrusive inspection measures.[1]

The events surrounding the resurrection of Open Skies were quite similar to those that attended its birth in 1955. In both cases, it was a "top-down" initiative, conceived by a small group of advisors and foisted upon the larger bureaucracy. In neither case was the bureaucracy particularly impressed.

Upon assuming office in January 1989, President Bush had ordered his national security team to conduct a wide-ranging strategic review "designed to respond to the emerging shifts in the global security environment."[2] As part of this review, U.S. arms control policy was to be thoroughly re-examined.[3] To a certain extent, the review was motivated by President Bush's concern at the possibility that the Reagan administration had invested too heavily in Gorbachev, and that the underlying nature of the U.S.-Soviet relationship remained fundamentally adversarial.[4] The Bush administration was also concerned that the Soviets were claiming the international public's attention with a series of well-timed initiatives on arms control and security matters. In particular, the Soviets were actively exploiting the differences that existed within the alliance as to whether its aging stock of short-range nuclear weapons in Germany should be modernized.[5] President Bush thus sought potentially popular initiatives of his own.

After an internal study lasting four months, however, the review team was unable to present any new ideas to the White House, a situation that caused considerable frustration among many in Washington and many allies as well.[6] In his memoirs Bush would later respond to these critics by speaking of his concerns at this moment in history:

> I wanted to be careful. The traumatic uprisings in East Germany in 1953, Hungary in 1956 and in Czechoslovakia in 1968 were constantly on my mind through these tumultuous months. I did not want to encourage a course of events which might turn violent and get out of hand and which we then couldn't—or wouldn't—support, leaving people stranded at the barricades. I hoped to encourage liberalization as rapid[ly] as possible without provoking an internal crackdown—as had happened in Poland in 1981—or a Soviet backlash. The problem was figuring where that line was and what was likely to be seen by the Soviets as provocative.[7]

On the arms control front, the first drafts of the review process proposed a "status quo plus" formula for dealings with Moscow. Essentially, State was proposing faster movement on the arms control negotiations already under way.[8] President Bush did not accept this conclusion, and ordered the National Security Council (NSC) to come up with new proposals. Bush ordered the NSC team "to demonstrate the new administration was not wedded to the *status quo* in Europe and was ready to seize the emerging opportunities for decisive change."[9]

Another source of pressure was the looming fortieth anniversary North Atlantic Treaty Organization (NATO) Summit, scheduled for late May. Concern existed that the ongoing debate over whether to modernize the alliance's stock of Short-range Nuclear Forces (SNF) would turn the summit into a public relations problem.[10] These fears were realized when the Soviets placed additional pressure on NATO on the eve of the summit by offering to withdraw a substantial number of SNF weapons in return for a pledge from the alliance not to modernize.[11] Much speculation existed that the Soviets would do something like this as the NSC worked to come up with new initiatives.

Thus, in an atmosphere of some tension, Robert Blackwill, special assistant to the president for European and Soviet affairs, and Philip Zelikow, NSC director for European security affairs, conceived the idea of reviving Open Skies.[12] A reintroduction of the Open Skies proposal was only one of several such initiatives examined, however, and it was by no means universally popular. Other initiatives on the list included the idea of reopening the question of German unity, and proposals for changes to NATO. Moreover, the study discussed Open Skies as a possible bilateral U.S.-USSR initiative only.[13]

Open Skies was attractive to the NSC for several reasons.[14] In addition to diverting attention from the SNF debate at the NATO Summit, Open Skies offered the chance to test Gorbachev's commitment to *glasnost.* The regime also held out the prospect of preventing tragedies such as the shooting down of a Korean airliner by Soviet air defenses in 1983. Finally, "the NSC staff believed that bringing the (Soviet) military establishment out of the shadows would promote wider changes in domestic politics as well as foreign and security policy."[15]

But Open Skies did not enjoy universal favor. Powerful elements within the U.S. intelligence and military communities were opposed because they felt that it could compromise U.S. assets in return for modest intelligence gains (given the other surveillance systems available). Moreover, these groups disliked Open Skies for precisely the same reason that would interest many countries: the ability for smaller states to exercise an independent data-collection ability. Although the NSC had placed Open Skies on a short list of proposals for the president, its acceptance was uncertain in the face of opposition from other bureaucratic agencies.[16]

Open Skies faced more than bureaucratic opposition, however. Some senior officials in the administration were concerned that it would be seen as retrograde and unimaginative. As National Security Advisor Brent Scowcroft would later remember:

> To me, the Open Skies proposal smacked of gimmickry, and would wrongly give the impression that we did not have the brain-power to think of something innovative and had to reach back 30 years for an idea. After all, we now had satellites to do such surveillance work.[17]

At this juncture, in late March 1989, Canadian officials first became aware that Open Skies was under consideration.[18] The two Canadians most directly involved, Ralph Lysyshyn (director of Arms Control and Disarmament Division of the Department of External Affairs) and John Noble (director general of International Security and Arms Control Bureau and Lysyshyn's superior), were both familiar with the policy-making process in Washington. Lysyshyn had served in the Canadian embassy in Washington earlier in his career, and he knew many of those conducting the NSC review personally. Noble dealt frequently with the Americans on a wide range of security issues.[19]

Noble and Lysyshyn were intrigued at the prospect of a revival of Open Skies for three reasons, which were to remain remarkably stable over the next three years.[20] They were convinced "that an Open Skies regime would enable the smaller participants, which do not have access to sophisticated National Technical Means (NTM) of surveillance, to exercise an independent capability to monitor areas of particular concern. In a very real sense, Open Skies would 'democratize' relations both between and within states of the two groups by allowing the smaller countries to 'see for themselves what [was] going on.'"[21]

Second, they believed "that an Open Skies regime would provide an opportunity for the North American Allies to demonstrate their willingness to shoulder some of the intrusive monitoring which the era of greater political openness and conventional arms control will require of [their] European Allies."[22] Finally, they felt "that Open Skies would represent a practical way of translating the current atmosphere of goodwill in East-West relations into something concrete . . . . Open Skies could further allow President Gorbachev to demonstrate his commitment to *glasnost* in a dramatic and practical manner."[23]

As they began to explore the issues with contacts in Washington, Noble and Lysyshyn became aware of the uncertainty facing Open Skies.[24] It was quickly decided to mount a high-level campaign to enhance the proposal's chances of acceptance using an upcoming trip by Prime Minister Mulroney and the Minister of External Affairs Joe Clark, who were scheduled to fly to Washington for consultations with President Bush and Secretary of State Baker.[25] Part of the meeting was to be devoted to security and arms control matters, with particular reference to the upcoming fortieth anniversary NATO Summit.

Canadian officials saw this meeting as the greatest opportunity both to convince President Bush that Open Skies was an idea whose time had come, and to persuade him that it should include all of the nations of NATO and the Warsaw Treaty Organization (WTO).[26] The latter condition was, of course, a prerequisite to Canada's involvement in any regime. It would have been possible to conclude an Open Skies regime between Canada, the United States, and the USSR, of course, but Canadian officials strongly favored an agreement involving all of the members of the two alliances because they saw Open Skies as a way to reinforce Canada's role in European security matters.[27]

Shortly before the meeting, Mulroney sent Bush a letter outlining his thoughts on the issues.[28] After discussing the need to avoid public difficulties over the SNF issue at the upcoming summit, Mulroney stated that, even if that issue could be sidestepped, NATO required an initiative if it was to be seen as possessed of the imagination necessary to counter Gorbachev's recent public relations coups. An initiative well suited to this objective would be an Open Skies agreement negotiated between the nations of the two alliances.

In arguing the practical benefits of an Open Skies regime, the PM's letter noted all of the reasons that had attracted Canadian interest in the proposal, carefully stressing that even the United States could gain useful information from Open Skies overflights. He then advanced a new reason for supporting the Open Skies: its possible utility in assisting in the verification of various arms-control and confidence-building regimes then under negotiation. Finally, the letter raised the point that Gorbachev might put his own version of Open Skies on the table in the near future, thus forcing the West to react once again. There was no evidence that Gorbachev was considering such a move, but Western officials had been burned in this very way before and the fear of it happening again was real.[29]

As expected, Mulroney and Clark raised Open Skies with the president and Baker. Bush encouraged an in-depth discussion.[30] As the issue was explored, the Canadians pressed the idea that Open Skies could be negotiated multilaterally, and would be particularly useful as a NATO initiative in the context of the upcoming NATO Summit. The PM concluded this part of the meeting with an assurance that, if the initiative was launched, Canada would actively support it. The president agreed, and the next day he told his staff that he had decided to launch the Open Skies initiative. A few days before his May 12 speech at Texas A&M University, the president informed Mulroney that he intended to propose multilateral negotiations on the subject of Open Skies to include all of the nations of NATO and the WTO.[31]

The president's thinking was largely influenced by the potential for Open Skies to test Gorbachev's commitment to *glasnost*. He was also aware that an Open Skies regime, though not without some risk for the United States, would return far more information on the USSR than the United States would have to give up,

> I didn't feel the Open Skies was such a bad idea—it looked like a no-lose proposition from our side. Gorbachev, committed to Glasnost, would find it hard from a public-relations standpoint to reject it. It was old-hat, but given the new openness offensive by Gorbachev, I thought we had a lot to gain. I knew there would be some hand-wringing in Defense about what could be overflown here in the United States, but I did not feel it would amount to much. Our country is so open already that I believed the Soviets would gain little additional knowledge about us. In contrast, I thought they would have some problems with unrestricted overflights of their territory. If Gorbachev could agree to it, we could only benefit—as we had much to learn about the Soviet Union.[32]

In retrospect, the Canadian intervention appears to have been critical. As one U.S. official would later say, "The letter and Mulroney's visit came at an extraordinarily opportune moment. We had a short list and there were mixed feelings about a number of the ideas on it. The visit tipped the balance."[33] In his memoirs, President Bush also acknowledges the part played by Mulroney.[34] But the point must be made that very little consultation had taken place over the initiative *within* the U.S. government. Instead, it was a top-down initiative. Shortly after Bush's announcement, an unnamed official flatly stated that "the bureaucrats are not guilty in this case."[35] This lack of interagency consultation and support was to have serious consequences once the job of translating the initiative into a detailed proposal got under way.

The Canadian action was the result of many factors. In addition to the reasons already outlined, an understanding of the internal culture of the Department of External Affairs at this moment is necessary. The department had invested heavily in research and expertise on verification throughout the 1980s.[36] This research was the consequence of a decision made at the beginning of the decade to identify verification as an aspect of the arms control process in which a middle-size country could make a substantial impact on multilateral arms control.

The Verification Research Unit had been established within the Arms Control and Disarmament Division (thus reporting to Lysyshyn) with a broad mandate to explore all manner of questions related to verification. Thus, when Open Skies surfaced, Canadian officials were comfortable with verification matters generally. Moreover, a high degree of expertise was present within the Canadian government, which could quickly analyze the idea and determine that Canada had an interest in pursuing it.

On May 12, 1989, President Bush launched the Open Skies initiative in a speech to the graduating class at Texas A&M University.[37] Bush's speech was billed as the first major exposition of his administration's view of foreign policy. The existence of the internal review process was widely known, and the press was waiting for a major statement. After referring to the momentous changes that had occurred in the Soviet Union, Bush challenged Gorbachev to go further. He spoke of the need for Moscow to continue on the path of reform if it were to be "welcomed back into the world order" and stated that the USSR would have to "earn" the right to a warmer relationship with the West. In this atmosphere, President Bush launched the Open Skies initiative with the following words:

> Thirty-four years ago, President Eisenhower . . . proposed a plan called Open Skies, which would allow unarmed aircraft from the United States and the Soviet Union to fly over the territory of the other country . . . . President Eisenhower's suggestion tested the Soviet readiness to open their society. And the Kremlin failed the test. Now, let us again explore the proposal, but on a broader, more intrusive and radical basis, one which I hope would include allies on both sides. We suggest that those countries that wish to examine this proposal meet soon to work out the necessary details, separately from other arms control negotiations. Such surveillance flights, complementing satellites, would provide regular scrutiny for both sides. Such unprecedented territorial access would show the world the true meaning of the concept of openness. The very Soviet willingness to embrace such a concept would reveal commitment to change.[38]

To the irritation of the White House, the public reaction to the speech ranged from uninterested to negative.[39] Both the press and the arms control community were lukewarm to the idea, with some accusing Bush of failing to meet Gorbachev's recent arms control offers with a realistic response.[40] In particular, the arms control community could see little to be gained from Open Skies in the era of surveillance satellites, and argued that its primary purpose was to put the Soviet leadership in an embarrassing position.[41] An administration official would later say of this period: "[We] were a little bemused by the way the press reacted to the initial announcement in the (Texas) A&M speech . . . . The general tenor of the community was: a) that it [Open Skies] was anachronistic; and b) that it was pretty much superseded by the advent of satellites."[42]

The reaction of the Soviet press was decidedly cool. *Pravda* labeled the speech a "disappointment," full of "old clichés" and displaying a "poverty of ideas." With respect to Open Skies, the Communist Party paper labeled the idea "senseless" in an era of satellites and mutual on-site inspections.[43] Other major papers in the USSR followed *Pravda*'s lead.[44]

Despite the fact that the initiative did not receive widespread support, both the U.S. and Canadian governments began to lobby in its behalf. The targets of their initial efforts were the members of the NATO alliance. Few of these governments had been briefed prior to the president's May 12 speech.[45] Canadian diplomats at NATO headquarters and in NATO capitals were instructed to make a series of high-level demarches on the subject, and were given extensive briefing notes for the purpose. These papers had been prepared some weeks before in anticipation of a lobbying campaign.[46] The U.S. government undertook a complementary round of demarches in what became a loosely orchestrated campaign.

Although they were not completely sure of the practical implications of the proposal, the allies were supportive of the basic concept. Many of the smaller allies were especially receptive to the argument put forward by the Canadians as to the utility of Open Skies for smaller countries without their own means of monitoring events in neighboring states.[47]

Thus, when the sixteen alliance leaders met in Brussels in late May, all of them were prepared to accept a mention of the Open Skies initiative in their communique. Ironically, the issue that had partially motivated the search for a face-saving initiative, the SNF debate, was overcome without public incident. In the communique issued by the NATO leaders on May 30, the alliance leaders stated:

> We consider as an important initiative President Bush's call for an "Open Skies" regime intended to improve confidence among states through reconnaissance flights, and to contribute to the transparency of military activity, to arms control and to public awareness. It will be the subject of careful study and wide-ranging consultations.[48]

The speed (about six weeks) with which Open Skies was brought from a vague idea for a possible bilateral initiative to a multilateral initiative announced by the U.S. president and endorsed by the NATO leaders was astonishing. However, the pressures generated by the upcoming summit that had caused U.S. policy-makers to embrace Open Skies receded into memory during the hectic summer of 1989. Those within the U.S. bureaucracy who had reservations about Open Skies may have been unable to block its adoption, but they now had an opportunity to play a significant role in fleshing out the proposal.

In particular, the speed with which the Open Skies was adopted had a marked impact on its subsequent prospects. As in 1955, it was a "top-down," political initiative that lacked significant support within the bureaucracy and was made public before the necessary interagency groundwork could be done. In the absence of such a "ground-up" appraisal of the proposal, the process of developing a consensus between strongly divergent internal positions was rendered far more difficult over the long run. Certainly, this is what happened to the Open Skies initiative once the various concerned agencies of the U.S. government turned their attention to it away from the glare of presidential politics. But this problem is not unique to the bureaucratic infighting that was to mark the interagency debate over Open Skies. As Talbott mentions in his analysis of the internal politics that surround U.S. discussion of the initial INF position, "It is an age-old adage of bureaucratic politics that no decision is final except for those who like the way the decision came out."[49]

Perhaps even more important, the lack of a clear and agreed need for Open Skies deprived the subsequent negotiation of a clear and agreed *goal*. In particular, a top-down initiative, launched to address the political needs of a specific moment, may suffer from a lack of agreed focus such that it will encounter divergent interpretations of its basic purpose when the practical aspects are addressed. In the case of Open Skies, the objectives of the regime, as outlined by President Bush and the NATO Summit statement, were so vague that they did not provide a clear set of criteria on which to design the practical aspects of the regime.[50] This was to become a significant problem throughout the first rounds of negotiations.[51]

On the other hand, it would be too easy to criticize those whose efforts gave birth to Open Skies. Of course the initiative would have ultimately profited had its proponents worked out the details before launching it. But, had they taken the time to do so, the possibility exists that the proposal would have missed its moment and never been launched. It may be the case that the opportunity for reflection upon the details of an idea does not exist in the rough and tumble of policy-making against deadlines until the idea has an institutional constituency. Only then are the resources devoted to thinking a proposal through, as scarce hours of examination cannot be given to every potentially good idea.

It is an irony of the bureaucratic and policy worlds that the maneuvering required to get an idea on the agenda can precede the reflection required to make the idea ultimately work. Rather, the birth of new proposals, such as Open Skies in 1989, is attended by a cursory examination of the pros and cons, and a keen appreciation of whether the initiative fits the particular political needs of the moment. If it does, speed is often the best weapon in any attempt to get the idea on the agenda before its opponents can muster the arguments to defeat it. As Newhouse noted in his assessment of the internal debate over the initial position of the United States in the Strategic Arms Limitation Treaty (SALT) talks:

> The typical bureaucrat, once his project becomes operational, tries to generate great impulsion . . . . The haste, combined with irregular procedures, adds respectively to the impression of a patchwork operation propelled along in a dizzying rush of activity.[52]

This "dizzying rush of activity" may be crucial to the survival of a proposal, but it can have a detrimental impact once the hard work of putting flesh on the ideas begins. Within the U.S. government, this task began in earnest on June 22, 1989.[53] On that date President Bush issued National Security Directive (NSD) 15. The directive ordered the bureaucracy to examine Open Skies and develop a coherent position. The directive did provide some guidelines for this process, but they were quite broad. The purpose of the regime was defined as "serv[ing] both political and intelligence purposes by increasing the transparency of the Soviet military establishment." In order to accomplish this, "the Directive called for an overflight regime that could be intrusive enough to test Soviet willingness to move towards greater transparency, yet would include sufficient restrictions to protect sensitive US national security assets."[54]

Each interested agency of the U.S. government began to examine Open Skies on the basis of this directive. The State Department had already prepared an options paper that contained four possible structures for an Open Skies regime.[55] These were: (a) "Highly Intrusive," allowing the overflying country to use any sensor on an uncontrolled aircraft with no territorial restrictions; (b) "Moderately Intrusive"; (c) "Narrowly Intrusive"; and (d) "Restrictive." These options became the focus of the discussion within the interagency process.

State Department officials, though somewhat skeptical of Open Skies, were nonetheless interested in negotiating a new agreement with the USSR. Their analysis was much the same as the earlier Canadian one in that they saw utility in reinforcing North American–European security ties at a time of considerable change in East-West relations. The State Department was also interested in testing the limits of *glasnost* and saw some benefits from Open Skies as an adjunct to other means of verifying various arms control agreements. State thus favored the "moderately intrusive" option.

The Arms Control and Disarmament Agency (ACDA) was less enthusiastic. ACDA was primarily concerned with the negotiations to develop a dedicated aerial inspection regime for the ongoing negotiations over a Conventional Forces in Europe (CFE) Agreement, which would significantly cut the conventional forces arrayed by the two alliances in the European theater. Accordingly, Open Skies was viewed as (at worst) something of a threat to a "real" arms control negotiation, and (at best) a nuisance that would simply consume time and resources. ACDA took the view that any Open Skies regime should "be limited to broad, low-resolution coverage for confidence-building purposes, and that CFE verification would require a separate and more intrusive aerial-inspection regime with shorter timelines and a superior sensor package."[56]

The views of the intelligence community were split between the concerns of those who *collected* intelligence for the United States and those who *protected* U.S. secrets (sometimes known within the community as the "hiders" and the "seekers"). The U.S. intelligence community is a far-flung group of institutions and interests. Prominent among them are the Central Intelligence Agency (CIA), the Defense Intelligence Agency (DIA), the National Security Agency (NSA), the intelligence branch of each of the armed services (Army, Navy, Marines, and Air Force), and the National Reconnaissance Office (NRO), which manages satellite programs for others.[57] The CIA's Arms Control Intelligence Staff was given the responsibility for coordinating the position of the U.S. intelligence community as a whole.[58]

The *collectors* soon came to recognize the potential of Open Skies as a means of gaining inexpensive wide-area coverage of the USSR (compared with equivalent satellite coverage). The differences between aircraft and satellites involve such factors as the huge development and purchase cost difference, the predictability of satellite orbital paths as opposed to the ability of aircraft to fly erratic routes and to loiter over or quickly revisit sensitive sites, and the ability of aircraft to fly under clouds.[59] The collectors were concerned, however, over the costs involved in running Open Skies operations and analyzing the data. They did not want these costs to come from their budgets, which was likely, unless the regime was able to return significant material of demonstrable intelligence value. Accordingly, they pressed for as intrusive a regime as possible and sought to protect the ability of the United States to use its most sophisticated sensors, motion-stabilizers, and digital processing techniques. Since these were not available to Eastern states, the United States and its allies would have realized a significant advantage.

The *protectors* took the opposite view.[60] The most concerned was the NSA, which is responsible for electronic interception of foreign communications, but also for the protection of U.S. facilities from such eavesdropping. NSA was quite worried about communications security and electronic signals intelligence (ELINT). Meanwhile, the branches of the intelligence community that operated reconnaissance satellites worried that the funds required to operate the Open Skies regime would come from their budgets. Finally, some intelligence officials worried that the wide availability of high-quality intelligence data would deprive the United States of an advantage of being one of only two countries with access to such information—the very idea of "democratization" that was of such interest to Canada and others. These groups thus favored a regime with a low degree of intrusiveness, even though it was pointed out by many that the coming age of commercial satellite imagery was about to erode much of their advantage.[61]

Civilians within the Office of the Secretary of Defense (OSD) in the Department of Defense (DOD) generally favored a highly intrusive approach.[62] They pointed to the fact that opportunities for intelligence collection would be greater for the United States under such a regime, as the USSR was a closed society, while a tremendous amount of information on the United States was already in the public domain. The possibility of embarrassing the Soviets, should they have rejected the idea, may also have been a factor in their support for the scheme.

The policy office of the Joints Chiefs of Staff (JCS/J-5) took the opposite view.[63] They favored the moderately intrusive option and wanted special measures to protect highly classified programs and areas. The JCS, for example, proposed that certain areas be held off-limits to overflights. Large exclusion areas were drawn up around Groton, Connecticut, the home of the Electric Boat Co., which manufactures nuclear submarines for the U.S. Navy; Colorado Springs, home of the U.S. Space Command; and areas in the Southwest, where several test ranges and sensitive weapons facilities were located.

Although this debate was conducted in private throughout July, selective leaks were made by various factions in order to gain support for their views. One article, of July 18, 1989, appears to have been based on leaks from those in favor of the moderately to slightly intrusive view. The article cites a source stating that off-limits areas would likely be established and wondering whether intrusive sensors would be allowed.[64] In fact there would be no off-limits areas in the final U.S. proposal, and intrusive sensors would be sought.

By the end of July the interagency process agreed on the broad outlines of a moderately intrusive regime, but several specific questions remained.[65] These included such matters as: whether exclusion areas would be permitted; what sensors would be allowed; whether the overflight would be performed by a host-country aircraft or one belonging to the country requesting the overflight; how many flights would be permitted per year and the duration of each flight; and the length of the prior notification period. Obviously, these specifics were at the heart of just how intrusive the eventual regime would be.

By mid-August several of the questions had been narrowed down to a few basic choices that tended to be interrelated. On the questions of permitted sensors and exclusion areas, for example, one option held that a ban on all sensors capable of collecting Signals Intelligence (SIGINT—essentially the ability to eavesdrop on radio, telephone, and radar emissions) would allow for a regime without territorial restrictions. If SIGINT were included, territorial restrictions would be required. It was therefore decided to drop SIGINT.[66]

Other measures were included to soothe the fears of the protectors within the intelligence community.[67] Advance notification of the exact flight path, to allow sensitive facilities to be shut down, was incorporated into the proposal in the form of a twenty-four-hour period between its filing and the overflights, as were restrictions on the ability of the aircraft to loiter over a target. An inspection of the aircraft for the presence of illegal SIGINT sensors was agreed, even though it was recognized that this could mean that the United States would not be able to use its most sophisticated sensors, as they would be subject to inspection by Soviet experts. Finally, it was agreed that the overflying country could bring its own aircraft, but that the host country could have monitors aboard to ensure that the flight path was followed.[68]

With all of these restrictions, the final package was sent to the White House where President Bush approved it in August 1989. Nevertheless, several elements of the intelligence community retained misgivings about the final package. Accordingly, they had "viewed their role as one of damage limitation, and (had) dug in their heels when it came to crafting a negotiating proposal likely to lead to swift agreement."[69] State Department representatives flew to Brussels to brief the allies on August 31.

As all of this activity was going on in Washington during the summer of 1989, the allies had heard very little officially. The deafening silence was something of an embarrassment to Canada, which had gone out in front of the United States in lobbying in behalf of Open Skies.[70] In an attempt to fill the void and to keep the initiative moving, Ottawa conducted both a public campaign in behalf of Open Skies and some private lobbying in NATO and WTO capitals.[71]

The public campaign centered on newspaper articles such as the one submitted to the *New York Times* by the Canadian foreign minister Joe Clark.[72] The article made public many of the points that had led Canada to push the idea in the first place. In particular, it sought to dispel the notion that aircraft were less capable than satellites, or had been made redundant by them. The article also drew attention to the fact that "[o]nly large countries have satellites" and argued that all nations require the ability to independently monitor events of concern. Finally, the article alluded to the fact that Open Skies constituted a test of *glasnost*.

The private campaign featured extensive demarches in the capitals of both alliances. By mid-July, however, the situation had become somewhat difficult for Ottawa.[73] Several countries asked why it was that Ottawa was running with a

U.S. presidential initiative. In an interview with *Isvestia* in October, Viktor Karpov, who would lead the Soviet delegation to the Ottawa and Budapest conferences, stated: "[It] is Canada that has come up with the "Open Skies" idea. Prime Minister Mulroney invented it and presented it to President Bush .... *But it is the Canadians who gave us all the explanations.*"[74] In a mid-July interview with a Canadian defense policy specialist, Karpov noted that "the US had not formally transmitted the proposal to the Soviets, but that Canada's ambassador in Moscow had already taken the initiative in explaining the concept to the Soviets."[75]

Although they pointed to the need for the interagency process to develop the proposal in Washington, the Canadians were increasingly frustrated in being on their own in promoting Open Skies.[76] Moreover, as they heard what was being considered in Washington, the Canadians became apprehensive. The idea that exclusion zones might be permitted was seen as unacceptable in Ottawa. The Canadians stressed to their U.S. colleagues that the regime in 1989 had to be at least as open as the one that Eisenhower had proposed in 1955, or it would be a public relations disaster.[77]

Once the United States came up with a proposal in August of 1989 in-depth discussion could go ahead, but the trade-offs that had been required to achieve that proposal became something of an impediment over the long term. Put simply, the intelligence community accepted Open Skies only because it was potentially useful to them in a certain form. If that structure were compromised, the utility of Open Skies as an adjunct to U.S. National Technical Means would also be adversely affected and the gains to be had from the Open Skies would disappear. The intelligence community would thus oppose any changes vigorously.

Over the longer term, then, the U.S. intelligence community's conditional acceptance of Open Skies imposed a straitjacket on U.S. flexibility once the negotiation began. This impact of the U.S. interagency process on the question of setting negotiating instructions is well known in both the historical[78] and the theoretical literature.[79] Unfortunately, the U.S. interagency approach to formulating negotiating instructions, or any committee-based approach in which very different views must be reconciled, means that strict instructions are likely to be issued to protect the positions of various committee members. Unless a strong figure can cut through and order a more flexible position, this makes it likely that negotiations will begin with a tough approach.[80] Raymond Garthoff's experience of the SALT negotiation bears out this observation:

> [T]he greatest problem of the American side in the SALT I negotiations has been the absence of a consensus on our own negotiating objectives. Challenging as is the

> task of negotiating with the Russians, our greatest difficulties in doing so have arisen from the attendant burden of continual negotiation and maneuvering among various elements within the American government.[81]

In the case of the Open Skies position developed by the interagency process in the summer of 1989, the result was a set of instructions that placed a premium on toughness in the expectation of a negotiation that would feature a series of concessions leading to a process of convergence. Moreover, since the U.S. position was at least partially driven by the need to acquire "useful" information, it is not surprising that the United States would seek to achieve some advantages over potential "adversaries" within the regime. Basically, the U.S. sought to draft the agreement in such a way as to preserve material advantages over the USSR, and others, in terms of the sensors that Washington might employ.[82] In early September, however, this problem lay in the future. The immediate concerns were to develop an agreed alliance approach to the subject, and to find out whether the Soviets were prepared to negotiate.

The Americans briefed NATO on their internal position on August 31. At the same meeting the allies decided to develop a unified position on the Open Skies initiative. Accordingly, they tasked the Senior Political Committee (SPC) of the North Atlantic Assembly (NAC) to begin consultations aimed at creating a consensus among the allies on the main points at issue. The SPC is composed of the deputy ambassadors of the allies. (The SPC's deliberation on Open Skies will be discussed in the next chapter.)

As the SPC began its work, tentative efforts began to determine whether the Soviets, and their WTO partners, were actually prepared to negotiate an Open Skies treaty. Incredible as it may seem, there had been relatively little contact with officials in the USSR, or any of the WTO countries up to this point. Although there had been some,[83] the Soviets had been listening rather than offering their own thoughts. Interestingly, the Hungarians had displayed considerable interest in the scheme and had asked the Canadians to keep them abreast of developments.[84] This nascent Canadian-Hungarian link was to have a significant impact upon the Open Skies process. Indeed, the Canadians and the Hungarians would keep the initiative alive after the failure of the Ottawa and Budapest rounds.

As with the Canadians, the Hungarians saw Open Skies as a means of providing an independent monitoring capability to the smaller countries of the two alliances. Of course, the nature of the relationship between the superpower and the rest in the WTO was quite different to that which prevailed within

NATO. Moreover, Central Europe was at the beginning of a process of extraordinary change in 1989, and the Hungarians were looking ahead to the day when they might be free of the WTO.[85] The Hungarians thus had much more to gain from an Open Skies regime than the Canadians.

Personalities and the bureaucratic culture of the moment also played a role in forging what was to be a crucial relationship between Canada and Hungary. The Hungarian most involved in bringing Budapest on board was much like his Canadian counterparts in that he was searching for an initiative that could be used to attract attention within an environment that encouraged "new thinking."[86] As in Ottawa, Open Skies thus fitted the institutional and bureaucratic needs of the moment in Budapest.

But if the Hungarians had expressed considerable interest and a desire to become involved, the Soviets had not. To the extent they had responded to the earlier Canadian briefings, the Soviets had simply asked questions. Would their aircraft be able to use bases in North America for refueling purposes after long transit flights? Would there be any areas in which Open Skies flights would not be permitted?[87] The Soviets were assured that their aircraft would be able to use refueling facilities in Canada, and were told that Canada favored a regime with no restrictions as to where aircraft could fly, save those necessary for flight safety.[88] Beyond these questions, however, the Soviets gave no insights as to their own views. They were waiting to see whether the idea could survive. Certain sectors of the Soviet bureaucracy were extremely hopeful that it would not, for largely the same reasons as some sectors of the U.S. bureaucracy had been opposed to Open Skies.[89]

Once the United States had come to its own internal position, the American ambassador to Moscow met with Soviet officials on September 11, 1989, to brief them on the outlines of the American concept of Open Skies and invite them to negotiate an agreement. It should be noted, however, that he did not ask them to outline their views, nor was he empowered to.[90] He received a noncommittal response but was promised an answer during Foreign Minister Shevardnadze's scheduled meeting with Secretary Baker at Jackson Hole, Wyoming, in late September. At this meeting, Shevardnadze informed Baker that the Soviet Union would participate in a conference on Open Skies.[91] He also handed over a letter from Gorbachev that marked the first Soviet comment on the issues to be decided at a conference. Gorbachev expressed three concerns.[92]

First, he insisted that steps had to be taken to ensure that the "information collected from the overflights could (not) be misused to harm the security of the observed party." Second, he argued that "there had to be full equality in access to information regardless of the differences among the parties in geography and technological know-how." Finally, he insisted that agreed constraints would have to be imposed to ensure that the first two conditions were met. Gorbachev suggested that these constraints might take the form of "a multinational pool of aircraft and sensors and the sharing of the collected data by all parties."[93] These Soviet concerns were to remain remarkably consistent throughout the Open Skies negotiation. They also indicated that the USSR had a fundamentally different concept of Open Skies from that which underlay the West's evolving position.

Interestingly, many aspects of the Soviet position were similar to their reaction to the 1955 proposal. Under the banner of equality, for example, the Soviets would insist that they be allowed to overfly bases belonging to the United States in Japan and the Philippines, even though those countries would not be members of the Open Skies negotiation. They had made the same claim during the fitful talks over the 1955 proposal. One Canadian official would later say, "Their initial criticism was exactly the same as in 1955. It was as if someone just opened the file on Open Skies and restated the position."[94]

Nevertheless, the Soviets had publicly agreed to negotiate. Prime Minister Mulroney offered to host the first round of the talks, and suggested November.[95] It was also agreed that the opening of the meeting would be at the level of the foreign ministers of the NATO and WTO members. This date was soon changed to February because of scheduling difficulties for the twenty-three foreign ministers. Shevardnadze met the Canadian minister, Joe Clark, a few days later at the United Nations and reaffirmed the USSR's willingness to negotiate.[96] And so, an international arms control negotiation had been agreed, a host had come forward, and dates had been set.

## CONCLUSION

Thus an idea had been proposed by the U.S. president and brought to an agreement to hold a major international conference, but virtually no actual prenegotiation had taken place on substance. It is often during this phase of prenegotiation that the sides explore the idea in sufficient depth to determine whether a successful negotiation is possible. The Gorbachev letter delivered by Shevardnadze indicated that significant differences existed between the nascent positions of the two superpowers, but no effort had been made to explore these differences.

Open Skies had been imposed upon an unwilling bureaucracy by a political decision. A general and widely held agreement among all of the internal actors on the U.S. side that negotiations should be explored as a policy option was missing. Moreover, in the weeks leading to President Bush's Texas A&M speech there was no problem to solve, except for a perceived public relations question within NATO that had nothing to do with Open Skies as such.

Examination of possible negotiating options had been undertaken in at least two countries (the United States and Canada), but it had been truncated and somewhat artificial in that the U.S. bureaucracy found itself examining options against the background of a publicly launched presidential commitment to negotiate. Nevertheless, the examination of possible options had resulted in the development of a coherent position. That this position would have the effect of forcing the negotiations to begin as a Concession to Convergence exercise was a problem for the future. Also problems for the future were the facts that the position would not be sufficient to achieve an agreement, and that the U.S. bureaucracy would have difficulty agreeing to changes once the negotiation got going. In retrospect, the fact that the president had already committed the United States to negotiations was the key aspect of the search for options phase in the U.S.: "Because it was a Presidential initiative, no agency could openly oppose it."[97]

Another way in which the Open Skies negotiation was affected by the events of this period was that little effort was given to establishing the interests of the other likely participants in the negotiations, especially the USSR. There was no attempt even to try to identify the other side's interests, let alone discuss them. This problem would be compounded in the next phase of the development of Open Skies, in that what prenegotiation was done during these phases was done almost entirely within one of the two coalitions that would be participating in the negotiation: NATO.

The deliberations within NATO consumed virtually all of the attention of Western diplomats in the period leading up to the Ottawa Conference. Despite the fact that they were increasingly aware that NATO's evolving position would not be acceptable to the USSR, they were unable to approach the Soviets until they had established their own position. This position was not to be agreed until the very eve of formal negotiations. Moreover, the process by which the NATO position was established was to become a negotiation in itself, involving a great deal of complexity and many difficult trade-offs.

# 3 The Issues Explored

NATO's Senior Political Committee (SPC) set to work in mid-September 1989. Their goal was to produce an agreed Basic Elements Paper (BEP)—a framework of the alliance's approach to Open Skies. The allies recognized that the BEP would have to be completed before the opening of the Ottawa Conference, scheduled for early February 1990, if the Warsaw Treaty Organization (WTO) states were to have any time to respond to it prior to the negotiations. A desire also existed to launch the BEP at an appropriately high political level. Accordingly, the allies identified their upcoming ministerial meeting scheduled for mid-December as a target for completion of the BEP.[1]

The work was facilitated by an American "straw man" paper.[2] The basic outlines of the regime proposed by the Americans were:

— The country undertaking the observation flight would be entitled to use its own noncombat aircraft, or to choose an alternate;

— Twenty-four hours' notice would have to be given before the arrival of the observation aircraft at a designated Point of Entry in the country to be overflown. Upon arrival, the crew would have up to six hours to file a flight plan. A twenty-four-hour period would then begin, during which the flight plan would be cleared and the aircraft could be subject to an intrusive but nondestructive inspection;

— There would be no restrictions as to where the flight could go, except for standard air safety regulations applied to civilian aircraft, but loitering would not be permitted;

— There would be no restrictions on sensors, with the sole exception of Signals Intelligence (SIGINT) devices, which would be banned;

— Data resulting from the overflights would be the property of the nation conducting the overflight, which could share it with any other participant if it so desired;
— Overflight aircraft would have to be capable of carrying host-country observers;
— The regime would be open to the twenty-three members of the European security alliances in the first instance, though increases in membership could be discussed once the regime was in operation;
— Open Skies would be a "stand-alone" regime, though the results of overflights could be used for the purposes of verifying other arms control agreements;
— A yearly quota of overflights would be agreed for each country; and
— States of the same alliance would not be permitted to overfly each other (resulting from a fear that the USSR would have its own allies conduct overflights of itself, and thereby "consume" a large portion of the Soviet quota of such overflights).

Although the allies were in broad agreement with the Americans on the overall shape of an Open Skies regime, many of the details would be disputed during the SPC's deliberations. Several of these difficulties would be over technical issues, such as how much advance warning of an overflight would be necessary. Others would be of a more political character, and involved rather basic differences as to the membership of the proposed regime. For the sake of clarity, and since this is the first time they have been discussed at any length, each of the main issues will be analyzed separately. Of course, the issues were interrelated in many respects, and these interrelationships will also be discussed as appropriate.

## THE ISSUES

### Aircraft Ownership

The allies were in agreement over the question of who should own the overflight aircraft. The country performing the overflight should be entitled to either use its own aircraft, or make arrangements for another.[3] The critical element of choice would thus lie with the country performing the overflight. Although the Soviet preference for some sort of a pool of aircraft was known, as a result of Gorbachev's letter,[4] the allies were not sympathetic to the idea for several reasons.[5] The creation of such a pool, it was reasoned, would involve an entirely new bureaucracy. Quite aside from the expense of establishing such a body, questions arose as to who would pay what and who would contribute what in terms of aircraft and crew. Since most countries already had suitable aircraft in their national inventories, or had allies who did, the SPC believed that the expense and trouble of establishing a pool was unjustified.

Moreover, a pool of aircraft would reduce the intrusiveness of the regime by standardizing all observation flights. The potential for states to use extremely intrusive sensors, if they were willing to have them subjected to inspections, would be eliminated. Instead, the pool would use a standardized set of sensors that would probably be of a lower quality than might be available to many states. Thus, the U.S. desire to obtain an advantage would be negated. Of course, the Soviets were interested in a pool for exactly these reasons.

## SENSORS AND DATA-SHARING

The allies were comfortable with the U.S. proposal on sensors. The idea of banning SIGINT did not raise any objections, and all looked forward to cooperation in mounting overflights with a variety of sophisticated sensors.[6] The related position on data-sharing was also broadly accepted, and the allies quickly reached an understanding that they would share the data from overflights among themselves. In response to a question on the eve of the Ottawa Conference regarding data-sharing, Hawes stated: "It is our view that the eventual regime will be most useful to everyone if we can have intense data-sharing among friendly countries. Obviously, the procedures for that will have to be worked out . . . . [T]here are discussions going on about this."[7]

### Timelines

Many of the allies were not comfortable with the American proposal for up to fifty-four hours from notification of a flight to the actual conduct of the flight.[8] This was viewed as too lengthy a period, and threatened to make a mockery of the idea of openness. It was pointed out that the Stockholm Document mandates that thirty-six hours may pass between the notification to conduct a challenge inspection and the beginning of that inspection. Given that one of the purposes of Open Skies was to demonstrate the willingness of the North Americans to accept the same intrusiveness as the Europeans, the fifty-four-hour period was seen in Canada as unworkable politically.[9] Several European countries also objected to the fifty-four-hour preflight period. They were motivated by a desire to begin their overflights as quickly as possible, and were not worried about allowing the Soviets to fly over them with a minimum of notice.[10]

The objection to the fifty-four-hour period was thus primarily political. Few of those working on the BEP were aware of the technical details of flight planning. When the actual negotiations over timelines took place in the context of the end-game, it would become obvious that a timeline that stressed a short-notice philosophy would present those who would actually have to fly the missions with considerable problems. In particular, a concern was to arise among flight crews that they would not be able to perform all the steps required of them in the allotted time and still have time for the crew-rest required by various national flight safely regulations. This problem was largely in the future as the BEP was under discussion during the autumn of 1989. Those flight crew members who did raise the problem in the autumn of 1989 were told that it was important to stress the alliance's desire to promote a short timeline for political reasons, but that the practical aspects of the issue would be thoroughly discussed once the negotiation began.

The Americans were reluctant to alter their proposed timeline, however.[11] It was clear that they were having difficulty with the idea of accepting the same degree of intrusiveness over their own country as the Europeans had accepted in the context of the Stockholm Document. More specifically, the protectors within the intelligence community argued that fifty-four hours was the minimum required for the security of the U.S. mainland. Under some pressure, it was eventually agreed to shorten the first twenty-four-hour period to sixteen. It was also agreed that individual nations could unilaterally shorten this period if they wished. The second twenty-four-hour period was retained. This was the more crucial of the two, as it was the period after which the country to be overflown would have been given the flight plan. The protectors within the U.S. intelligence community, as well as the operators of certain bases and systems, were adamant that they needed twenty-four hours after receipt of the flight plan to protect their most sensitive installations.[12]

### Mission Operations

The questions of flight safety and ensuring that Open Skies overflights were not overly disruptive of busy European air traffic corridors caused great concern at first. It quickly became obvious, however, that flights envisaged under an Open Skies regime would cause no problem for air traffic control. Indeed, the air traffic controllers who were asked to examine Open Skies assured SPC members that they could live with far less than twenty-four hours as the period after the flight plan had been filed.[13] Thus, although the North Atlantic Treaty Organization (NATO) countries would continue to say publicly that the twenty-four-hour period had been selected at least partially in the interests of air traffic control requirements, this was not the case. In fact, it was the insistence of the U.S. intelligence community upon a twenty-four-hour period after receipt of the overflight plan that drove this point.[14]

The Mission Operations section of the completed BEP also stipulated that overflights would begin "from pre-designated points of entry and terminate at pre-designated points of exit."[15] These points would be listed in an annex to the completed treaty, and normal fueling and maintenance facilities would be available at them. The larger countries were also to be obligated to provide extra locations for refueling stops along the route of the overflight. These ideas were not controversial. It was also widely agreed that Host-Country Monitors would be on board the aircraft during its observation flight. These monitors would have the right to move about the aircraft without restriction, to check that it was following the agreed flight path, and to monitor the operation of the sensors.[16]

In keeping with the position adopted by the United States in August, it was agreed that no areas would be permanently closed to overflights. This did not mean that certain areas might not be closed temporarily, or that certain altitudes might not be restricted on a temporary basis, if flight safety considerations required such steps. But if a country wished to close an area off temporarily, it would have to make an announcement well in advance, and notify all other regime participants. It would be impossible to close an area shortly after receiving the proposed flight plan. As a general rule, the BEP stated that "presumption shall be on behalf of encouraging the greatest degree of openness consistent with air safety."[17]

Finally, the Mission Operations section of the BEP contained this rather cryptic statement: "The operations of the Open Skies regime shall be without prejudice to states not participating in it."[18] This language evolved from a Turkish concern that flights too near its border with Syria might result in friction. Civilian aircraft that had flown too near this area had been shot at in the past.[19] The statement was intended to give the Turks an escape clause. Should a country request an overflight too near the Syrian border, Ankara could then simply say that such a flight plan would be prejudicial to the interests of a non-participant.

### Participation

This area of the SPC's discussions was difficult, and exposed very different concepts as to how Open Skies fit within the rapidly evolving European security dynamic. It was well recognized that Europe was on the verge of dramatic changes in the early autumn of 1989. President Gorbachev's willingness to accept profound changes in Eastern Europe had been demonstrated that summer when Hungary had opened its borders without protest from Moscow, allowing thousands of East Germans to escape to the West. Indeed, the fact that these changes were under way was one of the reasons Open Skies had been relaunched in the first place. But the Canadians and Americans driving the Open Skies initiative did not foresee the speed or the extent to which events in Europe would move in the autumn of 1989.[20]

The U.S. position on the participation question was that only the twenty-three countries of the two alliances should be involved in the negotiations. Although the United States said publicly that it would be willing to consider the expansion of the regime once it was up and running,[21] privately it was in no hurry to do so.[22] The Americans also took the view that the eventual regime should be a stand-alone one, not formally linked to any other confidence-building or arms control regime (though it was, of course, recognized that information picked up by Open Skies flights would be of use in the verification of arms control treaties, most notably the Conventional Forces in Europe [CFE] Treaty then under negotiation).[23]

The U.S. position was the result of several factors. First, the United States believed that the negotiation would be facilitated by restricting participation.[24] As Hawes would say on the eve of the Ottawa Conference, "We believe that this is strictly a practical consideration . . . that it is easier to develop the actual regime with a smaller group."[25] Second, the United States was leery of the idea of including a number of smaller European neutrals, as these countries were, in Washington's eyes, sometimes inclined to relationships with other countries that the U.S. was not prepared to allow to acquire data about itself. Third, some question existed over whether all of the neutrals were ready to embrace the concept of openness to the degree required of an Open Skies regime. The attitude of some of them toward transparency had struck many as "disappointingly modest" in recent Conference on Security and Cooperation in Europe (CSCE) discussions.[26]

Finally, the United States worried that placing Open Skies within the rubric of the CSCE would create confusion over the relationship of the regime to the CSCE as a whole. This concern was related to the traditional American desire to limit the scope of CSCE Confidence-building Measures (CBMs) to Europe only. Moreover, the United States worried that the application of any CSCE-related CBM to the United States could be the start of a "slippery slope" that might eventually lead to pressures to accept a host of CBMs regarding American activities not related to European security affairs—such as U.S. activities in space and on the high seas. Indeed, the Soviets would make half-hearted attempts to exploit this fear by proposing that Open Skies negotiations be accompanied by similar talks on "Open Seas" and "Open Space," though they never defined either concept in any detail.[27]

France took the opposite approach. Paris was eager to ensure that the Open Skies negotiations not become a bloc-to-bloc affair.[28] French resistance to placing European security negotiations within the context of the two alliances was well known in 1989. They had raised similar concerns during the negotiations over the CFE mandate,[29] and had refused to participate in the Mutual and Balanced Force Reduction (MBFR) talks in Vienna because of objections to their bloc-to-bloc nature.[30] Essentially, the French wished to reduce the primacy of the bloc-to-bloc structure of European security. The motivation of this stance was a desire to diminish the stature of NATO in European affairs.[31] If the goals of French diplomacy were long-standing, the weakening of the WTO under Gorbachev provided new rationales. With the WTO disintegrating by the day, ran the French argument, why insist that it be given a new breath of life by "forcing the East Europeans to rely on Soviet coordination"[32] for Open Skies overflights? Moreover, the exclusion of the other CSCE members struck France as anachronistic in an era when the East/West structure of Europe was eroding.

At a workshop on Open Skies held in Ottawa in November 1989, for example, the French participant argued strongly that Open Skies be negotiated within the framework of the CSCE. He also wanted the eventual treaty to take account of the emerging CFE Treaty in terms of its quota structure.[33] These were reasonable points, and would grow in relevance as the negotiations unfolded over the following three years. In the autumn in 1989, however, France was still in the minority (though it did receive some support from Spain and Italy).[34]

The participation issue was complicated by another factor. If the European neutrals were to be admitted, the question arose as to who would represent Cyprus. Greece and Turkey had very different views over this issue. Athens argued that the Greek-Cypriot government was the internationally recognized representative of the island. Turkey insisted that the break-away "Turkish Republic of Northern Cyprus" was equally legitimate, and should also be admitted to the talks if any other neutrals were. The dispute between Greece and Turkey over the status of Cyprus, though utterly unrelated to Open Skies as such, was destined to become the greatest single impediment to bringing the European neutral countries into the negotiations.

In practical terms, the dispute over participation had an impact on the preparations for the Ottawa Conference. The French insisted that the CSCE countries be represented in some way. Many of these countries themselves put the Canadian hosts of the first meeting under some pressure to make an arrangement for their participation.[35] The United States, on the other hand, would not accept any official status for these countries. With the conference only weeks away, the Canadians made a unilateral decision to invite the neutrals to Ottawa in the capacity of observers, with rights to attend the public sessions, and with the promise of weekly briefings from the host of the conference. Although not popular with the French, the Americans, the Greeks, the Turks, or the neutrals themselves, this formula was the beginning of the process whereby the neutrals gradually gained access.

The fact that the conference was able to proceed only by essentially ignoring the differences over the participation issue was a harbinger of things to come on this front. Although the participants would attempt to deal with the problem many times, they could not succeed in devising a formula whereby the negotiations could be expanded to include Europe's neutral states. On the eve of the Ottawa Conference the issue was not seen as particularly important to the discussion of the practical aspects of the regime. But the changes under way in Europe would force many to revisit their original policies. Unfortunately, the difference over Cyprus would block all attempts at compromise.

### Relationship of Open Skies to the Conventional Forces in Europe Treaty (CFE)

Here, once again, France differed with its allies. In particular, Paris wished to see the Open Skies Treaty specifically mention the relevance of Open Skies as a verification mechanism for the emerging CFE Treaty. As one French official stated, "CFE must take into account Open Skies, because the overflights in CFE would likely be the same, except perhaps in terms of the request-overflight delay and other rules. Although we accept the need to discuss Open Skies on a separate basis, there is a link that needs to be defined."[36] Although it might appear that a desire to link Open Skies to both the thirty-five-nation CSCE negotiations and the twenty-three-nation CFE talks was a bit schizophrenic, it should be remembered that France also wanted to include the neutrals in the

CFE process. Thus, the attempt to make Open Skies a CSCE process, and then link it to the CFE was at least partially motivated by a broader desire to expand the CFE process and then subsume it within the CSCE negotiations.[37]

Not surprisingly, the United Sates resisted this attempt. In addition to its traditional concerns over the application of either CSCE or CFE measures to U.S. territory, Washington sought to craft an Open Skies regime without any reference to a particular arms control regime because such references might serve to limit Open Skies to that regime.[38] The United States wanted to be free to use the results of Open Skies overflights to assist in the verification of a variety of arms control treaties (START and the emerging Chemical Weapons Convention were often discussed in this regard), as well as for other purposes.

Moreover, Open Skies was not seen by Washington as a verification measure, although its utility to verification was obvious, but rather as a regime with a variety of purposes. As the head of the U.S. delegation to Open Skies would say on the eve of the Ottawa Conference:

> The results of Open Skies will be available to all the participants for any use they want, including understanding the forces remaining in Europe after the CFE. We have not seen—NATO has not seen—Open Skies as a verification regime, we've seen it much more as a broad confidence building measure and as a complement to whatever specific measures you could have in the CFE.[39]

## Quotas

The difficult political questions of participation and of the relationship of the Open Skies regime to the CFE Treaty had their practical counterpart in the discussions of the quota structure of the regime.[40] Once again, the main protagonists were the French and the Americans, although several others also had questions about the quota structure.

The U.S. straw man paper argued that geography be the principal unit in the development of a quota structure for the regime.[41] Based on their desire to receive no more than one overflight per week, the Americans had divided the yearly number of flights they were prepared to accept (fifty-two) by the total size of their country and come up with a proposal that each country accept one overflight for every seventy thousand square miles of territory. As Hawes would explain on the eve of the Ottawa Conference:

> Obviously the quotas of flights will be a subject for the negotiations. We have put out a ballpark figure. We have said that, for the purposes of calculation, we would be prepared to receive one flight per week. And then have projected that across all the

other initial participants on the basis of their geography and pro-rated up and down . . . working off of a hypothetical standard of one flight per week over the United States.[42]

It is important to note that this figure was not based on a "scientific" assessment of the number of flights that would be required to monitor particular types of events, but rather on an assessment of how many overflights the United States was prepared to accept before they became too much of a nuisance.[43] There was thus no definition of exactly why these overflights were taking place, beyond the general "increase in confidence" rationale. This fact would be important in the negotiations, as the USSR would advance far lower quota proposals, and the NATO countries would be hard pressed to explain why it was so important to stick to their own, higher, figures. Simply put, there is no objective criterion against which one can measure the number of flights required to increase one's confidence.

In practical terms, the U.S. arithmetic had some interesting results when applied to the other potential participants. The USSR was required to accept slightly more than twice the number of overflights the United States was, while Canada would also have taken more than the U.S., based on its larger size. The totals for North America as a whole and the USSR were thus roughly equal. Everyone else could accept far fewer flights. Indeed many smaller European countries would have suffered no overflights at all, as their territory was less than seventy thousand square miles. Because of the need to ensure that all participants were subject to at least a few overflights, the United States refined its proposal to include the provision that every participant had to accept four overflights per year, regardless of size.[44]

Two problems arose from this situation.[45] First, even though the number of flights over North America was roughly equal to that over the USSR, the Soviets would have been forced to conduct more than half of their North American flights over Canada, a county of far less interest to them than the United States. Second, the fact that many of the European countries would have incurred only four flights per year, despite the fact that Europe was the most heavily armed region in the world, called into question the confidence-building utility of Open Skies in this area.

It also presented some European countries with a problem in that their right to perform a high number of overflights over the USSR and its allies (their active quota) would have been linked in some way to the number of flights they were compelled to receive (their passive quota). There was a general agreement within NATO that the active and passive quota entitlements should be linked.[46] Accordingly, several European countries sought means of increasing their passive quotas in order to increase their potential active quota. One conceptual tool that was examined was the idea of using some combination of territorial size and military strength as the triggering mechanism for an overflight, at least in the European area.[47] The Europeans also argued that overflights of a much greater duration would be required to adequately cover very large countries than those necessary to cover the small European states.[48]

However, the allies were divided on the rather basic question of whether active and passive quotas should be reflected in the treaty, or just the passive quota.[49] Canada and the United States argued that the treaty should seek only to outline passive quotas (the number of flights each country would be obliged to accept). They believed that the allocation of passive quotas could be undertaken within each alliance. This approach would have allowed for the more technically sophisticated alliance members to conduct the majority of the flights, and share the data with the rest. It would also be much simpler to negotiate passive quotas only, rather than trying to link all of the passive and active quotas in the treaty.

France believed that both the active and passive quotas of each participant should be enshrined in the treaty.[50] The French were motivated by a fear that the establishment of only passive quotas, on the understanding that active quotas would be worked out in each alliance, would mean that the two superpowers would dominate their respective alliances. This was viewed as problematic at a time when the WTO was breaking up. And, of course, leaving the allocation of active quotas to the internal process of the two alliances would have been a de facto recognition of the primacy of the bloc-to-bloc approach that Paris was so dead set against.[51] Finally, the approach would have made it difficult to eventually integrate the neutral countries into the Open Skies quota structure because they could not have belonged to either of the blocs, and thus would have lacked a coordinating mechanism for the distribution of their active quotas.

Another aspect of the quota debate reflected the extent to which the bloc-to-bloc approach was increasingly unworkable as the WTO unraveled. The U.S. proposal had argued that states of the same alliance not be allowed to overfly each other. This was done to prevent allied countries from using up each other's passive quotas, thereby denying states of the other alliance the opportunity to overfly each other. The danger that allies might use up each other's passive quotas had been recognized by those who framed the Stockholm Document. They had agreed that they could not do so, and that agreement had been publicized in a Chairman's Statement attached to the final document.[52]

As the WTO came apart, however, it was clear that most of its members would want to overfly each other. In particular, the smaller WTO states would want to overfly the USSR.[53] Given the fact that the purpose of Open Skies was to provide its members with a sense of confidence in their neighbors, and that the increasingly independent Eastern European states harbored far greater historical fears of their soon-to-be former allies than they did of most NATO countries, the regime would not address the real security concerns of these countries if it prevented them from overflying each other. The French thus argued within the SPC that the treaty should not prohibit states of the same alliance from overflying each other.[54] Their position may have owed more to their desire to prevent the final agreement from being a bloc-to-bloc arrangement than to any obligation to the Eastern Europeans, but it was a valid point.

### The Alliance Negotiation

These differences formed the substance of the SPC's debate during the autumn in 1989. As the autumn wore on, and as the pace of change in Europe intensified, the French became more attached to their positions, while the United States could not entertain changes to its positions, lest the fragile interagency consensus be upset.[55] By early December, the structure of the disagreements was clear to all, as was their relationship to each other in political terms. But the allies were no closer to solving their disputes.

With their self-imposed ministerial deadline approaching, the allies began searching for ways out of the impasse. The deadline was seen as important in that the WTO states were aware that NATO was working on a document, and that the alliance intended to release it on the margins of the December ministerial meeting. Failure to have done so would thus have been seen as a signal that the allies were in trouble on their own initiative on the eve of the Ottawa Conference, a potentially damaging development.[56]

Finally, on the margins of the ministerial meeting, the allies reached a compromise. In return for agreement that the technical sections of the final BEP would largely reflect the U.S. view, the French insisted that a lengthy preamble be added.[57] This preamble outlined the French views with respect to the changes under way in Europe. It was also worded in such a way as to leave the door open to an evolution in the technical aspects of the BEP. In other words, the compromise that the allies reached over the political aspects of the BEP was to agree to disagree. Once the negotiations began in Ottawa, it became clear that the French and the Americans had every intention of adhering only to those sections of the BEP that accorded with their views.

Although the allies were able to publicly announce their position on schedule, the BEP was essentially a document that papered over the cracks. The twin facts that many of the BEP's technical aspects (such as the timelines section) would be seen as unworkable once the technical negotiations began in earnest, and that the allies harbored significant political differences, hardly augured well for the upcoming negotiation. Indeed, they reflected the fact that the speed with which Open Skies had been brought from concept to negotiation had not allowed sufficient time to overcome these very basic differences.

### The Emerging Soviet Position

As the NATO Basic Elements Paper was under debate, very little was heard from Moscow about the USSR's position. Informal contact with other WTO states, primarily Hungary, kept NATO abreast of the fact that Open Skies had come up within WTO discussions but had been passed over quickly pending the announcement of further details from NATO. Hungary tried to raise the idea at several WTO meetings through the autumn of 1989, but the Soviets did not wish to discuss it.[58] At the conclusion of a meeting of WTO deputy foreign ministers and chiefs of staff in Sofia, Bulgaria, in early November, for example, the only comment from the Soviets was to restate the relationship between Open Skies and confidence-building in space and on the seas, both known to be unacceptable to the West.[59]

To be fair, the states of the WTO had a great deal to contend with during the autumn of 1989. Governments were toppled throughout Eastern Europe during this period. Open Skies could hardly have been first on anyone's list of priorities under the circumstances. But one or two veiled signals did come in. Unfortunately, NATO was so preoccupied with its own internal deliberation that it was unable either to respond to them or to integrate the concerns into its own evolving thinking at the time. In their few public statements in the subject,[60] for example, the Soviets called for the creation of a multilateral fleet of aircraft to conduct Open Skies missions. Such a fleet, they argued could have been a cooperative confidence-building measure in itself. Moreover, the fact that the aircraft could be jointly maintained would ensure that illegal sensors were not secretly placed on board, thus obviating the need for lengthy preflight inspections. As a part of the multilateral approach, the Soviets advocated that all data be processed by the central organization and be made available to all participants.[61]

Interestingly, however, during the extensive consultations undertaken in late 1989 by Canadian officials in Eastern Europe, the Non–Soviet Warsaw Pact (NSWP) countries failed to enthusiastically parrot the emerging Soviet line.[62] While a few of them put forward novel ideas of their own, the mere fact that they allowed the Soviet positions to go completely unsupported was a dramatic indication of the changes under way in Eastern Europe.

A more troubling Soviet position was Moscow's call for the right to overfly all of the military bases of regime participants, even if they were located in third countries that were not members of the regime.[63] This would mean, for example, that American bases in countries such as the Philippines and Japan would be subject to overflights by Soviet aircraft. The Soviets maintained that such a provision was a necessary one in that the equipment at the U.S. bases in these countries was targeted against the USSR.[64]

This position was rejected by the NATO nations. They argued that they did not have the right to negotiate overflight rights on behalf of sovereign nations that would not be a part of the negotiation. Interestingly, the Soviets were isolated in this position within their own alliance.[65] Moreover, some years later Western officials would learn that the Soviet military had been the champion of this stand in the interest of putting an utterly unacceptable position on the table in order to derail the Open Skies talks.[66] Indeed, the Soviets had asked their own allies outside of the territorial scope of Open Skies (Cuba and Vietnam) in which Moscow had bases if they would accept the same types of overflights as Moscow was insisting upon over U.S. bases in Japan and the Philippines. These countries said that they would not accept such flights under any circumstances.[67] Thus, had the West agreed to this Soviet position in 1989, Moscow would have been acutely embarrassed.

The NATO countries failed to heed these Soviet pronouncements in the autumn of 1989. To the extent that they were examined, many believed that they were largely opening positions in what was to be a difficult negotiation. As Noble would later say:

> We had, of course, heard about the Soviet bureaucracy's positions prior to [the] Ottawa [Conference] .... [T]hese discussions had revealed a cautious approach, which had sought to raise more questions than it answered. I should stress, however, that these contacts were few and, when juxtaposed with the enthusiasm displayed by politicians, such as ... Shevardnadze, we felt that they were negotiating tactics rather

than a true insight into Soviet thinking on the issues. During the negotiations . . . we found that we were wrong.[68]

The statements that were made by representatives of the USSR during the autumn of 1989 were accurate reflections of the positions which that country would take and hold fiercely once the negotiations began. To a large extent, the failure of the NATO countries to recognize the fact that the Soviets were serious in their statements may have been a reflection of the fact that they were so busy discussing their own position that they failed to use the opportunity for prenegotiation in the weeks leading to the Ottawa Conference.

Throughout the autumn of 1989 the opportunity to at least partially rectify the situation would be missed as the need of one of the alliances (NATO) to attempt to attain internal cohesion would dominate. This left the discussions over the conference procedures and protocol as the one opportunity to seriously come to grips with some sort of prenegotiation. But even this was not to be. Instead of the usual lengthy discussions over such questions as the division of costs, the procedures and matters of protocol,[69] the Canadian hosts simply decided much of it either unilaterally or with very little consultation.

This extraordinary departure from normal conference practice was the result of two factors.[70] First, if the opening date of early February 1990 was to be met, the schedule was so tight that extensive negotiations over the procedures were not believed to be possible. Second, in order to avoid last-minute difficulties over what were seen in Ottawa as largely peripheral issues, the Canadians decided to pay the entire cost of the Ottawa Conference. Because they were paying, the Canadians felt "entitled to take certain liberties"[71] in order to speed the process along. While this step may have kept up the momentum, it robbed the participants of the chance to discuss substantive differences under the guise of procedural negotiations. The Canadian desire to force the pace, which had been important to the development and survival of the Open Skies idea, hindered the achievement of a proper prenegotiation.

Of course, some discussion of the procedures was undertaken. But this was more in the nature of bilateral consultation as Canadian officials traveled to the various capitals to brief the participants on Canadian plans for the conference. These plans were arrived at as a result of an examination of the basic rules of procedure of the CSCE and CFE conferences, which were adapted by the Canadians to suit the needs of Open Skies. As Mr. Francis would later recall, "Although the Open Skies Conference was not formally linked to the CSCE process, the fact that all prospective participants were familiar with these rules was thought likely to make them acceptable."[72] The exact procedures and their impact on the efficiency of the conference will be reviewed in the next chapter, but the point to be made here is that they were never really discussed at any length prior to the start of the negotiations.

While the goal of avoiding last-minute complications during the countdown to the conference was thus met, the final chance for any prenegotiation was eliminated. The only multilateral preparatory meeting to take place before the Ottawa Conference was a three-day meeting in Budapest from January 30 to February 1.[73] The organizational arrangements made by Mr. Francis were agreed without substantial comment at this meeting.[74] Once again, however, the Soviets held firm to their positions on aircraft ownership, sensors, data-sharing, and third-country bases.[75] It was thus clear that the Soviets intended to maintain a hard line. Nevertheless, even after the preparatory meeting, Western officials continued to believe that the USSR's stance was primarily a tactical one.[76]

Interestingly, a number of participants at the Budapest meeting pointed out that arms control negotiations "usually required several years" to prepare and complete.[77] By the time of the preparatory meeting, however, the Canadians and the Hungarians had announced that they expected the treaty to be signed by May 12, 1990—exactly one year after President Bush had announced the Open Skies initiative. The setting of such an ambitious deadline is an interesting example of both the speed with which the initiative was moving and the extent to which its champions believed it would ultimately prove acceptable.[78]

The May 12 deadline was suggested by Lysyshyn in October for purely symbolic reasons and quickly endorsed by his superiors. It reflected the belief of the Canadians that the Open Skies negotiation would be relatively trouble free once the serious bargaining began.[79] The Hungarians quickly endorsed the one-year deadline, and the two announced it to their partners. On the whole the other countries did not demur, but there were no extravagant statements of agreement either. Months later, when the Budapest negotiating round was only three days old and in obvious trouble, Karpov would criticize the deadline as having been "not reasonable" from the start.[80]

The fact that a deadline had been tentatively set for a negotiation even before the negotiation began is somewhat singular. Usually, deadlines are not set until the negotiation is advanced, and the structure of the required trade-offs is both clear and acceptable to all. Certain types of negotiations have deadlines at the outset, but these are often negotiations that are begun in response to a political crisis which must be resolved by a certain point. If the setting of a deadline marks the shift to the beginning of the end-game of a negotiation, it seems clear that the organizers of the Ottawa Conference believed the negotiation would begin with the end-game. This indicates the extent to which they felt that the technical issues of the regime could be solved quickly, and that the political differences were largely tactical rather than real.

Although it did not ultimately kill the Open Skies negotiation, the setting of an unrealistic deadline, which was then not met, did contribute to a sense of failure after the Budapest Conference that was greater than it might have been otherwise. Then again, the fact that Canada announced dates for the beginning of the negotiation prior to extensive prenegotiations was itself something of a departure from the norm.

### Other Initiatives

While the BEP was under debate, other activities took place in support of Open Skies. Two of these in particular were to have a significant impact upon subsequent negotiations. Canada's trial overflight of Hungary, which took place on January 6, 1990, was to prove conclusively that NATO's concept of flight operations would not pose obstacles to air safety. Secondly, the draft treaty text, initiated by Canada and then taken over as a cooperative Canada-U.S. project, meant that the ensuing negotiations were provided with a single negotiating text, and forced the alliance to further refine its ideas.

The trial overflight idea arose during the Workshop on Open Skies held in November. Discussions on the margins of the workshop sought ways in which the initiative might be advanced prior to the Ottawa Conference. The idea of a trial overflight was suggested by the Hungarian participant.[81] The announced purpose of the flight was to test the potential impact of short-notice overflights on air traffic control in Europe.[82] This was only partly true; concerns about the impact of Open Skies on air traffic control had largely been laid to rest by late autumn. The larger reason for the flight was that it was felt that a demonstration would have a dramatic public impact—especially on the eve of the conference. It was quickly agreed that an unarmed Canadian Armed Forces aircraft would stage a trial overflight in early January 1990. It was also agreed that the aircraft would carry no sensors.[83]

Because this was the first flight, the planning was more cooperative than it was anticipated would be the case under an actual regime. A complicated flight route was deliberately chosen, one that cut in and out of military areas normally off limits to civilian air traffic. Two of the military bases to be overflown were not Hungarian, but Soviet bases in Hungary. Interestingly, the Hungarians did not ask Moscow's permission. Indeed, the Soviets received final confirmation that the flight was going ahead from the Canadian ambassador in Moscow.[84] The flight demonstrated conclusively that existing air traffic control procedures could easily cope with the demands of Open Skies with only slight modifications,[85] though this was already known. The test also validated NATO's approach to Open Skies, proving that a multilateral fleet of aircraft was not necessary from the point of view of flight safety. Finally, the first ever surveillance flight by a NATO military aircraft over a WTO nation generated a high degree of media interest, which had always been a primary purpose of the exercise.[86]

The Soviets, however, were not impressed. Despite the fact that the Canadians and the Hungarians had given a glowing briefing on their experience, the Soviet head of delegation at the Budapest preparatory meeting reported:

> Many difficulties of a technical nature emerged during the (Canadian-Hungarian) test flight . . . . Most significant of these were the system and methods of checking apparatus aboard an aircraft, the procedure for notification of observation flights, and coordination of the system for gathering and processing the information so that neither side gains an advantage.[87]

The draft treaty was another example of the Canadians forcing the pace. As the BEP was going through various drafts during September and October, the task of keeping track of dozens of suggestions being made on each item became increasingly difficult. Purely for my own organizational clarification, I decided to draw up a matrix of proposals on each subject and update it continuously as decisions were made. This having been done, it was a relatively simple matter to convert each of the proposals into treaty-type language. Finally, I began to add ideas of my own to the existing proposals with the encouragement of my superiors.[88] Thus was born, in the space of a few days, a draft treaty text. The text was passed around to the officials within the Canadian government working on Open Skies for their comments.[89] By the end of November, the draft was in its fifth revised edition as various government departments submitted comments and decisions reached in Brussels were incorporated. For the officials who would subsequently represent Canada, the process was a particularly useful one, as they would enter the negotiations possessing some experience of translating various proposals into legal text.[90]

Canada indicated to the United States that it had developed a draft treaty. Those in Washington keen to advance Open Skies were enthusiastic, while others argued that the alliance should go into the first conference with the BEP in order to elicit a Soviet response to that.[91] Canada replied that, as host, it would prefer to see a draft treaty introduced to give the gathering a single negotiating text to organize its work around. Ottawa indicated that it would prefer to table a fully agreed NATO draft treaty, but was prepared go alone if required.[92] Lysyshyn and Noble thus used the fact that Canada had an almost complete text to pressure Washington to move on to what the Canadians regarded as the next logical step in the development of the idea.

Shortly thereafter, the United States suggested that Canada and the U.S. work together to develop a draft.[93] Canada gave its draft to the United States in mid-November to serve as a basis for discussion. Messages and suggestions went back and forth between Ottawa and Washington throughout December, and the U.S. prepared its own draft. This process culminated with two meetings in Washington in early January during which the two sides developed a joint draft. On January 17, the two sides agreed on a joint text that substantively reflected the points in the earlier Canadian draft, though the U.S. legal team had insisted on a more stringent, less flexible text.

The final draft was thus more detailed than the original Canadian version.[94] The United States insisted upon spelling out rights and obligations for all possible contingencies. In some respects not all of the detail was welcome. The Canadians, for example, had argued that a degree of flexibility should exist in areas such as mission planning in order to allow the flight crew and host-country controllers to decide among themselves the best way of meeting the requirements of the flight. The Canadians believed that such flexibility would permit the planners to overcome in a cooperative manner such last-minute problems as air congestion or bad weather.[95] The United States saw this approach leading to an endless series of negotiations prior to each flight. Perhaps because of their experience dealing with the Soviets in other arms control regimes, the Americans believed it best to spell out every right and obligation in detail to prevent ambiguities over what could or could not be done.[96] Canadian protestations that it would be impossible to provide for every contingency in advance, because each flight could take place in different weather, produced some changes in the text. But the final text was still very detailed.

In many respects the different styles to the two drafts reflected the different approaches of the two nations to Open Skies.[97] The Canadian draft was shaped something like a statement of fundamental principles and guidelines reflecting the manner in which the regime would work, but which could be interpreted as experience was accumulated. The Americans wanted a firm, all-encompassing statement of rules that would not be subject to revision or interpretation by the operators on an ongoing basis.

But this difference over the draft text also reflected a fundamental divergence of view on the approach that the two wanted to take into the negotiations. The Canadians were prepared to begin the negotiations by putting forward a text that outlined a general formula of how the regime should work and then enter into a discussion of the details. The United States stuck rigidly to the position of their interagency process that the opening text should reflect a firm set of positions that they would then bargain over. Although it was ultimately the approach advocated by the Canadians which produced a breakthrough, it was not possible to initiate it at this time. In fairness to the Americans, once the negotiations began it would quickly become obvious that the Soviets were not ready for the approach favored by the Canadians either. The Canadian approach may well have reflected a degree of naivete as to how these types of agreements were negotiated and implemented. On the other hand, the U.S. draft reflected the fragile nature of the interagency consensus on Open Skies, and was unwieldy as a result. It also strait-jacketed the U.S. delegation in the subsequent negotiations.

The final joint text was submitted to the allies in the third week of January and enjoyed their basic approval.[98] Because of individual sensitivities over various issues, however, certain areas of the treaty were left blank. The article dealing with accession was not filled in, as all attempts to do so proved fruitless because of the Cyprus dispute.[99] Other sections were not filled in because the allies wished to see whether the WTO nations would have proposals of their own. The annex dealing with quotas was devoid of any numbers, for example. It was not possible for the allies to complete their discussion of the draft treaty in time for the opening of the Ottawa Conference, and the NATO Caucus at the conference was left with the job of finalizing it in the first week.

## CONCLUSION

The experience of bringing Open Skies from vague proposal to agreed alliance position, to largely agreed Allied draft treaty on the eve of a major international conference, lasted nine months. Given the pace at which these types of processes usually occur, this was very rapid progress indeed. But the same speed that enabled Open Skies to run a gauntlet of internal U.S. opposition and alliance differences meant that some difficult questions were either deliberately bypassed or inadvertently overlooked.

Moreover, things happened so quickly, and at such a dynamic moment in the history of postwar Europe, that there was virtually no prenegotiation between the members of the two blocs. Those signals that were sent by Moscow were often contradictory ones. The Soviet Union's political leaders gave rhetorical support for Open Skies, while its bureaucratic officials were far more cautious.

Had they not been so preoccupied with their own internal deliberations, the NATO countries might have given more consideration to the troubling discrepancies emanating from Moscow. As it was, the NATO nations were so busy attempting to sort out their own positions on the various issues that a detailed consideration of what the Russians were saying was never undertaken. This shortcoming is not unique to the preparations for the Open Skies conference. During the period leading up to the bilateral U.S.-USSR SALT talks, for example, the internal, interagency debate that raged within the U.S. government was almost entirely inward looking. As Newhouse reports, "Little of the preparation for SALT had much reference to Moscow's attitudes . . . . The concern was not what might be negotiated with Moscow, but what could be negotiated within the Pentagon."[100]

Furthermore, though the NATO nations may have appeared to present a unified approach to Open Skies, and in many respects did, a significant degree of latent discord existed over several aspects of the proposal. The BEP papered over the cracks on a number of important issues, such as participation by the neutral countries of Europe. Indeed, it is doubtful if the negotiation would have begun in February of 1990 had not the Canadians come up with the rules of procedure and paid the cost in order to avoid the need to settle the participation question prior to the beginning of the conference. This, in itself, was something of a departure from the norm of international conferences, which routinely begin with an intensive negotiation over a set of agreed rules of participation prior to the start of the conference. This matter, and the participation of the neutral countries of Europe, would become the subject of a growing controversy as the negotiations unfolded.

While all sixteen NATO allies agreed with the principle that transparency was good in itself, significantly different objectives would surface over what this transparency was to be in aid of. This difference was exposed during the upcoming negotiations. The French would return to the charge on all of their concerns without delay once the negotiations began in earnest. The fragility of the U.S. internal consensus on Open Skies meant that their delegation was to have difficulty in adapting its positions to the dynamics of the negotiation.

Once again, it is legitimate to argue that the initiative was brought to full negotiations far too quickly. In retrospect, it is quite true that the time devoted to prenegotiation between the alliances, and even within them, was extremely limited. This resulted in the USSR arriving at the Ottawa Conference with a fundamentally different concept of the operation and purpose of the regime. But even the NATO allies had some differences. While these shortcomings in the preparation of the Ottawa Conference are quite obvious, however, one should be careful before laying too much blame on those who pushed a short timetable. It seems clear that many interests within the U.S. intelligence community were quite prepared to allow Open Skies to die a quiet death after President Bush had proposed it at Texas A&M. Although they could not openly oppose a presidential initiative, they were in no hurry to embrace it either. The one thing they could do was to use the intricacies of the U.S. interagency decision-making system to ensure that the U.S. delegation arrived in Ottawa with a hard-line, rigid position and a requirement to refer all requests for modification back to the interagency process.

Those whose exuberance for the idea pushed it along at breakneck speed may well have been guilty of bringing the idea to the negotiation stage before sufficient groundwork had been done to ensure its success. But, one may fairly ask, would the initiative have reached negotiations at all had its champions not forced the pace? Indeed, some doubt may be entertained as to whether it would have been embraced by the president had not the Canadians championed the cause. Once the initiative was launched, the skepticism of many in the U.S. government deepened and had to be overcome. Forcing the pace, as the Canadians did over the summer and autumn of 1989, was one means of compelling the U.S. bureaucracy to engage in the development of a position. Certainly, those within the U.S. bureaucracy who favored Open Skies quietly encouraged the Canadians during this period to keep the pressure on as a means of forcing their own internal process to come up with a position.[101]

Thus, if there were any over-riding reasons why the initiative was able to survive its critical initial period they probably had to do with the twin facts that the president had publicly linked himself to it, and that it had an external champion willing to expend the capital to keep the pressure on once the political heat of the announcement began to fade. Unless both of these conditions had existed, it is possible that the initiative might not have been launched, or that it might have died within the U.S. security bureaucracy when attention focused elsewhere.

Whatever the case may be, the shortcomings of the process by which the initiative was brought to the table were to become very obvious as the Ottawa and Budapest conferences unfolded. In particular, the lack of an agreed basic conception of the purpose of the proposed regime, both between and within several delegations, meant that the negotiation was to suffer from a lack of agreed goals. This, in turn, meant that it quickly degenerated into an argument over widely differing positions.

# 4 The Ottawa and Budapest Conferences

The Ottawa Conference began on February 12, 1990. The ministers arrived the day before, and the North Atlantic Treaty Organization (NATO) ministers spent part of the evening in an alliance caucus. The primary focus of their attention had been on Conventional Forces in Europe (CFE) issues. A select group of ministers and their senior staffs were also working secretly on the question of German reunification and would announce a breakthrough formula in Ottawa. The breakthrough on the German reunification question would be the event for which the conference would be most remembered.[1]

Attention turned to Open Skies the next morning, however, as the ministers began making their public statements. All of the statements made reference to the revolutionary changes that had swept Europe in the autumn of 1989.[2] They also praised the Open Skies initiative as a dramatic indication of the new direction of European security affairs. But the speeches were more interesting for their differences than their similarities.

The U.S. Secretary of State, James Baker, stressed the need for an open, effective and workable regime. He then went on to argue that effectiveness meant "openness even at night, or on cloudy days, and that meant the right to use any technology that will do the job, understanding that these devices can be inspected by the country being overflown."[3] Workability, in Baker's view, meant "[no] unwieldy bureaucracies . . . . If countries want to share resources, that would be fine. If they want to fly their own unarmed aircraft . . . that is also fine."[4] Baker's comments were obviously in line with the NATO Basic Elements Paper (BEP). All of the NATO foreign ministers would echo his sentiments over the technical issues in their opening remarks to the Open Skies conference.

The only significant differences among the NATO countries regarding national position over any specific aspect of Open Skies came from France and Turkey. The French foreign minister spent a considerable portion of his speech arguing that "the Open Skies negotiations should not define a new state equilibrium from alliance to alliance" but should offer "the opportunity of concluding national commitments that reflect the wish of each state to foster transparency and reduce tension."[5] He then made a strong plea that the negotiations be opened up to all members of the Conference on Security and Cooperation in Europe (CSCE) process: "All the European countries have the task of participating in this vast movement (Open Skies) . . . the neutral and non-aligned as well . . . . On what basis could one possibly deny them the right?"[6]

The Turkish minister outlined his concerns regarding the expansion of the regime to include the other CSCE states. While agreeing in principle to such expansion, he warned that it would have to wait until "after the regime is well established" and that "the decision to invite them (must be) taken on a case by case basis and by consensus."[7] This was an obvious reference to Cyprus, and Turkey's desire to ensure that the Greek-Cypriot government not be accorded the position of sole representative of the island.

The Soviet foreign minister, Eduard Shevardnadze, after calling for negotiations on naval confidence-building (Open Seas) and increased transparency in outer space (Open Space), laid out the Soviet view of the essential characteristics of an Open Skies regime:

> The Open Skies regime must rest on the principle of comprehensive and full equality—equality in the acquisition of, and access to, information which must not be used to the detriment of any of the sides; equality as regards the area of application of the regime covering the state's military activities not only on their national territories but also outside; equality as regards flight quotas, the use of airplanes and monitoring and data processing equipment.[8]

Although seemingly innocuous, this statement outlined the wide gulf separating the Soviet delegation from many others. Shevardnadze was calling for a pool of equal aircraft, overflights of military bases belonging to regime participants but located in third countries, and a uniform data-processing capability. These views were diametrically opposed to the type of regime outlined in the NATO BEP.[9]

Interestingly, Shevardnadze's Warsaw Treaty Organization (WTO) colleagues failed to back him up. Instead, they put forward their own views and concerns. In sum, these concerns were: that the regime's benefits be equally available to all participants regardless to their technical capabilities; that the regime be as cost effective as possible; and that the regime treat all of its participants as sovereign states, rather than as members of blocs.[10] The Hungarian foreign minister was the last of the WTO ministers to speak. At the conclusion of his speech he tabled a WTO version of NATO's Basic Elements Paper.[11]

The WTO BEP came under intensive scrutiny by the NATO delegations. One of their first conclusions was, as Noble later stated, that "the document had some internal inconsistencies."[12] In particular, the document appeared to be at odds with several of the statements made by the Soviet foreign minister. Where Shevardnadze had insisted upon the right to overfly bases in countries, the WTO BEP merely said that:

> Given the occurrences of military operations outside the national territories, those participating countries with military bases abroad would enter into negotiations, as far as possible while the agreement is still being worked out, with the aim of deciding whether the regime should extend to their military bases in third countries not participating in the regime, with the agreement of those countries.[13]

This was less categorical than Mr. Shevardnadze's statement. In later conversations, NATO delegates were informed that the other members of the WTO had insisted that this language be inserted in place of the much stronger Soviet views. NATO delegations were also to learn that the WTO had tried to develop its own treaty text but had been unable to do so because of the differences between the USSR and the rest.[14]

The WTO BEP fed a misunderstanding of the depth of the Soviet's commitment to their positions that existed within the NATO delegations.[15] Many allied delegations still believed that the Soviets would soon compromise once the hard bargaining began.[16] The fact that the WTO BEP appeared to lay less emphasis upon the inclusion of the right to overfly bases in third countries seemed to back this up. Once the extent to which the WTO BEP was out of step with the realities of the Soviet position became known, however, the document "was quickly forgotten in the ensuing negotiations."[17]

But the fact that this confusion could have existed at all seems to indicate that the dissolution of the WTO was, even at its early stage, adding to the complexity of the situation. One of the solutions to the problem of complexity in multilateral negotiations is the ability of the more powerful members to influence the outcome through the use of sheer power. The Soviets, however, were unable to use their power to force their erstwhile allies to accept a common position. Of course, one could argue that the WTO was in the process of dissolving at this time. It might therefore be expected that differences would exist in the positions of its members.

But such an explanation does not adequately address the situation. Up until the late 1980s, for example, the USSR did not seem to have any difficulty in using its power to command consensus within the WTO. Moreover, the military power of the USSR relative to that of its allies was the same in 1989 as it had been for many years. What had changed by 1989 were the conceptions of legitimate use of power as a tool of coercion within the WTO. Gorbachev himself had allowed, and even encouraged, the sweeping liberalizations that had so altered the European landscape in the autumn of 1989.[18]

If one has eschewed many aspects of the use of power, as the USSR had done in its relations with its allies by 1989, power becomes a far less effective tool in a diplomatic setting. The existence of power in itself, then, is not the determining factor in calculations of its utility as a force for order in complex negotiations. What really matters is whether those against whom the power could be used really believe that it will be should they step out of line. In this case, the primary variable was whether absolute Warsaw Treaty Organization cohesion in the Open Skies negotiations was sufficiently important to the USSR in early 1990, given everything else that was going on in Europe at the time, that Moscow was willing to use its power against its increasingly independently minded allies. The answer was, clearly not.

Of course, the USSR's bargaining power remained intact in one important sense, despite the fact that Moscow could no longer command a favorable consensus within the WTO. As other delegations were soon to learn, it did not really matter that the Soviet delegation stood alone; their positions on the key issues remained unchanged. In other words, the USSR's ability to use its power in a proactive sense, to make others conform to its will on Open Skies, was considerably diminished by the beginning of 1990. But its ability to use its power in a negative sense, to prevent the signature of a treaty that did not conform to its conception of its interests, remained. So long as one of the key goals of the regime was to open up the USSR to overflights, the Soviets were in a position of considerable, if largely negative, power.

Another issue that affected the negotiations at this early point was the psychological inability of negotiators to recognize evolving situations. The ability to internalize subtle and complex messages can be eroded by a desire to impose order on a chaotic situation. In this case, the NATO nations failed to recognize that the WTO BEP was a document that suffered from considerable internal tensions in the same sense as their own BEP had been. This fact may have led to the confusion that the WTO BEP caused.

NATO diplomats largely failed to recognize that the "internal inconsistencies" of the WTO BEP were not signals of a Soviet willingness to consider more "realistic" positions, but evidence of the inconsistencies that the increasingly moribund WTO was experiencing in coming to a unified position. Conditioned by a lengthy history of watching the WTO achieve unified positions, NATO diplomats were unable to accept that a paper bearing the signatures of all of the members of that alliance was not, in fact, the view of any of them; that they would produce a document that papered over the cracks in exactly the same way NATO's had. The WTO BEP was the dying gasp of that organization so far as Open Skies was concerned, and it reflected such a torturous mixture of incompatible positions that it was bound to raise questions unless understood through this prism.

## THE COMMUNIQUE

The confusion did not last long. As the ministerial speeches were under way, senior officials met in seclusion to consider a communique on Open Skies to be issued by the ministers. Although a communique was not absolutely necessary, the NATO countries were keen to have one for two reasons.[19] First, a communique would provide an outline for the negotiations from the highest political level. Second, NATO diplomats felt that they could get Mr. Shevardnadze to agree on an ambitious communique, since he was known to sometimes get ahead of his bureaucrats. Hard-liners within the Soviet delegation would then have great difficulty in repudiating his position once the discussion began over the details of the regime. This tactical decision had been taken by the NATO delegations on the eve of the conference.[20]

If there were any hopes about the USSR's willingness to consider compromises, they were quickly dashed during the negotiations over the communique.[21] These negotiations began early on the afternoon of the 12th of February. A draft text was tabled by the NATO countries, and it was recognized that a communique would have to be agreed by the afternoon of the next day, as many of the ministers would be leaving. Although they did not know it as they gathered, the delegates would be in session until three o'clock the next morning and their efforts would not produce an agreed text. As Noble would later write:

> It was during the negotiations over the communiqué that we got our first substantive look at Soviet officials' attitude toward Open Skies. We also got our first look at how the new dynamic of the WTO would play out at an international conference. In both cases, the results were fascinating . . . . Before our eyes we saw the Warsaw Treaty Organization dissolve during negotiations among officials over the communiqué.[22]

The Soviet representatives in the communique discussions adopted a hard line on all of the substantive issues.[23] They insisted on a primitive sensor suite, consisting of cameras with very low resolution capabilities. They insisted on a data-sharing agreement and a common data-processing facility. They refused to back down over the issues of bases in third countries. To this end, the Soviets presented draft texts on each of these points, and requested that it be included in the chairman's text in brackets.[24] The Soviet positions were rejected by the allies, who were surprised at the vehemence with which the Soviet delegation argued its position.[25]

Equally surprising, however, "was the extent to which the Soviets were essentially isolated in their positions."[26] The other members of the WTO did not remain silent; they joined the criticism that the NATO nations were heaping upon the Soviets.[27] During the discussion of overflights in third countries, for example, the Romanian made an impassioned statement that the idea of assessing an obligation against a sovereign country that was not a party to the negotiation was contrary to all norms of international law. He concluded by stating that such a discussion would be viewed by Romania as a gross insult were it a country so affected.[28]

As the discussions dragged into the evening, the non-Soviet WTO members outlined a common position on several issues. Their stand had been alluded to by their ministers, but this was the first time it had been discussed in any depth. Basically, these countries were prepared to accept the NATO BEP in its entirety, but they had certain conditions. Essentially, they were worried that the regime would prove vastly discriminatory unless they were guaranteed access to sensor systems of a much higher quality than those to which they had access at the time.[29]

The NATO countries were quick to notice this. Sensing an opportunity to further isolate the Soviets, a tentative deal on sensors was proposed at around ten in the evening.[30] The deal called for an agreed sensor package, including a day/night, all-weather capability, to be made available to all. The package would have been far more capable than the Soviets had indicated they were prepared to accept, but not so capable as the NATO nations would have been able to use had they been left with unrestricted sensor capabilities. Although many did not know it at the time, this proposal was not without its own difficulties. The question of what constitutes an equal sensor capability is difficult to define in purely technical terms. Such definitions can be manipulated to preserve an advantage. This fact would become apparent later.

Nevertheless, the NATO countries were prepared to accept the idea in principle if it locked the Soviets into a day/night, all-weather sensor capability. The Soviet Foreign Ministry official present was also prepared to accept it, and it looked as though a major issue might be tentatively agreed. As soon as they received a translation of what had been a fast-moving conversation in English, however, the Soviet military representatives in the room (who were arrayed behind the diplomat and soon became known among the NATO participants in the discussions as the "nyet chorus") vetoed the deal. Accordingly, the NATO countries went back to their position in unrestricted sensors.[31]

Not all the discussions pitted the Soviet delegation against the rest. On the question of the future membership of the regime, the French insisted that reference to accession by the CSCE countries be included. This raised the Cyprus issue. The Greek delegate insisted that all CSCE members be entitled to join en masse, without the possibility of veto. The Turks argued that each member of the CSCE would have to apply separately, and insisted that all regime members have a right of veto over each application.[32] Such a mechanism would have given them the ability to refuse any request from the Greek-Cypriot government, unless the largely unrecognized Turk-Cypriot government were also allowed to join. These positions were to be the foundation of the debate over membership in the regime for the next three years. Debate over this issue took up considerable time that evening, and was thoroughly inconclusive.[33]

When the meeting broke up at three on the morning of the 13th, the text contained brackets around all of the major points. Even the language thanking the Canadian government for organizing the conference was bracketed.[34] The chair had asked all delegations to consider possible compromises and had suggested a meeting for eleven that morning. This meeting was a very brief affair, as no compromises were suggested.[35]

The bracketed text was sent to ministers that afternoon. To the surprise of many, the Canadian minister asked his colleagues to tackle the issues themselves, rather than referring the text back to their officials with new instructions. As Noble later noted, "This was a considerable risk on his [the Canadian minister's] part, as the remaining differences were considerable and there was no previous experience in such a forum."[36] The ministers debated the text for nearly two and a half hours. Once again, the WTO experienced sharp differences. The Eastern European ministers "openly undercut the Soviet position, often suggesting compromises which essentially favored the Western position in its entirety."[37]

Unfortunately for the NATO countries, however, Shevardnadze did not take part in the exercise. He was instead involved in a series of bilateral meetings concerning the emerging "two-plus-four" arrangement for the reunification of Germany. Thus the plan of exposing him personally to the criticism of his colleagues was not realized. Shevardnanze's place was taken by the head of the Soviet Open Skies delegation, Viktor Karpov, who spent most of the afternoon looking uncomfortable at the extent of his isolation, but unmoved by it. After an hour's discussion it was clear that a text would not be agreed simply by having delegations disagree with the Soviet position. Accordingly, the chairman called a break for informal consultations.

During hasty corridor conversations a series of compromises resulted in a text that "papered over the substantive difference between the NATO and Warsaw Pact positions."[38] The communique was claimed as a victory by the NATO countries, which drew attention to the fact that the Soviets were isolated in their positions.[39] But the communique did not resolve the issues. It was drafted in such a way as to allow each side to subsequently claim support for its position. The communique stated, for example, that:

> The Open Skies regime will be implemented on a reciprocal and equitable basis which will protect the interests of each participating state . . . . The regime will ensure the maximum possible openness and minimum restrictions for observation fights.[40]

But the question remained, What exactly was an "equitable and reciprocal basis"? The Soviets claimed this meant that military bases in third countries must be included. Further, "[T]he maximum possible openness and minimum restrictions" were not agreed. The maxima and minima of the NATO countries proved to be considerably different from those of the USSR.

On practical issues, such as overflight quotas and the sensor suite, the communique was similarly uninstructive. The relevant sections read:

> Each participating state will have the right to conduct, and the obligation to receive, observation flights on the basis of annual quotas which will be determined in negotiations so as to provide for equitable coverage . . . . The agreement will have provisions concerning the right to conduct observation flights using unarmed aircraft and equipment capable in all circumstances of fulfilling the goals of the regime.[41]

Once again "equitable coverage" had not been defined. Nor had "the goals of the regime," even though these goals would set the standard for sensor resolution. One victory for the NATO nations was Karpov's acceptance of the phrase "capable in all circumstances" in relation to sensors. Although somewhat vague, this was subsequently accepted as meaning that the sensor suite must be able to operate twenty-four hours a day, and in all types of weather.[42]

The problem of "Open Seas" and "Open Space" was solved by the inclusion of the meaningless phrase "The Ministers noted further that the establishment of an Open Skies regime may promote greater openness in the future in other spheres."[43] The Soviets did not return to this theme in subsequent discussions. The question of future regime expansion was similarly sidestepped with the following: "The participating states will favorably consider the possible participation in the regime of other counties, primarily the European countries."[44]

This eventual compromise was not won before "The Greek and Turkish Foreign Ministers had an on-going discussion of the status of the Government of Cyprus which lasted 45 minutes."[45] The final compromise to obtain this formula was that the names of the neutrals in attendance as observers be listed, at the insistence of Greece. Since the list included Cyprus, the Turks insisted that they be allowed to insert the phrase "Turkey reserves her position on the status and representation of Cyprus."[46]

Thus, instead of providing the NATO countries with a favorable framework for subsequent discussions, the communique solved very little. It was subsequently quoted in the negotiation by both sides as a vindication of their positions, but the frequency of the references to it soon diminished. It was rarely quoted publicly by either side.

The communique negotiation may thus be judged a failure from the perspective of the tactics that the NATO delegations had taken into it. The final document had not tied the Soviets to a more flexible stand, nor had it been possible to use the presence of Shevardnadze to force the military members of the Soviet delegation to adopt a more flexible position.

Many of the NATO delegates privately expressed disappointment that Shevardnadze had not participated in the ministerial discussion over the communique.[47] While the timing of his other discussions had denied this possibility, it may be that it was not the tragedy many thought. It is questionable whether Shevardnadze would have been able to display any real flexibility on the issues at this stage. The Soviet military was so adamant that no ground be given that Shevardnadze might have had difficulty over-ruling the military representatives present.

The communique exercise demonstrated an unwillingness on the part of the Soviet Foreign Ministry to expend political capital over the issues. This was to puzzle and frustrate the NATO delegations.[48] Many speculated that Soviet officials could not persuade their military leaders to accept an Open Skies agreement on top of all of the other pills they had been asked to swallow on conventional arms control and German reunification. One West German diplomat stated as much when he told a Western journalist that "there (was) a need for some face saving" within the Soviet military.[49] Even the Polish foreign minister was moved to publicly, if gently, remind the NATO delegates of the need to be sensitive "to the Soviet need for some Western concession. They have already conceded so much" on other matters of European security.[50]

Shevardnadze had himself hinted at this problem in private discussions with his colleagues in Ottawa when he reportedly informed one minister that "we too are developing constituencies" capable of exerting sufficient pressure on the government to "impede its plans."[51] Not surprisingly, Karpov would echo his minister's comments in an interview at the conclusion of the Ottawa Conference when he informed Western journalists that "I cannot sell" the West's Open Skies proposals to the Soviet military.[52]

Although the full dimensions of this impasse were not completely understood as the ministers departed Ottawa, astute participants were increasingly aware of the difficulties that lay ahead. It is in this context that one may argue that having forced Shevardnadze to endure the criticism of his colleagues would have accomplished nothing, other than publicly embarrassing one of the very moderates whose influence would be crucial to realizing any hope of an eventual change in the Soviet position.

## WORKING GROUPS FORMED

Once the ministers left Ottawa the working sessions began. It had been agreed that four working groups would be established. Working Group A was "initially tasked . . . to examine three main subjects: aircraft and sensors; inspection of aircraft and equipment; and the role and status of observers on board aircraft."[53] Working Group B "was initially tasked by the Plenary to examine four main subjects: Quotas; Combined Parties; (Territorial) Scope; and Limitations (on overflights)."[54] Working Group C "was tasked to examine three main subject, namely: Flight Mission (regulations); Air Safety Rules; and Transit (flight regulations)."[55] Finally, Working Group D was asked to deal with all of the legal issues in the negotiations.[56]

The groups maintained a rigorous schedule. Groups A and D met in the morning, while B and C met in the afternoon. It had been felt that this arrangement would allow senior political representatives to attend Group A and B, which were expected to be more politically sensitive. Groups C and D were believed to contain questions that would not require political guidance. This point was validated in the subsequent discussions of the groups.[57] The meetings were simultaneous, thus permitting all of the groups to meet every day. In addition, two plenary meetings were held each week, on Wednesdays and Fridays.

As discussed in the previous chapter, this schedule had been drawn up by Canadian officials and agreed after cursory discussions. Although it reflected a desire to accomplish as much as possible in a short time, the number of meetings called for in the schedule would eventually be regarded as overwhelming. In particular, the almost constant series of meetings placed the smaller delegations under a considerable strain. This was especially difficult for the smaller members of the WTO, as they had to act as virtual independents at the conference since the WTO had fallen apart. The smaller NATO countries were also affected by this phenomenon in that they also maintained a regular schedule of alliance caucuses. The NATO heads of delegation met each morning, and the NATO caucus of each working group met daily.

The schedule also restricted the amount of time available for informal consultations. With such a wide gap between the basic viewpoints of the USSR and the rest, it was vital that time be spent exploring the issues in a noncompetitive atmosphere. The schedule militated against this, however, by forcing the delegations to spend the majority of their time in the formal atmosphere of the working groups. This put a premium on the informal sessions that did occur. Indeed, it was during these few informal sessions that the basic structure of a compromise was eventually articulated. For much of the conference, however, the structure of the talks was perceived by many who took part as a brake on the efficiency of the discussions.[58]

This question of whether the negotiations labored under an inefficient structure is important to understanding the dynamic of the Ottawa Conference. Inefficiency can affect a negotiation if it hampers the negotiators' attempts to establish a control over the centrifugal pressures present in a negotiation. These centrifugal pressures may be thought of in terms of both the numerous interrelated issues that exist in a complex negotiation, and the different national positions that are present and must be reconciled. Failure to use the available time wisely, such that the necessary trade-offs can be identified and pursued in that time, constitutes inefficiency. Moreover, excessive attention to the details of the negotiation can cloud the "big picture," thereby making the process of identifying the trade-offs even more difficult.

If measured against these criteria, however, the Open Skies conference was not actually all that inefficient. In fact, the delegations were able to identify the basic trade-offs that would be necessary to establish the regime in their, admittedly few, informal sessions. What they were unable to do was to reconcile their differing positions. The question that must be asked as one examines the record of the Ottawa and Budapest conferences, however, is this: was this inability to reconcile the trade-offs the fault of an inefficient conference structure, or was it the result of an inability (or unwillingness) on the part of key delegations to approach the necessary compromises in a realistic spirit? An in-depth analysis of the performance of the individual working groups and of the informal discussions that were held is required before this question can be answered.

The working groups soon got down to their assigned tasks. Their activities were facilitated by the tabling of the NATO draft treaty on February 16.[59] The WTO nations agreed to use it as the working text of the negotiation. This provided the subsequent discussions with a single negotiating text. The draft was largely the same as that which had been submitted to the allies by Canada and the United States in the late autumn of 1989. It had, of course, been discussed in detail by the allies, and had only been agreed the night before.[60] It was later learned that the WTO had tried to come up with its own draft treaty, but that the non-Soviet members had refused to accept Moscow's ideas and had disassociated themselves from it.[61] The Soviets subsequently tabled an extensive series of amendments to the NATO draft that had to be incorporated into a new, heavily bracketed draft. This draft was published as *Amendments to the Open Skies Draft Treaty Text, ICO-CS-063*.[62]

Within NATO, the main stumbling block to agreement on the NATO draft treaty had been the problem of the accession formula to be adopted in the treaty. France, Greece, and Turkey had argued their traditional positions with their traditional inflexibility. After many hours of discussion, it was decided to put the draft forward with a blank accession article. This was not satisfactory, but it was the only way to get the rest of the draft agreed.[63] Some fear existed that the Soviets might seize this blank to introduce mischievous accession formulas in an attempt to drive a wedge between a few badly divided NATO allies on this issue. They did not, perhaps all too aware of their own alliance unity problems.

Not all of the problems within the alliance were caused by political differences, however. The U.S. delegation had some difficulty agreeing to fill in many of the blank spaces regarding such technical issues as how long the aircraft could be inspected by the host country. This difficulty was an internal U.S. delegation matter, and reflected the ongoing dispute between the intelligence community's collectors, who wanted a short inspection of their plane when it was in a foreign country, and the protectors, who wanted the right to do a lengthy inspection of a foreign aircraft when it visited the United States. After some pressure from the chairman of the caucus, the U.S. came to an internal compromise.[64]

With the draft treaty tabled, the plenary lost no time in assigning specific articles to the various working groups. As expected, the degree to which each group made progress was tied to the extent to which the issues they had been given were of a political or technical nature. Groups C and D, for example, dealt with generic air traffic control (flight safety) and legal issues, respectively. It was thus possible for them to agree without reference to the most political questions as to the degree of openness that the final regime would feature.[65]

Those political questions that were present by implication in the work of these two groups were either avoided, or simply explored in the abstract with a view to identifying possible compromises for future political decisions.[66] Perhaps as a reflection of their nature, the atmosphere in these groups was businesslike, and even cordial. It must also be said, however, that the personalities of the two chairmen (a Czech for Group C and a Dutchman for Group D) made a considerable impact in keeping the meetings friendly and productive.[67]

Groups A and B, however, were much more difficult. Most of the decisions confronting these groups were, by implication, directly relevant to the core issues of how open the regime would be. Questions such as the list of allowed sensors and their resolution capabilities, or the number of overflights and whether they would be subject to any territorial limitations, could not be sidestepped. Although they were able to identify and discuss the basic issues, these groups made relatively little progress toward resolving them in Ottawa.[68] Interestingly, the basic character of the two chairmen was quite different. The Canadian chairman of Group A was a dynamic individual, who continually attempted to stimulate his group's sometimes lethargic performance. By contrast, the Bulgarian chairman of Group B was content to allow his charges to fail to find their own way without much guidance on his part.[69] The fact that neither group made a great deal more progress than the other would seem to indicate that the problems faced by these groups were not capable of resolution by a particular type of chairmanship.

Of course, it could be argued that the issues faced by the two groups were completely different, and, thus, that such comparisons are not valid. This is true in a purely technical sense but misses the essential point. Although the questions related to the selection of sensors and the distribution of quotas were quite different, the underlying cause of the dispute in each case was a basic political difference over the purpose of the regime under negotiation.

## THE ISSUES

By the end of the Ottawa Conference the technical issues were well understood, as were the divisions between the participants. There were generally agreed to be five main issues, but it was recognized that they were highly interrelated. The five were overflight quotas; the territorial scope of the eventual regime; the aircraft ownership question; how capable the sensors would be; and whether data-sharing would occur on a voluntary or a mandated basis.[70] Each of these will be discussed, as will the differences between the USSR and the rest, and some of the subtle differences that emerged within the NATO alliance.

### Quotas

Based upon the U.S. willingness to accept one flight per week, the flights had been calculated using geography as a guide. The NATO states called for considerably more than one hundred flights per year over the USSR. But many of the European allies were not satisfied with the smaller number of flights they would be able to perform under a formula based solely on geographical considerations. Accordingly, they indicated a willingness to accept a higher number of flights than required under a strictly geographical formula. The larger European allies (France, West Germany, Italy, Spain, Turkey, and the UK) had all indicated a willingness to receive between ten and sixteen overflights per year. Most other countries were prepared to receive four to six flights per year.[71]

The Soviets indicated that they were prepared to receive fifteen flights per year.[72] Although they criticized the USSR for its unwillingness to accept a higher passive quota, the difference reflected a conceptual difference over the basic purposes of the regime. Essentially, the Soviets maintained that the fundamental purpose of the Open Skies regime was to allow participants to increase their level of confidence that surprise military activities were not in preparation. Since massive military activities require some time to prepare, slightly more than one overflight per month would suffice, according to the Soviet argument.[73]

The NATO countries, and the other WTO countries with them, argued that a high degree of access could, in itself, be a confidence-building gesture. They also argued that it was not necessary to give specific reasons for their overflights; it was enough that they wanted to come and take a look. Why they might want to do so would be their own business.[74]

The only other issue in the quota discussions was the French desire to ensure that the quota formula should not assign overflights on a bloc-to-bloc basis. Their primary motivation was to ensure that the final quota structure would not prevent the future accession of the other CSCE countries. Paris was also keen to promote the idea that the Eastern European countries be allowed to overfly their soon-to-be-former allies. Not surprisingly, the French were supported by the non-Soviet members of the WTO. Since Group B was in no danger of deciding anything, the French did not have to press the issue. They correctly reasoned that there would be time enough, and that pressure to see things their way would mount as events in Europe unfolded. But they never missed an opportunity to place their concern before the rest of Group B.[75]

### Territorial Scope

The second issue, territorial scope, was intimately related to the quota issue, and was also discussed in Group B. Again, the USSR differed from the rest in its desire to restrict certain areas from overflights. They maintained that these areas were "not relevant to the purpose" of the regime.[76] Many of these areas were defined in terms of safety regulations. The Soviets, for example, wanted to restrict overflights to very high altitudes in the vicinity of nuclear and chemical plants, and to forbid overflights of major cities such as Moscow. These restrictions were far greater than proposed by any other country for "air safety" reasons. More ominously, the Soviets indicated that some military facilities would be declared off-limits on "security grounds." In response to requests as to what these regions might be, the Soviets were geographically unspecific, but maintained that they would be military facilities that would have nothing to do with the purposes of the regime. They would not define what this meant, however.[77] Privately Western officials were told that these exclusion areas would include strategic facilities and sensitive communication posts.[78]

These were exactly the same types of facilities that the American intelligence community's protectors had wanted to declare off-limits in their restrictive approach to Open Skies during the interagency debate, before their concerns were overridden. The Soviets also stuck to their insistence that military bases in third countries belonging to regime participants should be subject to overflights. Western diplomats were privately told that this was not a real issue, that it represented the Soviet military stalling for time.[79]

### Aircraft Ownership

This issue also pitted the USSR against the rest. Every other country was prepared to allow aircraft belonging to the overflying country to conduct the overflights. The Soviets met this with a proposal for a multinational pool of aircraft that would be jointly owned and operated (even though they had not required this in the Stockholm Agreement). This was rejected as costly and complicated. The Soviets then proposed that overflights be performed by aircraft belonging to the overflying country, or to the overflown country, or to a third party, but that the choice as to which of these options would be exercised would lie with the country to be overflown. Privately, the Soviets admitted that they would routinely choose to supply the aircraft on every occasion.[80]

At heart, the Soviets were concerned that a foreign aircraft could contain hidden sensors that would not be identifiable during the "intrusive, but non-destructive inspection" called for in the NATO draft treaty. In a later interview, Karpov would argue: "The present development of electronics makes it possible to fit an aircraft with a tiny sensor which could collect a vast quantity of information having nothing to do with Open Skies and could be very difficult to detect by inspectors when checking someone else's aircraft."[81]

Although the NATO delegations argued that concealment would be extremely difficult, they could not offer categorical assurances that it could be impossible to cheat in this manner. Indeed, the fear of such concealed sensors had been the primary factor in the insistence of the U.S. intelligence community's protectors that a twenty-four-hour period elapse after the fight plan was handed in before the overflight began. The United States wanted the time to shut down sensitive facilities in case the Soviet aircraft was carrying hidden sensors that could not be detected.[82]

But the U.S. insistence that Signals Intelligence (SIGINT) sensors be banned gave the Soviets a logical opening. If one type of sensor could be banned because it would not contribute to openness as sought by the treaty, they pointed out, why couldn't other types? Indeed, what, exactly, were the kinds of sensors required to build confidence? It all came down to a question of one's conception of the type of openness being sought and why.[83] Although it was clear that the Soviet argument was purely tactical, it was a logical point that Western delegates were hard pressed to answer.

### Sensors

The fourth issue, sensors, further revealed the depth of the differences between the USSR and the rest. But it also contained the seeds of significant differences among the other countries. The NATO countries held that any sensors, other than SIGINT devices, should be permitted. The U.S. proposed an ambitious list that included both imaging devices and "measurement and signatures intelligence" (MASINT) devices. The list of imaging devices included optical cameras; electro-optical cameras (to improve contrast under hazy or twilight conditions); infrared linescanners (for use in clear but dark conditions); and synthetic aperture radar (SAR) (for use in cloudy conditions). The list of MASINT devices included air samplers (to measure radioactive isotopes and any chemicals that might have been in the air); and gravitometers and magnetometers (capable of detecting underground command posts and concentrations of equipment, and of producing extremely accurate topographic and geodetic maps).[84] The Soviets were only prepared to allow optical and electro-optical cameras with resolutions of two to three meters.[85] The non-Soviet members of the WTO were prepared to accept the NATO proposal, but on the condition that they be granted equal access to any sensor used by any other regime member.[86]

Basic philosophical differences underlay the positions. The Soviets, in keeping with their limited conception of the purposes of the regime, sought sensors capable only of detecting large concentrations of military equipment that might be used for surprise attacks. The U.S. position was motivated by a desire to be as open as possible. But, as a member of the U.S. delegation has subsequently written:

> [The U.S.]demands for intrusiveness . . . had been shaped by the needs of the intelligence services rather than a clearheaded assessment of what was both negotiable and essential for confidence-building . . . . [T]he long list of MASINT sensors clearly exceeded the core requirement of day/night, all-weather observation, and heightened the Soviet military's concerns that Western overflights might collect information harmful to Soviet security . . . (such as) . . . the vulnerabilities of the military command and control system and the deployment patterns of mobile missiles, precise topographic and geodetic maps for targeting purposes, and economic assessments of Soviet agriculture yields and mineral resources.[87]

Not surprisingly, the Soviet military could not accept this degree of intrusiveness. In an interview with *Pravda*, the head of delegation, Karpov, stated: "The main content of the position expounded by US representatives . . . boils down to the fact that the United States, taking advantage of its technological potential, intends to overfly other countries' territory, collect information, and tuck it safely away . . . . So where is the openness?"[88] A General Staff officer and member of the Soviet delegation at the Ottawa Conference later stated:

> NATO is proposing, in addition to (optical and electro-optical sensors), the use of infra-red equipment and synthetic aperture radar, multispectral equipment, and instruments to take air samples, magnetometers, gravitometers and laser detectors. The question inevitably arises: What is the need for all of this? To build confidence? Hardly. For intelligence purposes? Then we are talking about something quite different.[89]

As the sensor discussions unfolded, many U.S. allies grew uncomfortable. It was clear that the U.S. intelligence community was driving this non-negotiable stand. A suspicion arose that that community was prepared to see Open Skies fail unless it got what it wanted.[90] This would have left the non-U.S. allies without the enhancement in their own information collection capabilities that a more modest Open Skies regime would have provided. In addition, the U.S. stand was fundamentally incompatible with the willingness of the non-Soviet WTO to accept any sensor that could be made available to all. The one NATO delegation that supported the U.S. stand was the United Kingdom. It was widely rumored that the UK intelligence community was supporting its U.S. counterpart in return for access to U.S. technology and information should their view have prevailed.[91] Not all members of the UK delegation were comfortable with this view, however.[92] This split would become even more evident in Budapest, and then in Vienna.

Sensing that this was the path down which a compromise lay, several other NATO countries were prepared to explore the issues. The United States was not, and sought to prevent such discussions.[93] Many of the other NATO delegations experienced an increasing degree of frustration with the United States over this issue, and wanted to explore possible compromises. They were not yet prepared to break NATO unity over the issue, however.

To explore the possibility of compromise, the Canadian delegation asked the U.S. sensor experts to work with it in defining ways in which the equality in sensor capabilities required by the non-Soviet WTO could be obtained. The

Canadians took the lead, as the chairman of Group A was the Canadian head of delegation, and he wanted to move the discussions along. Also, the negotiations were in Ottawa, and so the resources of the Canadian government could be brought to bear on the U.S. delegation to stimulate the search for compromise.[94]

The exercise demonstrated to the Canadians the extent to which the U.S. intelligence community was driving the American position. The Canadians proposed that the only way to measure equality in sensor capabilities was to fly similar systems over identical ground targets under identical conditions and then measure the images to see if their "ground resolution" was similar.[95] The Americans argued that such steps were unnecessary. They maintained that one could ensure equality by measuring certain technical properties of the sensors to see that they were equal. While that was theoretically true, the Americans were selective in the numbers and types of technical properties they were prepared to measure. This would have resulted in systems that looked equal but were not. Although the results of the work were not presented at the Ottawa Conference, it was a useful exercise because this difference would become a critical aspect of the talks in Budapest and Vienna.

### Data-sharing

The final issue, data-sharing, was closely related to the differences that existed over sensors. The Soviets sought a jointly run data-processing center that would process all data and make it available to everyone.[96] This stand was motivated by a desire to retain control over the data in order to ensure that the final product conformed to the rather low standard of resolution sought by the Soviets. The Soviets were also concerned that superior Western processing techniques would enhance the quality of the collected data far beyond what they could achieve.[97]

NATO, led by the United States, maintained that data-sharing between the alliances was unnecessary and would be fundamentally incompatible with the requirements of openness.[98] It was, ran the NATO argument, up to the overflying country to decide what it wanted to take pictures of and with whom it wished to share them. Of course, the allies had already agreed that they would share the data among themselves.[99]

The United States was dogmatic on the issue. To a large extent, its stand was predicated on the belief that extremely intrusive sensors would be used, and on a desire to protect the true capabilities of those sensors from the Soviets. The

U.S. was worried that its intelligence collection strategies and capabilities would be compromised if the Soviets could see exactly what had been captured by the U.S. sensors. Finally, the United States argued that access to the data would permit the Soviets to discern whether any steps they had taken to camouflage sensitive areas had been successful. This would permit them to upgrade their concealment techniques.[100]

Although they officially subscribed to the NATO position, the other allies were prepared to consider some form of data-sharing, if only of the raw data. Canada took the lead, perhaps as a result of its work with the U.S. delegation over other sensor issues.[101] Raw data–sharing would have meant that each country would still have processed its own data, but that the overflown country would have been granted access to a copy of the unprocessed material directly off the aircraft after the overflight.[102]

This stand was predicated on a growing realization that it would be necessary to share sensor technologies with the non-Soviet WTO nations. In such a case, provided the shared technologies were equal, there was nothing lost in sharing the raw data. Indeed, such sharing would constitute a guarantee that the capabilities of the sensors were not in excess of those that had been shared. For this reason, even though they did not want or need shared data, many of the NATO countries were prepared to do so to make the non-Soviet WTO nations more comfortable.[103]

The non-Soviet WTO countries were keen to explore a data-sharing arrangement, though not of the type proposed by the USSR and not for the same reasons.[104] These countries, with Czechoslovakia and Hungary at their head, recognized that the amount of data they could acquire from their limited number of overflights would be small. Accordingly, they reasoned that access to the data-pool of the entire regime would serve to multiply the number of flights they could do. It would also give them access to at least some data on the USSR at a time when the regime was still officially being designed to forbid flights over members of the same alliance. These countries argued that a copy of the raw data from any overflight should be available to *any other regime member* that wanted to pay for it.[105] Since only raw data would be shared, and since their data-processing capabilities were limited, these countries also requested that they be allowed to purchase data-processing equipment from the West, along with the sensors.[106]

These were the main issues, and the main differences as explored by the working groups. Since each group concentrated on one or two sets of issues, the identification of potential trade-offs between them was difficult. In the few informal meetings that did occur, however, trade-offs were identified and discussed. Obviously, informal discussions took place between delegates, but the main vehicle for stepping back from the working groups and addressing the issues on a conceptual level were two informal heads of delegation meetings arranged by the conference hosts on successive Saturdays.[107]

## INFORMAL SESSIONS

The first took place at Meech Lake, about thirty minutes outside of Ottawa in the Gatineau National Park. The NATO draft treaty had been tabled the previous day, and it was the intention of the NATO countries to conduct a detailed "walk through." This intention was not realized, however, as the preliminary general discussion, which had been meant to last only about thirty minutes, consumed most of the meeting, with the NATO countries probing Karpov to determine what the limits of his positions were.[108]

In response to questions about the USSR's position, Karpov was evasive. He would state that a common definition of the purpose of the regime was required, before advancing the Soviet position and accepting no compromise. He laid particular emphasis on the need to ensure that the regime was capable of collecting material useful for confidence-building, stressing the need to avoid intelligence collection. Whenever an attempt was made to construct a package of trade-offs, however, Karpov shifted the ground. At one moment he claimed that equality in sensors was the crucial matter, and that the sensors should be unable to return data for any other purpose than confidence-building. When he was asked if that meant the USSR would allow foreign aircraft over its territory if sensor equality could be accomplished, Karpov replied that the right to insist on the use of its own aircraft was the only means acceptable to the USSR to ensure that agreed sensors would be used. Aircraft ownership thus became the critical issue.[109] The non-Soviet WTO countries used the Meech Lake informal meeting to advance their arguments concerning the need for an equal sensor package and some form of raw data–sharing.[110] Although the NATO countries were unable to agree to these positions at this point, many among them recognized the inherent logic in these arguments.[111]

The second informal meeting took place in the Ottawa Conference Centre on the morning of Saturday, February 24.[112] Once again, the meeting was aimed at an informal discussion of the larger issues. After a general discussion, the Czech head of delegation took the floor and outlined what subsequently became known as "The Grand Compromise." Essentially, it involved the following trade-offs: the sensor package would be restricted to imaging sensors but capable of acquiring detailed images and of twenty-four-hour/all-weather operations; these sensors would be of whatever capability the West was prepared to make equally available to all participants; some form of raw data–sharing, at the very least between the overflying and overflown nations; the overflying country would be entitled to use its own aircraft, but additional work would be done to ensure that mechanisms existed whereby these aircraft would be thoroughly checked for illegal sensors; some compromise figure on quotas would be found to strike a balance between the NATO and Soviet proposals; the USSR would drop its position on overflights of bases in third countries and would accept coverage of the USSR without any territorial restrictions.[113]

Virtually everyone present immediately endorsed this compromise package.[114] Its components had been discussed in the hallways for the previous week, but this was the first time anyone put it together as a proposal. The United States was enthusiastic, although it did not express unreserved support. For his part, Karpov quickly said, "I agree with you 100 per cent,"[115] but then left the room, thus forcing his deputy to step back from the compromise package.[116] Subsequent discussions focused on ways of improving the package. This proved pointless because of Soviet inability to accept it. But the package was on the table and its logic was understood by all.

Thus, the question as to whether the inefficiency of the conference procedures acted as a brake on the development of the necessary trade-offs must be answered in the negative; one has to say that it was possible to construct a package of trade-offs. That the "Grand Compromise" could be put forward and discussed in some detail indicates that the Ottawa Conference had achieved a degree of efficiency. What the conference had not achieved were the political conditions that would have allowed the participants to discuss these trade-offs in a manner that could have permitted them to manipulate the various concepts into an acceptable package. But this was not possible in the absence of a high-level political commitment to Open Skies in Moscow capable of overriding the objections of the Soviet military. In fairness, it must also be said that the U.S. intelligence community was displaying many of the same negotiating characteristics as the Soviet military, though that was less noticeable at this stage.

To the extent that negotiators experienced frustrations, these were not so much the result of any inefficiency of the conference procedures, but of the inability of the superpowers to pursue a realistic agreement.[117] It is difficult to see how the procedures of the conference, or even the tactics employed by the NATO nations, could have overcome a basic unwillingness to compromise on the part of the Soviet and, to a lesser extent, the American delegations, however.

There were areas in which simple bureaucratic problems led to a degree of inefficiency. For example, there were not enough translators on hand for the amount of work that materialized. It took a week to translate the NATO draft treaty into Russian, and the Soviets used that week to claim they could not make any final decisions on the text until they had a Russian copy.[118] Once the translation had been accomplished, however, the Russians moved no faster.[119]

The Ottawa Open Skies Conference ended on February 27, 1990. Although they agreed that their ministers should reserve May 11–12 for a possible signing of the treaty in Budapest, officials were not convinced that would happen. The U.S. head of delegation was quoted as saying that there were "very wide divergences" in positions that would require "quite a lot of work . . . . Everyone understands there are no promises for Budapest."[120] It was also recognized that a high-level political impetus would have to be given if the talks were to succeed. Some hope existed that Baker-Shevardnadze meetings, scheduled for April 4–6 in Washington, might provide the impetus. The upcoming NATO ministerial, scheduled for April 10, was also identified as an opportunity for a high-level push.[121]

## THE INTERSESSIONAL PERIOD

The intersessional period was occupied with a search for compromises within the Senior Political Committee (SPC), but little of substance happened between the United States and the USSR. In Brussels, several members of the alliance advocated acceptance of the non-Soviet WTO's position on sensor availability. They also chided the United States for excessive rigidity over such issues as data-sharing. Those in the forefront of this discussion were Canada, the Netherlands, and Germany.[122]

The U.S. accepted the need to meet the non-Soviet WTO on the sensor issue, to further isolate the USSR. Accordingly, Washington promised a paper outlining how equality in sensors would be achieved. The paper did not materialize until the eve of the Budapest Conference, and, when it did, confirmed Canadian fears that the United States would try to define equality in such a way as to preserve an advantage.[123] Instead of discussing "equality" in sensor access, the paper talked about access to "comparable" sensors.[124]

Nevertheless, the NATO countries did agree on the principle of equal access to sensors for all. This concession imposed some limits on the NATO sensor package. It also meant that the allies would have to seek a relaxation of the export regulations governing the transfer of these technologies to the WTO states. These transfers were, at this time, regulated by guidelines established by the Coordinating Committee on Export Controls, also known as COCOM. Although the NATO allies asked COCOM to examine the issues surrounding such a relaxation, movement was slow, partly because the promised U.S. paper failed to materialize.

In order to stimulate the examination of technology transfer, the Hungarians decided to stage an exhibit of surveillance equipment during the Budapest Conference.[125] The exhibit would itself have been a test of COCOM's willingness to approach the issues with greater flexibility, as demonstration permits would be required for Western companies wishing to exhibit their wares in Budapest. Although the Canadians backed the exhibit idea, and several European firms expressed an interest, the United States took a lukewarm view. Washington did not encourage U.S. firms to apply for the required permits, and the idea of the exhibit soon withered. This episode was a foretaste of things to come on the technology transfer issue.

The French also presented new ideas on quotas to the NATO caucus during the intersessional period.[126] Building upon their concern that the quota structure not be a bloc-to-bloc affair, the French proposed that each nation accept an extra number of passive quotas and reserve these for the use of members of the same alliance, or for the use of neutrals when they joined the regime. These extra quotas (unfortunately dubbed "Jokers" by the French) were received uncomfortably by the other members of the alliance. Many agreed with the French that some means of ensuring that a suitable number of flights remained for the neutrals and members of the same alliance had to be found, but they were loath to complicate an already confused quota discussion with an entirely new category of quotas.

The April 5–6 bilateral discussions between the United States and the USSR were similarly unproductive.[127] Some hope had existed, as the Soviets had asked that an Open Skies working group be established on the margin of the Baker-Shevardnadze discussions, hinting that a new position would be presented. The Soviets announced that they were now prepared to accept technologies necessary to achieve a twenty-four-hour, all-weather capability. They then agreed to add synthetic aperture radar to their list of acceptable sensors. Unfortunately, they went on to propose an extremely primitive SAR, with a resolution of ten meters. This would have been unable to detect, much less recognize or identify, any military equipment. By contrast, the SAR resolution capability that the NATO countries would later be prepared to transfer to the WTO was on the order of three meters' resolution.

As these various subjects were being discussed privately, little was heard of Open Skies in the public domain. What little discussion there was tended to be the two superpowers justifying their positions and accusing the other side of intransigence.[128] Interestingly, those very few Western analysts who were interested in the subject advocated a relaxation of the rather competitive approach taken by the United States on Open Skies.

Speaking before the U.S. Senate Foreign Relations Committee, for example, Michael Krepon, president of the Henry L. Stimson Center (a private think tank specializing in arms control and verification matters), warned: "To work effectively over the long run, Open Skies must be a true cooperative measure, not a method for some states to gain significant advantages at the expense of others."[129] He went on to argue: "If a public case cannot be made on behalf of a particular sensor, or if the equipment is too sensitive to sell to participating states, it probably does not belong on Open Skies aircraft."[130] Krepon's cautionary notes proved to be prophetic. As they gathered in Budapest to resume their discussions on April 23, however, the prospects for compromise seemed quite distant to most of the delegations.

## THE BUDAPEST CONFERENCE

The Budapest Conference began on April 22, 1990, under a cloud of rapidly diminishing expectations. Indeed, there had been some discussion in Brussels of canceling the Budapest session because it seemed so unlikely that the Soviets would be prepared to make the required compromises. In the end, the NATO countries decided to go to Budapest prepared to work hard and see what happened. Although few expected a treaty to result, a desire existed to demonstrate that it would not be for want to trying on the part of NATO.[131]

Each side presented its concessions on April 24 at the first meeting of Working Group A. The United States, speaking on behalf of the NATO allies, announced that the allies were prepared to "consider favorably requests for access to sensor systems with *comparable* Western technology" by all participants that did not possess them.[132] The Soviet representative, in turn, took the floor to announce that "his country was now prepared to accept additional observation equipment (synthetic aperture radar) which would make it possible to achieve the aims of an Open Skies regime in all weather circumstances, night and day."[133] The Soviets also announced that they were prepared to accept thirty centimeters as the resolution limit for all camera systems.[134]

Although these were welcome moves, they were not all they seemed. Intensive discussion of the Western proposal made clear the fact that the NATO countries had no agreed formula for measuring "comparability." On the one hand, several countries, with Canada at their head, argued that comparability meant equality.[135] Others, primarily the United States and the United Kingdom, adopted a more subtle approach that sought to manipulate the definition of "comparability" in such as way as to preserve an advantage.[136] Essentially, the United States proposed that comparability be measured by ensuring that certain characteristics of each sensor were identical, but these characteristics were carefully selected and did not include the full range of characteristics required to measure the full equality in sensors. In other words, the sensors would appear equal but would not necessarily return equal data.[137]

To take one example, a working document entitled "Technical Characteristics for a Selection of Sensors" was circulated by the NATO countries on April 26. For each sensor category the document listed the parameters by which comparability would be measured. In the case of SAR, for example, the listed characteristics were operating frequency and antenna length. A Hungarian document of the same date suggested that the following characteristics be used: frequency range (GHz)/Wave Length (m), effective range (km), and spatial resolution (m). A Czechoslovakian proposal of May 2 was even more detailed.[138]

The UK delegate attempted to clarify the situation by reading a statement reminding the group that "as a matter of principle, the Group of Sixteen Nations [NATO] sees no requirement for absolute limitations on sensor performance, and that parameters . . . should be used to indicate the performance of sensors, but not to impose arbitrary limits to that performance." He then spoke of "the rather dangerous trend in this group to treat the words 'parameters' and 'limitations' as having an identical meaning . . . with the predictable result that stated parameters have quickly been assumed to be acceptable limitations." He cautioned the non-Soviet WTO countries that "applications for access to (technologies) are considered on a case by case basis by a specially convened coordinating committee. None of the sixteen delegations to this conference has the authority to make preemptive decisions on access in place of that committee." He concluded with the assurance that "[t]he Group of Sixteen Nations . . . undertakes that we will abide by the technology access regulations developed for the Open Skies regime, by using only comparable sensors to which the other participants are granted access."[139]

This was a much more accurate reflection of the situation, which sought to maintain a Western advantage in that it did not bind the NATO countries to equality in sensors—just to equality in certain parameters of sensor capabilities. What the UK representative promised was that the West would do its best to make highly capable systems available to all, but that it would not allow itself to be bound by any restrictions that COCOM placed upon those characteristics which were *not* part of the agreed list of technical characteristics in the treaty. In other words, if the West could prevent all of the relevant technical characteristics from being mentioned in the treaty, it would be able to use greater capabilities than it was promising to try to transfer.

This was far less than the non-Soviet WTO had sought, which was across-the-board equality. The non-Soviet WTO reasoned that enshrining a much broader definition of equality in the treaty would have two results. First, it would make the treaty much more equal in its effects. Second, it would stimulate the NATO countries to release highly capable technologies through the COCOM process.[140]

Several allies made it clear that they disagreed with the U.S./UK approach. In informal sessions of sensor experts, Canada led a group that sought to establish comparisons of ground resolution as the defining characteristic of "comparability." This stand reflected the earlier work done at the Ottawa Conference. Toward the end of the Budapest Conference, Canada became the first to publicly break ranks with the NATO position on this issue, when the Canadian representative in Group A reserved his position after the U.S. had presented a NATO statement.[141] In his "Report to Plenary," the chair of Group A made references to these discussions, and to the differences that continued to exist:

> Experts did not agree on the approach for verifying sensor/observation equipment parameters. Some experts put forward specific technical parameters which they believed should be used for sensor/observation equipments, *in particular, ground resolution.* Other experts questioned that particular parameter, suggesting other parameters, for instance, focal length and lines per millimeter for optical systems.[142]

The Soviets were no doubt pleased to see the NATO countries having to defend their position. The Soviet delegation did not get away without criticism, however. In particular, their proposal that SAR be accepted, but at a resolution of ten meters, did not fare well.[143] Even though NATO's limitations on sensor transfer were becoming better understood, it was still clear to all that NATO was prepared to transfer a much higher quality of SAR than ten meters. Moreover, the Soviet insistence upon ten-meter resolution for SAR made no sense in the light of their willingness to accept thirty-centimeter resolution for cameras. "It was," as one NATO delegate was to say later, "tantamount of saying that the USSR would permit one kind of Open Skies regime under certain meteorological conditions, but quite another when the sun went down or the clouds rolled in." He went on to say: "The Soviet stance on SAR and other overhead imaging systems could only have been a bargaining position, and was viewed as such by the West."[144]

The only other sensor matter of consequence that was discussed at Budapest was data-sharing. The Soviets submitted a new annex to the draft treaty, Annex M, entitled "Procedures for the Processing of Data Obtained with the Aid of Observation Equipment."[145] Not surprisingly, the Soviet draft called for the "processing of the Observation Flight materials [to] be carried out in established ground facilities by mixed teams of specialists from the Observing and the Observed Party and with the aid of agreed equipment." The final data would be given to the Observed and Observing parties with the original to be sent to the data storage center.[146]

Although they did not agree to this proposal, an increasing number of NATO nations believed that some sort of raw data–sharing arrangement should be agreed.[147] In particular, the fact that they were prepared to share exactly equal sensors meant that these nations were unable to see any danger in making the raw data available to the overflown country. The United States and United Kingdom, mindful of their desire to use higher quality sensors than might be obvious, realized that sharing the data might alert the overflown countries as to the true capabilities of those sensors. Accordingly, they refused to consider data-sharing. They also wished to protect their lead in processing technology. As one U.S. Department of Defense official stated at the time, "On data sharing the problem quite frankly for us is one of technology sharing. We process better. If you share your data you reveal a lot about your processing and we're not willing to take that step."[148]

By the end of the Budapest Conference the ongoing disputes over sensor capability and data-sharing would prompt the Canadian chairman of Group A to sharply criticize the U.S. delegation in public: "The use of Open Skies as an intelligence gathering mechanism is unwarranted . . . and may reduce confidence, a point which some in the American bureaucracy seem to have some difficulty accepting."[149]

The other working groups fared no better than Group A. Group B, dealing with quotas, made no progress. The Soviets did indicate that they were prepared to increase their passive quota to twenty-five, but this was only on condition that the neutral states joined the regime.[150] Thus, in reality, it amounted to no greater degree of access for NATO countries. In an effort to stimulate the debate, the NATO caucus decided to propose a "game" in which each delegation would outline its desires for active quotas over all the others. However, "when they tallied up the totals . . . the totals for the Soviet Union were just astronomical, and the numbers for the other states were minimal except for Germany, and no one much wanted to overfly the United States."[151] The Soviets also stuck to their positions on overflying U.S. bases in third countries and on territorial restrictions for overflights within the USSR.[152]

Groups C and D continued to work in a cooperative spirit in Budapest.[153] Both made some progress in dealing with the purely technical issues but were increasingly frustrated by the fact that they were coming to the end of the list of subjects they could deal with that did not include the larger political differences of the negotiations. As the chairman of Group D put it in his final Report: "Solutions are still to be found for the remaining bracketed passages . . . . Most of these will not pose serious problems, but some . . . will have to await political agreement outside the scope of the Working Group."[154]

The Budapest Conference was structured in exactly the same manner as Ottawa. Once again, many delegates voiced frustration at the pace of the meetings and the relatively small amount of time allowed for informal consultations. Obviously, numerous informal discussions between small groups of delegates took place throughout the conference. What was felt by some to be lacking were organized informal sessions. As before, however, one wonders whether the lack of time for informal meetings made very much difference. The positions were so far apart, and the willingness to entertain compromises so markedly absent, that informal discussions were rather pointless. Moreover, everyone knew what trade-offs were required by this point. Further exploration at a senior level was unnecessary; what was required was the political will to act upon the trade-offs that had already been discussed.

Indeed, the trade-offs were so well known that individual delegates were capable of extensive and technically complex discussions on them. One member of the USSR delegation engaged a number of individuals from Western delegations in lengthy, informal sessions throughout the Budapest Conference.[155] These discussions consisted of detailed examinations of the potential impact of a variety of packages of trade-offs on the key issues. The discussions ultimately came to naught, as the political will was not present for action to be taken. This work was not entirely wasted, however, as the compromise packages achieved in these talks would eventually form the basis of the final deal, once the underlying political ground had shifted.

The essential outlines of the regime produced in these informal discussions were similar to those of the Grand Compromise from Ottawa, but contained a key difference.[156] This was the continued insistence that the USSR be allowed to supply the aircraft used during any overflight of itself. The Soviet delegate was willing to examine ideas for a Western sensor suite to be installed in a Soviet aircraft for use in such overflights, but he could not imagine the Soviet military agreeing to allow a foreign aircraft to overfly the USSR. On all of the other issues, compromise was possible. These conversations were discussed within the NATO caucus, but there was no hope of convincing many allies to move off their position that the country performing the overflight be allowed to use its own aircraft.[157]

The one informal session that did occur involving all of the delegations at a senior level was held over the first weekend at a Hungarian government retreat on Lake Balaton.[158] It took a matter of minutes to agree that the treaty would not be ready in time for the planned signing ceremony on May 12. In fact, Karpov had informed Hungarian radio before the Budapest Conference had begun that the treaty could not be ready for signature. He had gone on to say that the deadline had not been reasonable to begin with.[159]

With the decision to postpone the ministerial made, the Hungarians tried to attract support for setting a date for a third round, but the other delegations preferred to leave the setting of a date for signs of movement toward a compromise. Many of the European delegations also voiced some concern that the CFE end-game was about to begin, and they did not think the two negotiations could run concurrently.[160]

The requirements of a compromise were then quickly discussed, but everyone knew them quite well by this point. It was agreed that the remainder of the Budapest Conference could be devoted to going through the text and preparing language that could frame both approaches to the various issues. This language would be included in brackets to facilitate the selection of trade-offs once basic decisions had been made at a political level.[161] The ease with which these decisions were reached, and the lack of rancor that was present, indicated that the delegations had already reached this decision privately.

Thus the May 12 deadline for the signing of the Open Skies Treaty was revealed for what it had always been: a symbolic and arbitrary one. It was selected before any prenegotiation, or even extensive consultation had taken place. Neither Canada nor Hungary had any idea that the negotiation would prove so difficult when they set the target date. Its easy removal by the parties at Lake Balaton was an indication that it should never have been set in the first place, as Karpov had said earlier. The deadline question demonstrates, once again, the manner in which the spectacular lack of prenegotiation affected the Open Skies talks.

Fortunately, the fact that the deadline was not met did not, in itself, have serious consequences for the subsequent negotiation, though one might have expected a public failure to hold a previously announced ministerial meeting to have such an impact. There may be two reasons why the Open Skies process was able to survive this setback. First, little had been heard of the Open Skies negotiations by the wider public since the Ottawa ministerial session, and most of what was in the public domain dwelt on how unexpectedly difficult the negotiations were. Second, and perhaps more important, there was so much going on in East/West relations at this time, the Open Skies was one story among many. Had Open Skies been "the only game in town," its failure would have been widely reported. It was not the only game, and the public admission of failure was not treated with much fanfare. However, the fact that the Open Skies Treaty was not signed on schedule was taken in the context of what was seen as a shift to the right by Mr. Gorbachev as hardline elements within the Kremlin reasserted themselves.[162]

Finally, even if they had wanted to make compromises, the Soviets would have found it difficult, as the decision-making machinery in Moscow was affected by the decay of the Soviet system generally. Their actions in the Open Skies talks were being reflected in other arms control negotiations and came as no surprise. As one Western delegate said, the problems in Budapest fell into the "general political landscape . . . . I think most Western countries believe there has been a slowdown in the decision-making process in Moscow," and it "has affected not only this conference but also the negotiations in Vienna and maybe the negotiations in Geneva between the US and the Soviet Union."[163]

The Budapest Conference ended on May 10, 1990. The final plenary did not set a date for the resumption of talks but asked Canada and Hungary to maintain a watching brief on developments and convene another round when the moment was felt to be auspicious. There was some thought that either July or

September might be possible,[164] with the balance of opinion favoring the latter date. Several of the Europeans were concerned, however, that the Open Skies negotiation should not interfere with the CFE end-game.[165]

## CONCLUSION

In assessing the first round of negotiation, both in Ottawa and Budapest, one is struck by the extent to which the lack of an agreed conception of the regime's purpose dominated the discussion. Nor was there any real attempt by the superpowers to reach such an agreed conception during the formal negotiation. Instead, the superpowers approached the negotiation with fundamental differences. Their conference strategy was largely composed of a determination to engage in tactical ploys designed to isolate the other side, and ensure that the blame for failure was attached to it. The United States was much more successful in the latter goal, but even its position was wearing thin by the end of the Budapest round.

Essentially, the U.S. tactic was to isolate the USSR and then force the Soviets to concede through embarrassment. This tactic failed miserably for two reasons. First, the Soviets did not really care whether they were isolated enough to provide the Foreign Ministry with the leverage to force the military to concede its position. Second, the United States did not need to isolate the USSR from its WTO partners; Moscow was already thoroughly isolated as a result of the enormous changes that were under way. What the U.S. needed to do in order to win over the other WTO states was not to isolate the USSR but to offer the others something they could use: equality. But the U.S. delegation, under the influence of its own intelligence community, was not prepared to make this offer. Even if they had, however, it would not have changed the Soviet position.

The Soviet tactic was to sit back and allow the impatience of the European NATO countries to erode the U.S. position. But the European allies, though interested in Open Skies, were not sufficiently interested to mount a concerted challenge to the U.S. position during either the Ottawa or the Budapest rounds. Their primary concerns were over the rapidly approaching CFE end-game, and, in the case of the powerful German delegation, the reunification of Germany. In sum, the will to expend the political capital was not there.

Each superpower sought to prevent an agreement, if one could not be obtained on terms favorable to its interests. In both cases, powerful elements on the delegations of the USSR and the United States decided that an Open Skies agreement on anything less than their own terms was not in their interest. They were, accordingly, prepared to do without an agreement rather than make the compromises necessary. Both of the superpower strategies were thus essentially negative ones.

The conference procedures, though not particularly efficient, were not in themselves a cause of the breakdown of the negotiation. The negotiators were able to identify a set of trade-offs. They were also able to explore them in some conceptual detail. What they could not do, in the absence of a basic political agreement as to the purpose of the regime under discussion, was to make headway in the selection of appropriate trade-offs. Despite the complexity that appeared to bedevil the negotiators in their detailed discussions, the larger trade-offs were clear.

Nevertheless, the informal sessions that took place in Ottawa and Budapest did represent some cause for hope, as did the informal discussion between a member of the Soviet delegation and a few others in Budapest. Those who were undertaking these conversations lacked the authority to pursue deals. But the fact that they occurred at all indicated that deals could be envisaged at the working level once the political factors fell into place.

In the end, it would not be until the NATO allies had radically revised their position, and the Soviet Union had undergone significant internal change leading to its own demise, that the stage would be set for the resumption of the Open Skies negotiations. In the meantime, the hiatus that the negotiation entered into provided the chance for a degree of informal consultation which had been absent prior to the Ottawa and Budapest conferences.

# 5 Interim Negotiations

With the end of the Budapest Conference, Open Skies entered a lengthy hiatus. Negotiations would not resume until September of 1991. Although it did not appear obvious at the time, this period would be vital to the eventual success of Open Skies. The hiatus would allow time for a number of important political changes to occur that would permit the reconsideration of long-held positions. Political leaders would take charge of the process and direct their sometimes unwilling bureaucracies to find solutions to problems. Moreover, the events of this period gave the Open Skies delegations a chance to engage in the kind of exploration of positions that should have preceded the Ottawa and Budapest conferences.

## THE IMMEDIATE WAKE OF BUDAPEST

In the weeks immediately after Budapest there was little reason to hope that the negotiations would resume in the near future. An internal U.S. position paper, leaked to the press shortly after the Budapest Conference, insisted that the allies should not agree to set a date for future talks until "the Soviets demonstrate their willingness to negotiate seriously."[1] In other words, it would be up to the Soviets to make the first move.

This view reflected the desire of some within the U.S. bureaucracy to see Open Skies taken off the agenda. By linking any future talks to Soviet movement, and then giving the Soviets, who did not like the initiative anyway, no reason to make such a move, effective deadlock could be maintained until the issue was forgotten. This tactic was championed by many within the intelligence community in Washington.[2] It was thus clear that a high-level political push would be required to refocus attention on Open Skies.

This push came unexpectedly quickly, at the Bush-Gorbachev Summit in Washington from May 30 to June 3, 1990. The prospects for a political push on behalf of Open Skies were not believed to be great on the eve of the meetings. Indeed, during preliminary discussions of summit issues, the Soviets and the Americans had refused to modify their positions.[3] "As a result," officials said, "the two presidents were not likely to issue a joint statement on the topic [Open Skies] during the summit."[4]

The two presidents surprised their officials, however. During the portion of the agenda devoted to arms control, they "spent more time on Open Skies than any other arms control issue except START [Strategic Arms Reduction Talks]."[5] Although no formal joint statement was released,[6] the presidential discussions achieved a tentative identification of the issues that required flexibility on the political level. They also achieved promises from Foreign Minister Shevardnadze of Soviet movement if Washington also moved.[7] Despite the lack of a formal statement, President Bush did tell the press that he was "hopeful that the good discussions between President Gorbachev and [myself]—the ones we had about the importance of Open Skies—will revive these negotiations."[8]

Just a few days later, the North Atlantic Treaty Organization (NATO) foreign ministers also publicly endorsed the Open Skies initiative in a formal statement issued at their ministerial meeting at Turnberry, Scotland. Paragraph seven of the communique read:

> We will pursue the Open Skies initiative, convinced that such a regime would make a significant contribution to the openness and transparency we wish to encourage. We therefore regret that our efforts to reach such an agreement have thus far not been unsuccessful and look to the Soviet Union to join with us to make the steps necessary to create an Open Skies regime that will increase calculability, mutual confidence and the security of all participants.[9]

These statements produced some activity in NATO. Shortly after the summit, Canada submitted a paper to the Senior Political Committee (SPC) suggesting a re-examination of the allied position.[10] The paper outlined the compromises that would be necessary if the Open Skies talks were to be revived. Basically, the paper argued for the alliance's adoption of the Grand Compromise that had been outlined by the Czechoslovakian head of delegation in Ottawa in February. As will be recalled, the Czech version of this compromise involved a twenty-four-hour/all-weather-capable sensor package using imaging sensors only, made available to all on a commercial basis by the West; some form of raw data–sharing; a compromise on quotas; no off-limits areas and no overflights of bases in third countries; and the choice of aircraft to rest with the overflying country.

The Canadians believed that the political impetus that had been imparted by the Bush-Gorbachev Summit and the Turnberry communique offered the chance to isolate the hard-line elements within the U.S. bureaucracy by appealing to the other allies for a compromise. The idea showed some signs of working. The paper was well received by the majority of allies. The United States, as expected, was unable to officially endorse it, despite the fact that many in the U.S. bureaucracy had encouraged the Canadians to submit it to the SPC in the hopes of forcing the pace of decision-making in Washington.[11]

Before the discussion that the Canadians had hoped to initiate could be fully joined, however, the allies decided to give priority to the Conventional Forces in Europe (CFE) end-game. This decision reflected the much higher degree of importance that the Europeans, and especially the Germans, placed on CFE. A concern also existed that having the CFE aerial inspection talks going on at the same time as the Open Skies negotiations would confuse the situation, and might even provide the Soviets with an opportunity to play the two sets of talks off against each other.[12]

## THE CFE NEGOTIATIONS

Although quite separate negotiations, the issues raised in the CFE Aerial Inspection and Open Skies talks were similar. The differences between the two sides were also eerily familiar.[13] Basically, the allies believed that CFE aerial inspections should be wide-ranging affairs, within the CFE region (known as the Atlantic to Urals [ATTU] area), over both declared and undeclared sites using a variety of sensors for the purposes of identifying and counting various Treaty Limited Equipment (TLE). The Soviets argued that any flights conducted under the aegis of the CFE Treaty would be limited to overflights of declared storage facilities for the TLE using quite unsophisticated sensors. Disputes also existed over aircraft ownership, data-sharing, and quotas.[14] Although placed on the "fast track," the CFE Aerial Inspection Protocol negotiations were ultimately unsuccessful.

But some progress was made in the CFE Aerial Inspections negotiations, progress that would play an important role in subsequent Open Skies discussions. In particular, the U.S. CFE delegation displayed quite a different attitude to several key questions than that taken by the American Open Skies team.[15] On the question of sensors, for example, the Americans were prepared to accept a sensor suite composed of imaging sensors only, so long as a twenty-four-hour/all-weather capability was achieved. The United States was also prepared to accept the idea of raw data–sharing in the CFE context.

These two issues were key components of the Grand Compromise, and their acceptance by the U.S. CFE team led to the hope that their Open Skies negotiators would also embrace these ideas. This hope was predicated on the belief that "it would have been rather difficult to accept ideas in the CFE talks while rejecting them in Open Skies."[16]

The fact that agreements were achieved reflected the different conditions under which the CFE Aerial Inspection talks were conducted. First, the role of the U.S. intelligence community in the CFE negotiations was very limited. Second, CFE verification measures would not apply to U.S. territory. Perhaps most important, the CFE had a goal that could be translated into measurable technical characteristics. As one analyst wrote, "It can be determined, for example, what resolution capability is required to identify and count specific objects given the conditions."[17] Open Skies had languished under the weight of undefined goals, which had the effect of "lend[ing] themselves to considerable debate over the nature of confidence-building."[18]

## INFORMAL CONSULTATIONS ON OPEN SKIES

The CFE Aerial Inspection talks were conducted over the summer and autumn of 1990. There were no formal Open Skies negotiations during this time. Informal consultations were held, however. The first of these took place in Moscow in mid-July, when the U.S. Open Skies head of delegation, John Hawes, met Viktor Karpov. Although the two sides had "a detailed exchange of views on matters concerning the drawing up of agreements at the conference," they made no progress.[19] Their inability to achieve a breakthrough reflected the extent to which the bureaucracies of the two nations retained control over the detailed agenda, despite the fact that the two presidents had called for progress.

The next informal consultation was conducted at a very high political level, however, and produced better results. Meeting in the Siberian city of Irkutsk on August 1–2, Secretary of State Baker raised Open Skies with Foreign Minister Shevardnadze.[20] Baker argued that the Soviet desire to overfly U.S. bases in third countries was untenable in that it required NATO countries to make commitments on behalf of sovereign nations that were not at the table. Shevardnadze replied that the Soviet position on overflights of third countries was negotiable but that Moscow's insistence that flights over the USSR take place on Soviet aircraft was not.

Seizing the moment, Baker suggested an agreement that Moscow fall away from the third-country base issue and to allow overflight of all Soviet territory in return for the use of Soviet aircraft over the USSR, but with Western sensors and operators. This sensor option was the preferred fall-back of the U.S. intelligence community, which, if it could not use its own aircraft, would sooner use its own sensors at least.[21] The two ministers promised to further consider a package deal along these lines. This formula, which subsequently became known as the Irkutsk Formula, was a key breakthrough, though it was not to be acted upon for several months.

Indeed, many elements of the U.S. bureaucracy were "taken aback" when they heard of Baker's discussions in Siberia.[22] Their fears that action might be imminent were assuaged by the deep hiatus into which Open Skies soon entered. Moreover, when Open Skies did come up for discussion again, the USSR was undergoing radical change that briefly called into question the survival of the Irkutsk Formula. But a realistic compromise formula had at last been articulated by the two main protagonists in the negotiation. Although they might try subsequently to repudiate the Irkutsk Formula, opponents of Open Skies could not deny it existed.

The Irkutsk discussions and the trade-offs made in the CFE Aerial Inspection talks confirm the central importance of informal discussion or prenegotiation to provide a core of tentative conceptual agreements. It would be some time before these trade-offs could be pursued coherently. It would take further time still before the political situation would evolve to the point that the deal could be raised with any hopes of acceptance. But the combination of the trade-offs on aircraft ownership, territorial openness, and third-country bases that had been explored at Irkutsk and those on sensors and data-sharing that would come out of the CFE Aerial Inspection talks were the foundations of the eventual Open Skies Treaty. The previous rounds of negotiations had not benefited from such a series of tentative understandings.

The manner in which these compromises were achieved also demonstrates the fact that these were not prenegotiations in the commonly understood sense. There was no exploration of these issues from the perspective of trying to understand them for the first time. All of those engaged in these "interim negotiations" knew perfectly well what they were trading, and how the constituent parts fit together. When the formal negotiation eventually resumed, it would be on the basis of the Irkutsk Formula. Subsequent sessions would largely be concerned with drafting the details. Of course, political differences would remain over a variety of issues not discussed in Irkutsk. Moreover, subtle nuances would appear in the Russian delegation's understanding of certain aspects of the Irkutsk Formula. But when the negotiators finally got back to the table, it was with the broad framework of a deal already agreed at a very high political level.

## A DEEP HIATUS

Throughout the summer and autumn of 1990 little more was heard of Open Skies. Studies were performed in both Canada and the United States to determine whether it would be technically feasible to develop a Western sensor pod that could be placed abroad a Soviet aircraft.[23] Technically speaking, it was found to be possible, though significant engineering work would have to be done at some expense. Western sensors are calibrated to operate at peak efficiency on certain types of aircraft.[24] The Lockheed Corporation, for example, was developing a detachable pod of sensors, known as the Samson Pod, to be fitted to any of its ubiquitous Hercules series by attaching the pod to the wing strut to which extra fuel tanks are usually attached. For an operator of Hercules aircraft the benefits of the Samson Pod are obvious: with minor modifications, any of one's transport aircraft can become a surveillance platform. But Soviet aircraft are quite different, and each time the sensor pod was "mated" to an individual Soviet aircraft a lengthy calibration sequence would have to be undertaken to accommodate the different vibration pattern. Some concern also existed about the fact that the internal power supply on Soviet aircraft is different from that on many Western aircraft.

Although it continued to be discussed in the specialist press,[25] little was heard of Open Skies by the broader public through the summer of 1990. A few public references did appear, however, and these were uniformly supportive of the idea of relaunching Open Skies at the appropriate moment. Interestingly, all made the point that both the United States and the USSR would have to make compromises if the negotiations were to work.[26]

By the autumn of 1990, it became clear that CFE would be signed in November but that it would go forward without an Aerial Inspection Protocol.[27] Accordingly, the allies decided to defer this, and the other unresolved issue of limitation on military manpower, to a follow-on negotiation under the CFE I Mandate. These talks became known as the CFE 1A talks and ultimately failed to produce an Aerial Inspection Protocol.

## A REVIVAL

With CFE signed, however, attention returned to Open Skies. In the Joint Declaration issued on November 19 at the Paris Conference on Security and Cooperation in Europe (CSCE) Summit, at which the CFE Treaty was signed, the members of the Open Skies negotiation "Reaffirm[ed] the importance of the Open Skies initiative and their determination to bring the negotiations to a successful conclusion as soon as possible."[28] Later that day, Gorbachev was quoted on Soviet radio saying, "We are ready to continue the detailed negotiation about Open Skies without delay."[29] On December 6, at the initial meeting of the CFE IA Plenary, Canada's ambassador to the CFE negotiation (David Peel) proposed that the Open Skies talks resume in February 1991 in Vienna.[30] References to the idea of quickly renewing the negotiation began to surface in the press.[31]

These public references mirrored work under way at the official level. More specifically, the process of discussion Canada had hoped to initiate with its original compromise paper of May was under way.[32] The paper was now enthusiastically picked up by the allies, many of whom submitted their own views in written form into what soon became a fast-moving review of NATO's Open Skies position. In Washington, meanwhile, the State Department "sought to 'canonize' Baker's Irkutsk proposal"[33] in a series of interagency meetings in early December. Some headway was made, over the initial protests of the intelligence community, which had never agreed to the Irkutsk Formula. All of this effort soon came to a slowdown, however, over a dispute with the Soviets regarding the implementation of certain aspects of the CFE Treaty.

Shortly before the CFE Treaty went into force, the Soviets removed a great deal of equipment slated for destruction to storage east of the Ural Mountains. This effectively removed this material (primarily armored vehicles and artillery) from the CFE zone of application. Not only was it thus exempted from destruction, it was also beyond the range of CFE verification. The Soviet Army also reclassified three motorized rifle divisions as "coastal defense forces" under the command of the navy, thus exempting a significant number of troops and equipment remaining within the CFE zone from the provisions of CFE. These steps prompted a general slowdown in all matters related to arms control. The allies refused to enter into "business as usual" on other security matters until these CFE disputes had been resolved.[34]

Although it was momentarily slowed by this dispute, the resurrection of Open Skies gained long-term strength from it. For the Europeans, the fact that the Soviets had moved a considerable amount of equipment beyond the Urals, and that they were unable to monitor it without relying on the United States to provide satellite data, reinforced the desirability of an aerial inspection regime that would get them across the Urals. "And the only idea in play which could accomplish that feat was Open Skies."[35] The determination of the major European powers to achieve an Open Skies agreement was thus ultimately strengthened by the dispute over Soviet CFE holdings. But the cause of this dispute was itself to be a major stumbling block to reviving the Open Skies talks. By late 1990, the conservative elements within the Soviet bureaucracy were in the ascendant, led by the military. They were determined to stem the tide of what they saw as unrequited Soviet concessions of security matters. Open Skies was to suffer as a result.

In December 1990 the SPC began its review of NATO's Open Skies position. At the same time, it authorized the United States to conduct bilateral soundings of the Soviet's willingness to engage in realistic compromises.[36] The first opportunity came at the Baker-Shevardnadze ministerial meeting in Houston on December 11–12. The Americans presented Shevardnadze with an informal paper that sought to solidify the Irkutsk Formula. "The nonpaper expressed Washington's willingness to accept Soviet aircraft for overflights of the USSR (without reference to the use of US sensors) in exchange for Soviet agreement to drop all territorial restrictions and move closer to the NATO positions on quota numbers and types and quality of sensors."[37] Shevardnadze was unable to comment on the paper but promised to study it.

Eight days later Shevardnadze resigned as the Soviet foreign minister. In his resignation speech, Shevardnadze expressed frustration with the growing conservative influence over decision-making and warned of a possible return of "dictatorship" within the USSR.[38] In a specific reference to arms control, Shevardnadze repudiated the criticism that the military was heaping upon him for, as he put it, "making too many concessions in the area of disarmament without any concessions from the other side."[39] Shevardnadze's abrupt resignation, and the general tilt to the right that underlay his frustration, signaled that Open Skies would not be resumed for some time. Although the allies were under no illusions about the difficulties they faced, many smaller allies believed that an effort should be made in order to acquire at least some information about Soviet deployments east of the Urals. Though cautious about making a commitment to a future round of negotiations, the United States was interested in exploring the ground.[40]

By mid-February 1991, the Soviets had responded to the U.S. paper handed over in Houston. The response was thoroughly disappointing. The Soviets refused to acknowledge the Irkutsk Formula and actually backtracked on a number of ideas they had previously accepted, such as the inclusion of synthetic aperture radar (SAR) in the sensor package. At the next SPC meeting the United States argued that the alliance should shelve any plans of a resumption until Moscow was more forthcoming.[41] Once again, however, the Europeans were anxious at least to try to restart the talks. As one Western official was publicly quoted on February 15, 1991, "The need to know about the equipment withdrawn behind the Urals was in part of driving the NATO work . . . . Open Skies would give the . . . European countries the chance to go beyond the CFE parameters."[42]

Accordingly, the allies decided to formally develop a new position that could be put to the Soviets as an official proposal, rather than a nonpaper. Working from an American paper that sought to draw together all of the elements of the various proposals that had been made since the original Canadian compromise paper of the previous summer, the allies conducted a wide-ranging review through February and March.[43]

As the review continued, the U.S. interagency debate began to change. Despite the recent Soviet shift to the right, the world had changed so significantly since the original U.S. interagency position had been adopted that the collectors within the intelligence community no longer required as intrusive an Open Skies regime. It thus became possible for the State Department to push the political aspects of the regime as the primary goals of the negotiation. Thus "the balance of interagency opinion shifted in the direction of a less intrusive Open Skies regime that will still achieve the core political objective of greater transparency and confidence-building."[44]

The internal NATO consultation over the new Open Skies position saw the European members of the alliance come to the fore in the consideration of the outstanding issues.[45] Indeed, the French, Germans, and British now regularly joined the Canadians in taking issue with the U.S. desire to wait for a signal of Soviet flexibility before displaying their own compromise.[46]

In many respects, the late-1990/early-1991 alliance debate over whether to display flexibility, or await a Soviet indication of a desire to go forward, illustrates the final resolution by the alliance of the classic question of whether to make toughness one's primary negotiating strategy, or to propose compromises in hopes of getting negotiations under way. This dilemma had haunted all allied discussions of compromise since the beginning of the Open Skies negotiation. Proponents of compromise had argued that a move by the allies would increase the chances of resuming the talks. Many within the U.S. bureaucracy had taken the view that such a concession might increase the chances of achieving an agreement, but that the final agreement would not have been the type of regime they sought. A move would thus be counterproductive.

By March of 1991, however, the question was changing in a subtle and yet significant way. It was no longer a question of either getting an intrusive surveillance regime that would be asymmetrical in its benefits and competitive in its operation, or of being happy with nothing. The allies, for very different reasons, were now coming to the conclusion that a moderately intrusive, equal, and cooperative regime was desirable. The question thus became: What was the best way to tease the Soviets into negotiations?

When they argued against too rapid a development of an allied compromise position, the Americans (or at least, by now, most of them) were not arguing against the eventual development of a compromise, but rather against laying out NATO's hand too soon. There was a fear that the Soviets would pocket whatever the allies put forward without reciprocating. It would then be up to NATO to come up with a further round of compromises, and so on, until the Soviets deigned to reply.[47] Those allies who wanted to develop a compromise and lay it before the Soviets took the view that the elements in Moscow who wished to move forward needed some ammunition to use against the Soviet military's stultifying refusal to budge. But they were also motivated by the recognition that almost any deal would have significantly enhanced their ability to acquire information about Soviet military activities outside of the CFE zone.[48]

In the case of Open Skies, the decision was ultimately to proceed with the compromise option. It may be argued that the Europeans and Canadian had thus "won" the argument. But, once the Americans had accepted a less intrusive regime, its utility to the intelligence community was greatly diminished. The achievement of an agreement became a political exercise, and one that Washington could afford to have fail, so long as it had genuinely tried to achieve a deal. Washington's acquiescence to the desire of the allies may have reflected the fact that the United States was no longer quite so interested in the regime for its own sake, but the Europeans manifestly were. The internal NATO toughness dilemma was thus finally resolved by the fact that the allies' interests achieved a degree of congruence for a variety of reasons.

## A NEW ALLIED POSITION

On April 24, 1991, the North Atlantic Council approved a document outlining the new NATO position.[49] Canada's deputy permanent representative to NATO, Ralph Lysyshyn, and an official from the Canadian CFE delegation in Vienna, John Bryson, presented the paper to the Soviets in Moscow on April 30. The paper, entitled simply *Resumption of the Open Skies Conference*, offered a "conceptual outline for a compromise" according to a Canadian official.[50]

On the aircraft ownership question, the proposal asserted, "The principle that Observation Flights are to be conducted by aircraft selected by the Observing State should be preserved insofar as possible."[51] Where this was not possible the paper stipulated: "No country should be able to deny a requested overflight on the grounds that only its aircraft can be used but that no appropriately equipped host-country aircraft is available." The paper argued that participating states that did not own suitable aircraft should be granted access to such aircraft to enable "those states to participate fully in the Open Skies regime."

On sensors, the paper stated that "the aim should be to achieve an all-weather, day/night capability that will be sufficient to achieve recognition of military equipment and activity." The allies believed that the initial "minimum sensor packages designed to meet that aim should include, in particular, optical and electro-optical cameras, synthetic aperture radar and infra-red sensors." They further believed that the possibility of adding additional sensors should be preserved, and mentioned multispectral sensors and air-sampling devices as two sensors that could be considered after a regime had been achieved.

For each type of sensor in the package, the allies believed that "[t]he Open Skies Treaty should establish optimal maximum performance parameters for each category of sensors to be incrementally included in the Open Skies sensor package." The paper did not outline what these parameters might be, however. It will be recalled that some dispute had existed within the alliances as to how equality in sensors would be established, with the United States advocating some ill-defined measure of "comparability," while others had wished to use the most straightforward parameter of all: ground resolution. The paper then argued that "[s]ensors with capabilities up to but not exceeding those optical parameters could be immediately incorporated into the Open Skies sensor package as they became commercially available to all Open Skies participants. At all times the sensor package should consist of equipment available to all participants." Finally, the paper argued that "if an Observed State were to insist on the use of an aircraft of its choice for an observation flight over its territory, the Observing state should have the right to insist that the aircraft be equipped with a set of sensors meeting in each category all agreed performance parameters of equipment available to all . . . participants at the time of the observation flight."

Turning to quotas, the paper vaguely alluded to a desire to be flexible, provided the Soviets were also, but outlined no number. On the questions of the territorial scope of the regime, and overflights of third-country bases, the paper maintained the alliance position that all territory of participants should be open to overflights and that third-country bases would not be part of the regime. On data-sharing, the paper offered ("subject to agreement on the foregoing elements") the idea that "provision should be made for raw data collected by an Observing State . . . to be shared with the Observed State."

These specific compromises were preceded by a general assessment of the situation that indicated the allies' willingness to convene an exploratory session "to determine whether, and, if so, how, additional progress can be made at this time." The paper suggested dates in mid-May, and the use of the CFE negotiation facilities in Vienna for this session. The allies warned, however, that "[o]ur flexibility in these matters needs, of course, to be reciprocated by others, particularly with regard to Open Skies quotas, sensors, and territorial coverage."

The Soviets received the NATO paper without officially displaying any willingness to match its compromises.[52] Privately, Soviet Foreign Ministry officials intimated that the NATO paper was a significant step forward and deserved a serious reply.[53] Unfortunately, officials within the Soviet Defense Ministry were unwilling to show flexibility.[54] Instead, Karpov and his officials listened to the Canadian presentation and then reiterated their positions on such issues as third-country bases and territorial restrictions within the USSR. Nevertheless, the Soviets promised to study the NATO proposals and reply within a few weeks.[55] In fact, they were not to respond for several months as the decision-making apparatus within the Kremlin ground to a halt through the summer of 1991.

As the internal Soviet debate took place, the CFE implementation dispute was resolved. Moscow agreed not to "resubordinate" its forces in the CFE zone, and to compromise on the equipment it had removed from the CFE zone shortly before signing the agreement such that a strategic reserve of forces would not be created just beyond the Urals. Gorbachev's desire to secure an invitation to the London G7 Economic Summit in June may have played a role in his forcing the Soviet General Staff to accept the terms of the CFE Treaty.[56] With resolution of the CFE issue, the stage was thus publicly set for a resumption of in-depth discussions on other arms control matters. Gorbachev's compromise over the CFE question may have added to his difficulty in persuading the General Staff to move on Open Skies, however.

## A BILATERAL TREATY

Some additional pressure was placed on the Soviets during the early summer when the Hungarians and Romanians signed a bilateral Open Skies Treaty on May 11.[57] Shortly after the end of the Budapest Conference the Romanians suggested a bilateral treaty to Budapest. The Hungarians were leery at first, fearing such a move would detract from efforts to revive the multilateral negotiations. By January 1991, the Hungarians accepted the invitation, hoping that a bilateral deal might stimulate the multilateral discussions. There were also concerns that traditional antagonisms between the two countries, which had been covered up during the Warsaw Pact era, might resurface as the two countries left that alliance. A bilateral Open Skies deal was thus seen in both capitals as a practical way of addressing security concerns that might arise between the two, and a symbolic way of demonstrating both sides' desire for stable relations in the new era.

Using the draft text from the multilateral discussions as their base, the negotiations moved quickly. The bilateral treaty was completed in March. The Hungarian-Romanian Treaty drew from both Western and Soviet versions of the multilateral draft, though it did favor the NATO ideas to a much greater extent. No limitations were imposed on camera performance, for example, though only film and video cameras were allowed because of the desire of both countries to limit the regime to technologies to which they had equal access. On the other hand, full data-sharing was mandated through the use of dual recording techniques, with each side keeping a copy of the processed film at the conclusion of each flight. A demonstration flight was carried out over both countries on June 29, and representatives were invited from the other participants in the multilateral negotiation.[58]

Despite the Hungarian-Romanian announcement the Soviets were not able to respond to the NATO proposals in May, however. In early June, they informed the NATO countries that they would not have an answer ready before

September.[59] According to unnamed NATO officials the Soviet announcement meant that the treaty would not be finished by the autumn.[60] As the summer dragged on, German foreign minister Genscher, on behalf of the nine states of the Western European Union (WEU), appealed to the Soviets in early August to respond to the NATO proposal.[61]

## A NEW PROPOSAL

Although nothing was heard from the Soviets through the summer, the United States did make a proposal on aircraft ownership to the NATO allies in June.[62] The new American idea represented an astonishing about-face for Washington, and caught many of the allies by surprise. Basically, Washington let it be known in June that it was now in favor of a jointly operated, co-located fleet of aircraft. This was the original Soviet position, and had been anathema to the Americans throughout the negotiations.

The reason for the U.S. switch was a technical assessment performed by the collectors within the intelligence community. They reasoned that, if they would have to fly around the USSR on an aircraft provided by the Soviets, they would not know whether the sensors had been calibrated or maintained properly. A jointly run and maintained fleet offered the possibility of keeping track of the calibration and maintenance of the aircraft and sensors so that peak efficiency could be ensured on each flight. The United States proposed that the fleet be based at a disused Soviet airbase in Hungary, and that it be composed of aircraft "donated" by countries that could afford to provide an airframe for a lengthy period of time. The costs of each flight would be reimbursed, but the "opportunity cost" of losing an aircraft would not. Thus, only those countries with relatively large air forces would have been in a position to supply an aircraft over time.[63] In addition to the allies and the Hungarians, the Americans were rumored to have approached the Soviets with the idea. Interestingly, by the summer of 1991 Moscow was not enthusiastic about what had been its own idea. They simply did not have the cash to pay for their share of the costs of a pool located outside of the USSR.[64]

The allies had been over these arguments in their consideration of the compromise paper. Although the Americans were now prepared to commit to this idea, NATO decided that it would not be wise to revise a proposal that had already been pitched to the Soviets and upon which they were awaiting a reply.[65] Though the American idea ultimately came to naught, the episode is interesting in that it demonstrates the extent to which the Americans now tailored their conception of the regime to a search for compromises. It also illustrates the extent to which the Soviets had little interest in their ideas once the prospect of an agreement was real and costs were reckoned into the equation.

## THE SOVIETS RESPOND

A few days after Genscher's August appeal, the Soviets responded, through the Canadian embassy in Moscow, informing the allies that they would agree to attend a one-week exploratory session in Vienna to begin on September 9.[66] Their response to the NATO package fell well short of the flexibility sought by the allies. Indeed, the Soviets made no attempt to move off their earlier positions, much to the dismay of Western officials.[67] This placed the allies in a difficult position. They were loath to resume the negotiations in the absence of a Soviet signal of compromise, but worried that a refusal to attend the one-week session would cause the Soviets to break off altogether. Once again, the Europeans were keener to try to restart the discussions than the Americans.[68] Accordingly, the Canadian and Hungarian foreign ministers, acting in their capacity as joint hosts for the earlier Open Skies Conference rounds, issued a press release announcing the one-week session to begin in Vienna on September 9.[69]

## THE COUP

Before the delegations could gather in Vienna, however, conservative elements within the Kremlin staged a coup attempt between August 19 and 23. Although unsuccessful, the coup weakened Gorbachev fatally. It also weakened the Soviet military and the KGB, causing many conservative officers to resign in disgrace. Before the end of the year, the coup would prove to have been a significant contributing factor in the undoing of the Communist Party and even the Soviet Union itself.

The immediate impact of these dramatic developments upon the proposed Vienna Open Skies session was to rob the Soviet delegation of new instructions on the eve of the session. The extent of the confusion in Moscow was too great to have expected anyone to issue new instructions on Open Skies in late August.[70] Over the longer term, however, the removal of the communists was the decisive step in creating the conditions that would ultimately allow Open Skies to succeed.[71] When they gathered in Vienna on September 9, then, the NATO delegations did not expect to hear new Soviet positions. What they wanted to see was informal evidence of a willingness to move on Open Skies once order had been restored in Moscow.

## THE PARTICIPATION QUESTION

The first question to be dealt with, however, was the structure and membership of the informal session. Once it had become obvious that such a session was to take place, the Canadians and Hungarians, acting in their capacity as cochairs of the first round called upon the CSCE Conference secretariat to provide secretariat services.[72] As the meeting was to be an informal exploration of the NATO compromise package, it was quickly decided to dispense with the working group structure of the Ottawa and Budapest sessions.

Instead, the secretariat was asked to provide a setting in which the heads of delegation and their advisors could meet twice a day to discuss each of the issues. In asking for this structure, the Canadians and Hungarians were responding to informal consultations they had undertaken among the other participants, several of whom had indicated a strong desire to avoid the excessively structured environment of Ottawa and Budapest.[73] They were also motivated by the outcome of a new round of the participation debate. The old problem of admitting the other CSCE members arose yet again. This problem had been present throughout the NATO discussion of the compromise paper. The traditional positions on the question had been maintained throughout the winter and spring of 1991. That is to say, the French wanted the CSCE countries to participate immediately, the United States did not, the Turks refused to accept any formula that might have conferred any recognition upon the government of Cyprus, and the Greeks refused to accept any proposal that did not.[74] Although an agreement to admit the CSCE countries was not possible within NATO, a French suggestion to increase their rights as observers was accepted. Henceforth, these countries would have "active observer" status, with the right to attend and to take the floor at all plenaries (but not working groups), and to receive all conference documents and to circulate their own.[75]

The situation changed dramatically in the aftermath of the failed Soviet coup, however. With the declaration of independence by the Baltic countries, a new equation arose. Since these countries were former members of the USSR, they were entitled to participate as "successor states." This right was enthusiastically recognized by all at NATO for two reasons. First, the Soviets continued to maintain sizable forces in the Baltic countries. NATO was anxious to overfly and photograph them as part of the Open Skies regime. It was thus important that these counties be brought into the negotiations for the regime as soon as possible. Second, a desire existed to bind the newly independent Baltics to the emerging security structure of Europe as quickly as possible. This second consideration was predicated on a belief that other Soviet republics that were breaking away should be encouraged to submit to the arms control obligations of the USSR. If these new countries were to be enticed to place their weapons under the terms of these various treaties, they would also have to be granted membership in the fora that were responsible for negotiating them.[76]

Once the decision had been taken to invite the Baltics to participate, it was recognized that it would have been impossible to accept countries that were a few days old (the Baltics) while continuing to reject countries that had been members of the CSCE for years. Hence, those countries which had adopted a cautious attitude on the question of admitting the CSCE neutrals were now prepared to see them admitted to the Open Skies negotiations as full members. Unfortunately, the Turks continued to reject any idea that might allow Cyprus to join the negotiations. Since the Greeks could not agree to any formula that would not include Cyprus automatically, stalemate remained over the matter of letting anyone else in along with the Baltics.

The only way out of the impasse, without embarrassing the other CSCE countries by admitting the Baltics without them, was to admit the Baltics into an "active observer" category. This was profoundly unsatisfactory, but was just about possible in that the Baltics had never formally accepted their incorporation into the USSR in the way the other republics had done. It was thus possible to argue that the Baltics were not, in fact, quite so much successors to the USSR as liberated from it.[77]

Although this solution would work for the Baltics in the context of the one-week session, it was recognized that it would be invalid once a "real" successor to the USSR applied for membership. The non-NATO countries were increasingly frustrated with the alliance's inability to deal with its problem, and wanted to go ahead and admit everyone immediately.[78] The rule of consensus prevented the conference from doing so, however. The inability to admit the CSCE countries meant that the structure of the sessions would be affected. Since the "active observers" could not be admitted to any working groups, the decision was thus taken not to have working groups but to have such informal discussions as might be necessary outside of formal plenaries in a series of informal plenaries. The desire to avoid the working group structure had already been agreed, for procedural reasons, but the participation problem reinforced the decision.

Once again, as they had done from the start, the delegations were able to sidestep the issue of participation. But it was recognized that this would be increasingly difficult as the negotiations unfolded. The dramatic events that had taken place in Europe were now placing the Open Skies negotiation in the position of "catch-up" with respect to the question of participation. The one situation that had not changed, however, was the dispute over Cyprus, and it was this problem that would continue to prevent the expansion of the negotiations.

Because it was impossible to expand the talks formally, a mechanism had to be found whereby the expansion would take place in a de facto manner, and yet one that could protect everyone's political position. Expansion in itself was an important political issue, but none of the countries to which membership might be extended were of sufficient importance to the existence of the operation of the regime itself that any of the present members were prepared to sacrifice the negotiations to the cause of expansion. In reality, this had always been the case.

## THE DISCUSSION BEGINS

When the meeting got down to business on September 9, the discussion was somewhat anticlimactic. As expected, the Soviets did not have a new position to bring to the meeting, nor were they able to officially entertain any compromises.[79] The Soviet delegation was led by Yevgeni Golovko, a deputy of Karpov's at the Foreign Ministry, and its chief Ministry of Defense advisor was a Colonel Romanov.[80]

Informally, however, Golovko and other members of the Foreign Ministry team "sought to move the discussion along, praising the new NATO proposal and promising to revise their positions."[81] Significantly, Golovko put Romanov in the chair when the most contentious issues of third-country bases and territorial restrictions within the USSR came up for discussion. Thus, the Ministry of Defense representative was forced to bear the brunt of a heavy attack on these positions from both the NATO countries and the Soviet allies alike.[82]

For its part, the U.S. delegation made the ultimate signal of its willingness to accept an equal and cooperative regime. In advancing the NATO position on sensor equality, the U.S. delegation suggested that comparisons of the ground resolution capability of different sensor systems would be the best way to ensure equality of output (as opposed to "comparability"). It then offered to incorporate tests to measure ground resolution into the final treaty provisions.[83] In its desire to retain an advantage in sensor capability, the U.S. delegation had resisted such a definition of strict equality since the Ottawa Conference. Its willingness to accept true equality was seen by all present as the final indication that the United States was prepared to accept a truly noncompetitive regime.

After one week of discussions on the issues, the Soviet delegation promised to seek new instructions. Accordingly, it was agreed to resume the conference proper once these instructions had been obtained. Although they tentatively scheduled this resumption for early October, most of the participants were aware that somewhat more than three weeks would be required for the Soviet delegation to get new instructions. One Western official subsequently told the *Arms Control Reporter* that he did not foresee the resumption of discussions before early November.[84] Significantly, and despite the fact that the Soviets had to receive their instructions, the delegations did tentatively agree to establish the CSCE Ministerial Meeting scheduled for March 24, 1992, as the target date for conclusion of the negotiations.[85]

Of course, this deadline was tentative. Furthermore, it would not be confirmed until the Soviets obtained new instructions, which paved the way to an agreement. But the fact that the delegations were thinking in terms of a deadline indicates that they believed the issues were capable of resolution in the time available. This was a dramatic evolution, particularly since the negotiators had been disappointed by an overly ambitious deadline once before.

## CONCLUSION

Events during the period between the end of the Budapest Conference and the end of the one-week sessions at Vienna thus laid the ground for the breakthroughs that led to the Open Skies Treaty. Although many of these events were the result of a desire on the part of several participants to re-energize the talks, the eventual success of the negotiations owed a great deal to events that had little to do with Open Skies. The disgrace and dismissal of the hard-liners following the aborted Soviet coup; the increasingly active involvement of the Europeans seeking an independent means of monitoring events within the USSR; and the recognition by the Americans that the eventual regime could not be driven by the needs of their own intelligence community were all part of a pattern of events as Cold War structures deteriorated at breakneck speed.

That the Open Skies initiative benefited from these developments was in part due to its ability to reinvent itself in order to fit the needs of the moment. It is also, however, an indication of the extent to which the key issues and tradeoffs had been identified by previous rounds, and could be manipulated quickly once the political will existed to do so. The issues were well understood by this point, and little exploration of their underlying characteristics was required.

When the delegations met in Vienna in early September, they were negotiating on the basis of already understood problems and a new position.

Thus the events leading up to the revival of the Open Skies negotiation cannot be described as prenegotiation. But neither can they be described as a full negotiation in their own right. They were exploratory talks that fell somewhere between. Finally, and perhaps most important, the key to success in this period was the fact that political leaders on both sides took charge of the Open Skies file, much to the surprise of their bureaucracies, and pushed for change.

# 6 The First Vienna Round

The Vienna round of the Open Skies Conference began on November 4, 1991. At the first plenary it became obvious that the Soviet delegation had new instructions. Ambassador Golovko made a statement in which he thanked the other delegations for their patience and then outlined new positions on each of the issues. Gone was the Soviet insistence that they be allowed to fly over bases in third countries. Gone was their desire to hold certain areas of the USSR off-limits to Open Skies overflights. Finally a new passive quota of fifty-two flights per year was offered.[1] Significantly, Golovko went to some lengths to stress that the new position had the support of all the republics, whose governments had been extensively consulted.[2]

This was the statement that the others had been waiting for, and they responded enthusiastically. As the U.S. head of delegation said, "It's been a good day . . . . [Golovko] . . . made a very important and fundamental statement, in that confirmation that all Soviet territory is open to overflight makes it possible now to move rapidly to agreement. This has always been the central issue of these negotiations."[3] At the same meeting at which Golovko made his statement the delegations formally committed themselves to having the treaty ready for signature at the Conference on Security and Cooperation in Europe (CSCE) Summit scheduled for March in Helsinki.

## A DEADLINE

From the beginning of the Vienna round a deadline existed and all of the delegations agreed to it. The previous deadline had been established by the hosts of the first two conferences for symbolic reasons and with little discussion. The new deadline was based upon a structure of trade-offs that had been agreed in an extensive interim negotiation. In stating publicly that the March deadline was a realistic one, Golovko was later quoted as saying, "We do not have any issues of principle which divide us. I believe that now we have a common approach."[4] For these reasons, the new deadline was far more realistic and achievable. Moreover, because it had been agreed by all, the deadline had the effect of forcing the negotiators to begin making the psychological shift required if any negotiation is to move away from the endless exploration of the options and toward decision-making, or the "end-game" phase.

It would take time for the delegations to fully realize the practical implications of this shift. Not until after the Christmas break would the end-game begin in earnest. But the work done in the autumn sessions was marked by an increasing belief that a real negotiation was in progress, and that decisions reached would one day actually form the basis of real Open Skies overflights.[5] This was new to the Open Skies negotiation.

The fact that the delegations were about to negotiate on the basis of an agreed formula was also new. The negotiations would now be about filling in the details through drafting. Although this was to prove unexpectedly difficult, and though some of the basic aspects of the formula were to be called into question by the Russian military, it marked an important shift from the Ottawa and Budapest rounds.

## A NEW TEXT

Over the next few days the larger Western countries (France, Germany, the UK, and the United States) indicated the extent to which they had been working together during the interval between the September session and the beginning of the November discussions as they tabled texts for all of the articles and annexes. Before long, an entirely redrafted treaty was on the table.[6]

Indeed, the extent to which these four had been consulting looked ominous to some of the smaller countries who feared that their concerns and interests would be lost as the larger countries took charge of the negotiations and moved towards a treaty. Over the next few weeks, however, it would become apparent that the larger countries were not agreed on all of the substantive points, and the smaller countries were able to influence the negotiation where they were willing to do the substantive work required to make a contribution. In fact, considerable differences would surface between the larger countries over a variety of political issues. These differences would not prevent the technical parameters of the negotiation from ultimately being largely set by the bigger countries, however.[7]

Although this fact was to cause some concern among the smaller countries,[8] it was probably inevitable once the negotiations moved away from the larger conceptual trade-offs and into the technical details of the treaty. One of the most effective means of overcoming a situation in which a large number of participants in a multilateral negotiation reduces the efficiency of the discussion is to create smaller working groups. These groups must be composed of those delegations most able to deal with the issues, or most necessary to the formulation of a compromise.

Despite the occasional displeasure that existed over the actions of the larger countries, then, these events were perfectly consistent with the need to reduce the complexity of the negotiation, and to increase its efficiency. It also became apparent that only the larger delegations were prepared to keep technical experts (both in terms of the sensor technologies, and the legal and political issues) in Vienna. This enabled them to cover all of the discussions, and to do the work required to explore the necessary compromises in any detail.[9] Moreover, as will be discussed, the "inner circle" was not exclusionary. Other nations were able to join when they could contribute ideas to the discussion at the more technical level. Canada and Sweden made this leap on various specific issues as the negotiation unfolded.

All of this was in the future. With the gist of a treaty on the table, the conference began discussing it in detail. Meetings continued until November 22, when a two-week break was called to allow capitals to assess the emerging draft.[10] The conference reconvened on December 9 and ran until the 20th before breaking for Christmas.

## INFORMAL CONTACT GROUPS ARE FORMED

Even before the break it had become obvious that the formality of the plenary sessions was an impediment to progress. Among other problems, the plenary structure meant that the real experts could not discuss the issues, but had to communicate through their senior representatives who held the national chair during the plenaries, thus preventing a free-flowing discussion. In order to overcome these problems, it was decided to form working groups to deal with the various texts. Significantly, however, the working groups formed during the Vienna Conference were quite different from those created for the Ottawa and Budapest rounds.

These differences were the products of both a desire to avoid some of the structural rigidity of the earlier rounds and of the political events that preceded the Vienna round. Many delegations expressed a belief that the Ottawa and Budapest rounds had featured an unnecessarily large profusion of working groups and caucuses, which had made life difficult for the smaller delegations. Moreover, the formality of the earlier working group arrangement was felt by many to have inhibited a free-flowing discussion.

On the political level, the procedural problem of how to incorporate the neutral CSCE countries into the proceedings once again became a critical issue. These countries were allowed to attend plenary sessions, and to take the floor during formal plenaries. If working groups were to be formed, however the Turks were not prepared to allow the CSCE states to participate, as it would give Cyprus too great a status.[11]

After some confusion, the UK delegation suggested that individual delegations might wish to convene "informal contact groups" to deal with specific texts.[12] The idea was that these groups would not be organs of the conference per se, but rather meetings hosted by an individual delegation. As such, the meeting would include whomever the host invited and proceed on the basis of whatever rules the host established. The groups would take no decisions, but their deliberations could be made known to the plenary, which could then act upon them.

This was not the first time negotiators in Vienna had created of a set of relatively informal groups to discuss specific issues. During the Mutual and Balanced Force Reduction (MBFR) talks of the 1970s and 80s, a structure of formal plenaries and "informals" evolved for many of the same reasons. As in the Open Skies negotiation, most of the real work was done in the informals and subsequently endorsed by the plenary (though the MBFR informals were somewhat more structured).[13]

The British proposal was commended for its subtlety, and adopted. Neither the Greeks nor the Turks were happy, but they were prepared to live with the compromise. Those CSCE states that wished to take a full role in the proceedings were pleased that they would be able to participate in the contact groups on a more equal basis than they could in the plenaries. But they were still unhappy that they could not be admitted to the conference proper.[14]

The UK delegation convened a group on sensor issues, since they had put the sensor text forward and had a sensor expert on hand. These included all questions related to sensor performance and calibration, and data-exchange issues. The Germans volunteered to deal with the operational questions; these included such areas as flight procedures, emergency procedures, and the timelines for overflights. The French took control of the texts concerning legal issues. This included accession, entry into force, review mechanisms, and all of the legal and diplomatic privileges and immunities of the flight crews. The United States took over a grab-bag of texts, such as Article Two on Definitions, and promised to take charge of the conforming process once that was under way. This was to prove one of the most labor intensive areas of the entire negotiation when it began, after the Christmas recess.[15] Canada, the only other country to host meetings during the conference, hosted the groups that dealt with the Preamble and Article 1.

## THE LEADERS ARE ESTABLISHED

The fact that "custody" of all of the texts was left in the hands of the various countries that were seen as the leaders within the negotiation was a significant difference between Vienna and the earlier Ottawa and Budapest rounds. The working groups in the initial rounds had been chaired by Bulgaria, Canada, Czechoslovakia, and the Netherlands. This step had been taken as a means of ensuring that a degree of balance existed between the two blocs. It also reflected a desire to avoid situations in which the most powerful countries were seen as having too great a degree of influence on the proceedings. The structure of the Ottawa and Budapest rounds was mired in the negotiating traditions of the Cold War.

Although it is unlikely that this structure in itself prevented agreement (as the primary issue was the lack of agreement as to the basic purposes of the regime), it can be said that the practice of giving custody of the texts to the leading countries, which was adopted at Vienna, had a profound effect in stimulating the work there. As the issues became more and more technical, the fact that the leaders took control of the texts meant that their expertise was brought to bear from a position of authority.

Instead of presenting the rest with texts that had large blanks which were then filled in by committee discussions, as had been attempted in Ottawa and Budapest, the leaders in Vienna routinely presented the smaller delegations with texts that were largely completed and then invited comment and discussion.[16] Often, the technical aspects of the texts had been intensively discussed by the leaders before they were presented to the rest, and represented a measure of what the bigger countries were prepared to live with. This tactic cut down on the amount of extraneous discussion, and may be said to have substantially reduced the degree of complexity present by providing the negotiation with a focus.[17]

This did not prevent other countries from voicing opinions, or disagreeing with the texts presented by the chairs of the various groups, of course. Nor did it prevent one or two occasions when smaller delegations expressed consternation at the extent to which some of the leaders presented what appeared to be a fait accompli.[18] But it did provide a basis for the discussions in that the texts represented a realistic starting point. In sum, then, the procedure adopted at the Vienna Conference was an important component of the eventual success of that conference.

## NEW COALITIONS FORM

As has been said, the Vienna Conference featured a lack of coalition politics, since the Warsaw Treaty Organization (WTO) was defunct. The non-Soviet former WTO members had operated as an informal caucus during the Ottawa and Budapest rounds, particularly in pressing for sensor equality. With that point now agreed, however, these countries felt little need to coordinate their approaches to other issues and did not do so during the Vienna sessions. Accordingly, their earlier cooperation may be seen as having been an issues-specific "marriage of convenience." It did not translate into a broader coalition that was active across a range of issues.[19]

The North Atlantic Treaty Organization (NATO) countries, for their part, did not use their alliance caucus as a mechanism for the coordination of their positions to anything like the extent they had in Ottawa and Budapest. In the earlier rounds, each working group had featured its own daily alliance caucus, which agreed upon tactics for that day's meetings. In Vienna, by contrast, the allies met in caucus once a week, and even then it was usually to deal with general matters rather than to work out unified positions on every specific issue. Moreover, their positions in the individual contact group meetings had not been carefully worked out beforehand.[20]

To an extent, this was the result of easily explained factors. First, as has already been pointed out, the basic compromises had already been made. Second, the Vienna Conference was quite different from the earlier meetings, in that it was a more-or-less continuous session over several months, much like the CFE Conference that was taking place at the same time in the same venue. Understandably, the pace and style of work were quite different from the earlier, shorter conferences. Third, the fact that the alliance caucus was of less importance in the Vienna Conference may also be attributable to the fact that the political circumstances were radically different by late 1991. With the demise of the WTO, and the impending dissolution of the USSR itself, the need that the allies had felt for close cooperation on every aspect of the negotiation was now lessening. Finally, as the end-game began those technical issues that had been side-stepped in earlier rounds now had to be discussed. Since some of the allies had differing positions on these issues (such as the Franco-U.S. difference over the relationship of Open Skies to the CSCE process), disagreement was inevitable.

Interestingly, two other coalitions arose to partially fill this gap during the Vienna round: the informal grouping of some of the Neutral and Non-aligned (NNA) observers; and the Western European Union (WEU). To begin with the NNA, not all of these countries played a particularly intensive role in the talks, but those that did often coordinated their position on a wide range of issues. Sweden and Finland were by far the most active members of the NNA, taking strong positions on all of the issues.[21] Austria was not far behind, but on more specific issues having to do with their role as host country of the negotiation and, potentially, of the various bodies that would be created to oversee implementation of the regime. Switzerland and Ireland were primarily interested in the expansion question, taking little interest in the mechanics of the regime. The other NNA were seldom heard from, except of course for Cyprus.

The Finnish-Swedish coalition was effective in seeing some of its points adopted, though their early interventions caused a degree of difficulty.[22] Many of the positions that Sweden and Finland took were often seen as being out of step with the manner in which both Europe and the treaty were evolving.[23] More specifically, these countries were regarded as being overly worried about both protecting their own secrets and forcing the Soviets (and later the Russians) to provide iron-clad assurances that they would abide by the treaty's provisions. It many ways, the particular ramifications of the positions adopted by the Swedes and the Finns were regarded by others as being excessively and unnecessarily complicated in the pre-Christmas period.[24] Later events were to prove that their concerns had not been without justification.

Finland, for example, was determined that no Open Skies overflight that came near a border of another country should be able to record images inside the other country, whether it was a regime participant or not.[25] This stand was believed to be partially motivated by a concern that an Open Skies flight over

Finland that flew near the Finnish/Russian border and acquired images of Russia would contravene the Finnish constitution's provision that the territory of Finland not be used by a third party for any military purpose.[26] While everyone else was agreed that Open Skies flights not be used to look into the territory of non–Open Skies signatories,[27] there was general agreement, including on the part of the Russians, that spillover into the territory of other signatories would be allowed in the interests of efficiency.

In responding to the Finnish points, all of the others stated that they were prepared to live with the modest degree of overspill that the Open Skies sensors would return as a result of flights near borders.[28] The Finns, supported by the Swedes, were aghast at the idea and came up with a series of proposals designed to overcome what they alone saw as a major problem. Most of these revolved around extremely complex flight planning procedures, designed to prevent any overspill in border areas, combined with rigorous notification measures for participants in whose border areas flights might occur. The problem was that the different sensors had different swath widths and fields of view, which meant that staying at the outer edge of the synthetic aperture radar (SAR) width could have meant that the cameras could not operate up to the borders, as their field of view was considerably narrower under certain circumstances.

Operating only certain sensors near a border, on the other hand, such that the swath width would be regulated to ensure no overspill, meant that the overflying state would have to accept a diminution of its right to employ all of its sensors wherever it wished. Perhaps most problematic, however, was the simple fact that the types of rigid rules being proposed by the Finns and Swedes to overcome what they alone saw as a problem would have had the effect of complicating flight planning procedures at the time the rest of the participants were trying to simplify everything. The feeling was developing that this "rigidity, had it not been nipped in the bud, would have impinged on the validity of the Treaty as a CBM."[29]

After considerable discussion, the solution to this problem was to include in the Preamble the phrase "Seeking to establish agreed procedures to provide for aerial observation of all the territories of States Parties, with the *intent* of observing a single State Party or groups of States Parties."[30] While it satisfied honor, this language fell far short of the concerns raised by the Finns and the Swedes.

Another issue raised by these two countries was Sweden's concern that the Russians might not follow the flight path on flights where the Russians supplied the aircraft. This mistrust was part of a larger feeling on the part of the Swedes that the Russians would seek to stretch the rules to their benefit whenever they could.[31] It may have been motivated by the fact that Swedes saw little difference between the Russian Federation and the USSR in terms of Moscow's traditional military priorities and activities in the Baltic region.[32] The Swedes thus advocated that every aircraft be outfitted to allow the observing country representatives to carry handheld Global Positioning System (GPS) devices. In the case of a discrepancy between the aircraft avionics and the handheld GPS system, the latter would take precedence.[33]

This proposal would have meant that any host-supplied aircraft could have its own navigation system overruled by an onboard observer with a handheld system. It would have meant that states intending to provide the aircraft for flights over themselves would have to modify their aircraft such that a handheld GPS could be used. This was flatly refused by everyone present, even though only the Soviets intended to supply the aircraft.[34]

A third matter raised by these two countries was over the question of whether the host would be expected to provide calibration test targets prior to Open Skies flights. Such targets would consist of a series of stationary objects, of agreed and uniform dimensions, that would be overflown by the observation aircraft at agreed heights. The resulting data could then be used to ensure the sensors on the aircraft did not exceed the allowed capabilities. These targets had been discussed in the previous rounds, but as a means of assuring the Soviets that the sensors on foreign aircraft would not exceed the agreed capabilities. Both the Soviets and the Americans had rejected the idea when it had been originally raised for very different reasons. The Soviets did not want foreign aircraft over their territory, while the United States wanted to retain the capability to use more capable sensors than might be apparent to the casual observer. Test targets would have taken some of the wind out of the Soviet argument, on the one hand, and would have forced the U.S. to use equal sensors on the other.[35]

With the agreement that the host could supply the aircraft, test targets were seen as redundant at the beginning of the Vienna Conference. The Swedes and the Finns argued that the test targets would be required to ensure that the sensors on an aircraft supplied by the Soviets fulfilled the terms of the treaty.[36] Although this argument was not seen as compelling before the Christmas break, a number of delegations came around to it during the end-game when Russia's position on sensor calibration was revealed and proved that the Swedes and

Finns had been correct in their suspicions of the willingness of the Russian military to accept Open Skies.

Finally, both Sweden and Finland were concerned that transit flights could be used to take clandestine images of the transited country.[37] Despite the fact that these flight could only be allowed in areas permitted by the transited country, usually civilian Air Traffic Control routes, the Swedes and Finns insisted that sensor covers be fabricated and placed on the aircraft during transits. This was eventually agreed. The language calling for the use of sensor covers may be found in Article IV, paragraph 4 of the treaty. Various regulations regarding the inspection of the sensor covers after transit flights are located throughout the treaty where appropriate.

The other coalition that arose in Vienna included the states of the Western European Union. There were several reasons for this.[38] Practically, the idea of cooperation between the WEU members made great sense. Given the relatively limited number of overflights that would be on offer, especially over Russia and the states of Eastern Europe, the purchase of an aircraft and sensor package by each of these countries would be difficult to justify. Moreover, pooling the number of overflights that could be performed, and the resulting data, would allow each state access to a much greater number of flights.

Politically, strong forces existed in favor of WEU cooperation.[39] Open Skies was an entirely new regime. Accordingly, cooperation between the WEU states would not fall afoul of previous procedures for cooperation within NATO. Open Skies was thus an opportunity to "put the WEU on the map,"[40] without coming into conflict with pre-existing arrangements. Other reasons also existed. The Germans, for example, held the rotating chairmanship of the WEU caucus in Vienna, and "wanted to make something of it."[41] France was keen on promoting a WEU role in Open Skies as a means of strengthening European cooperation.

During the pre-Christmas period, the WEU states concentrated on the idea of a common fleet of aircraft for their overflights. Basically, two options were under consideration.[42] The first would have created a centrally located pool of sensor pods that would have been compatible with different national aircraft from WEU states. Each state, in turn, would contribute a national aircraft for a set period to carry the commonly owned pod on behalf of all of the others. The second option was for the straightforward purchase of a specially equipped aircraft to be commonly owned and operated. Interestingly, the Russians were curious about the WEU's plans in this regard, and went so far as to informally suggest that Russian aircraft be used, with Western sensors and engines.[43] The WEU's discussions did not result in a firm plan for an aircraft pool during the Vienna Conference itself. They did, however, signal the desire of the WEU to carve out a role.

The NNA coalition was an example of a group of smaller countries attempting to use their collective weight to compensate for their relative lack of individual power. On the whole, those of their ideas that were ultimately successful were the ones which tapped the mood of the rest of the conference. The NNA were eventually successful on such things as sensor calibration test targets, once the others began to recognize the unwillingness of the Russian military to accept the spirit of Open Skies. Given the fact that these countries were not full participants in the discussion, their coalition was an effective means of multiplying what influence they did have.

The WEU, meanwhile, was positioning itself to become a force for order within the negotiation in two important ways, though this was not apparent before Christmas. In practical terms, the WEU countries' desire to combine their aircraft in some way would lead to a logical desire to approach the quota discussion from a united standpoint. This would prove vital in the bargaining over the quota distribution. In political terms, the WEU, and particularly the German leadership of it, would provide a counterweight to French tendencies toward confrontation with the United States over such matters as the Open Skies/CSCE link.[44]

## THE INFORMAL CONTACT GROUPS

The daily work in the contact groups prior to the Christmas break was characterized by an informal atmosphere.[45] In retrospect, it is apparent that much of the work done prior to Christmas was not of a lasting nature. It would become obvious after the Christmas break, for example, that many of the texts would have to be extensively revised.[46] While this need to revisit texts that had already been considered might be viewed as evidence of inefficiency, at least three mitigating factors are present.

First, though the broad trade-offs between the issues were well known, the majority of the participants in the Vienna negotiation were not sufficiently familiar with the technical issues to make final judgments on workable texts. Second, the extent to which decisions made in one group would affect the results of the others was not sufficiently appreciated. Finally, certain issues were seen as so politically charged—such as the questions of regime expansion, costs, and quotas—that a conscious decision was made to avoid intensive discussion of them until final stages of the end-game, when they could be taken up at a very high political level.[47]

The first two considerations were especially true with respect to the operational aspects of the treaty. Time and again, both before and after Christmas, the delegations were forced to revisit Article VI, dealing with mission operations, in order to correct paragraphs that were supposed to have been set aside.[48] Although some of this was the result of hasty initial drafting, much more resulted from the need to modify operational decisions already made to conform with decisions subsequently made by other groups regarding the types and capabilities of the sensors that would be allowed. The question of the timelines to be followed during overflights was not raised until relatively late in the game. This omission was the result of a conscious decision to establish a conceptual outline of flight procedures before filling in the actual details. It was felt that negotiating the details at the same time as the basic concepts would only muddy the waters, as had happened in Ottawa and Budapest.

On sensors, the majority of the participants required some education. Moreover, as the negotiations proceeded, it became clear that the Russian military sought to ensure that the final sensor package would be considerably weaker than had been expected.[49] Because so much of the early negotiation on these issues was conducted either at a general level, or with only the representatives of the UK, U.S., Germany, and Russia present, the majority of the participants were unable to clearly distinguish what would become a general Russian desire for a less effective sensor package until after the Christmas break. But some signs were there. The Russian military representatives, for example, held that their methods of calibrating individual sensors were the only methods acceptable. These were quite different from those of the majority, and were somewhat less effective.[50] This issue would become one of the key problems of the post-Christmas end-game.

On legal issues, the autumn was spent dealing with such matters as the immunities of the flight crews. The more political areas, such as the question of the accession of other CSCE states to the regime, were touched upon, but it was recognized that these would be critical end-game issues.[51] No one expected any compromises in these areas until the eleventh hour, and little effort was expended on finding compromises until after Christmas.

The question of costs was also not resolved during the autumn. The original NATO position had held that, if the overflown country chose to supply the aircraft, it should bear the costs.[52] The Soviets were not pleased with this idea and served notice that they would seek a change. The issue was not debated intensively during the autumn, but several NATO nations saw it as a possible concession to be held in reserve.[53]

Another idea raised during the autumn session was that of the "joker" with respect to the quota formula. This was originally a French idea from the Budapest round, and sought to make extra flights available, both for use in crisis situations and for use by nations of the same alliances when overflying each other. Canada put the joker back on the agenda with a nonpaper released in mid-November.[54] The paper arose from a concern that the evolving regime would be too restrictive with respect to the number of overflights that could be done by the smaller countries of Eastern Europe. The concern was that the small passive quota of each of these countries would not be enough to satisfy the larger countries and leave anything for these small countries.[55] Obviously, this fear arose from the fact that the bloc-to-bloc aspect of the negotiations had been abandoned, and the former WTO states would now be able to overfly each other. Since these countries were seen to be located in a region in which tensions were highest, the paper argued that their neighbors might be precisely the ones requiring flights. Accordingly, the paper proposed that a variety of means should be explored to place a higher number of active quotas at the disposal of neighboring countries.[56]

First, it was proposed that these countries accept more overflights (their passive quota), in order to increase their active quota, but that a proportion of these extra overflights be reserved for the use of regional neighbors. Second, special flights during periods of tension were proposed. These flights could count beyond the normal quota entitlements and should be reserved for use between neighbors, with no right of refusal. It was also proposed that consideration be given to the utility of such flights being conducted on behalf of the CSCE's Conflict Prevention Centre (CPC).[57] Finally, the paper proposed consideration of a series of bilateral, regional arrangements within the overall framework of the multilateral treaty. These bilateral arrangements would follow the Hungarian-Romanian Treaty and would allow the states of a region to increase their coverage of each other.

Informal consultations on the idea were organized by France and included Canada, the United States, Hungary, and the Netherlands. The final country was included because it held the chair of the European Community at the time and France wanted its backing in placing the joker flight within the purview of the CSCE.[58] During these consultations it became obvious that many were in favor of the joker idea in principle. There were worries, however, that Canada's emphasis on these flights being available only to neighbors would tend to "localize" security problems that might be of concern to all the countries of Europe. It quickly became apparent that the joker should be available to all. Another concern over the original formula was that the absence of a right of refusal would create a limitless loophole in the quota structure. Canada had argued that any state requesting a joker overflight would have to be prepared to receive such a flight itself, and that this reciprocity would keep the number of mischievous requests to a minimum.[59] It was believed that the Soviets would be unwilling to accept this idea, however, sensing correctly that they would be the target of most of these special overflights.[60]

The French introduced another idea to the debate, however, by insisting that any joker flight be organized and run on behalf of the CPC of the CSCE.[61] This was a sign of things to come in the end-game, as the French would try to make the CSCE the altar upon which Open Skies must be laid. Their desire to link Open Skies to the CSCE was to set them on a collision course with the United States, and, to a lesser extent, Canada. The Americans, still unable to entertain a CSCE confidence-building regime that incorporated their territory, argued that some practical link between the Open Skies regime and the relevant CSCE bodies would no doubt be forged for reasons of efficiency. But they could not accept any "organic" link that made Open Skies a part of the CSCE process.[62] As with other issues, this was not to play itself out in earnest until the end-game. What the pre-Christmas discussion of the joker issue did accomplish, aside from putting the joker itself back on the agenda, was to raise in people's minds the concern that the treaty was becoming too rigid. A concern was arising that the eventual regime would not be sufficiently flexible to respond to unique situations or to evolve.[63]

## THE SECOND TRIAL OVERFLIGHT

One final development during the pre-Christmas period was the Canadian-Hungarian discussions concerning a second trial overflight.[64] As will be recalled, the Canadian Air Force had conducted a trial overflight of Hungary on the eve of the Ottawa Open Skies Conference. This flight had been designed to test the air traffic control procedures necessary for short-notice overflights. The flight had also been intended to arouse public and media enthusiasm for the Open Skies initiative. It had succeeded on both counts. Hungary had been invited to a reciprocal overflight but had not done so because it did not have a suitable aircraft. The Canadian Chief of Defence Staff had offered the use of a Canadian Forces aircraft while on a visit to Budapest during the summer of 1990.

With the negotiations now in high gear, both delegations thought that another trial overflight would demonstrate solutions to various problems. As with the first test flight, the Canadians and Hungarians deliberately used the flight to push the envelope in terms of some positions that others were still resisting. The Soviets continued to balk at the idea of overflights that passed over nuclear power plants, for example, and so the Canadian/Hungarian overflight deliberately passed directly over a Canadian nuclear power station. The Americans were not entirely sure that they were prepared to authorize the sale of digital Synthetic Aperture Radar for technological transfer reasons, so the flight deliberately used a digital SAR. Although some difficulties were encountered over the question of who would pay for the provision of an aircraft, the flight did take place shortly after the New Year and was a considerable success in demonstrating that compromises were possible on all issues.[65]

## CONCLUSION

As the pre-Christmas session moved toward a close, several different trends were apparent. The delegations had managed to get through an enormous amount of text in a very short period. They had even managed to set a great deal of it aside as uncontested. This led to a feeling of considerable accomplishment that was misleading. After Christmas, much of the text had to be reopened in response to events in other areas of the negotiation.

Another striking feature of the pre-Christmas period was the stance taken by the United States on several issues. With the intelligence objective of Open Skies having been abandoned, the U.S. delegation adopted a much more flexible attitude to many of the technical questions. This trend had begun several months earlier. At the same time, the U.S. delegation was unable to compromise on one of the political issues that was arising: the French desire to formally link the Open Skies regime to the CSCE.

The overwhelming political issue during this period was the Cyprus question. Intimately linked to this was the business of how to incorporate the CSCE countries into the regime. A mechanism had been established whereby these countries could take part in the negotiation, but there were no new ideas as to how to get them into the regime proper. This issue had dogged the negotiations since the beginning, and there was no reason to expect that it would now go away.

Although the delegations were making some progress, it was already apparent that a degree of confusion was creeping into the technical discussions. This confusion was usually not over the basic political compromises, which had been set before the Vienna round. Rather, it was increasingly a matter of the many technical details of the negotiation interacting in a complex way. Many of the relationships between very different aspects of the text were proving troublesome and were regularly forcing the delegates to go back and reopen texts they thought they had dealt with. This problem would grow in the post-Christmas session. There were, however, at least some issues that the delegates thought had been agreed at the political level which were still to require further discussion. Most significantly, the Russian military's desire to degrade the actual capabilities of the sensors that would be allowed was not entirely apparent to all before Christmas. It would become so after the Christmas break.

Against the confusion that was felt by many to be creeping into the discussions, the activities of the larger countries, and, to a lesser extent of the WEU coalition, were becoming a force for order. The fact that the larger countries often worked out basic texts between themselves on a range of complex issues meant that the discussion at least had a starting point. The larger nations were not infallible, but they did provide some semblance of structure. The WEU coalition had yet to hit its stride. It would become a moderating force on French objectives during the end-game, however.

# 7 End-Game

After a short break for Christmas and the New Year the negotiation resumed in Vienna on January 13, 1992. From the beginning a different atmosphere prevailed. An awareness was seeping in that much remained to be done before the March 24 deadline. The biggest single change in the post-Christmas period was the fact that the USSR had ceased to exist as of December 31, 1991. The USSR seat was taken by the Russian Federation. Most of the individuals who represented the new country were the same as those who had bargained on behalf of the USSR, however. Indeed, shortly before the break, Golovko had predicted that he would return as the representative of Russia.[1]

If the dissolution of the USSR had been correctly anticipated, however, changes in several of the positions taken by its representatives were not. Many Western delegates believed that the USSR's insistence that the host be allowed to supply the aircraft if it wished to do so would be abandoned by the Russian delegation. In an article written shortly before the Christmas break, the head of the Canadian delegation speculated on the possibility of such a change in this position. He went on to argue that such a change "would certainly simplify the negotiations considerably."[2] This comment was not idle speculation. Several Russian delegates had informally mentioned their hopes that the position might be modified once the USSR had been disbanded.[3] This step was not to be taken, however, signaling the fact that the military still retained a powerful influence.[4]

## THE PARTICIPATION QUESTION

Although Russia's positions did not change appreciably, the disappearance of the Soviet Union did raise the question of how to incorporate the former

Soviet republics into the negotiation. As they would have significant military holdings, and could be a source of instability, it was vital to incorporate these countries into the fabric of the European security system as quickly as possible. In theory, they should have been able to assume a seat by virtue of their status as successor states to the USSR. This is the position that the majority of the other participants took.[5]

In practice, however, problems existed with this approach. Several of the newly independent republics were not immediately recognized by all because of their human rights records and the lack of a clear government. Most of the Open Skies delegations were prepared to live with some confusion in the short term in order to get these countries to the table and to bind them into the European security process.[6]

The French, however, took the position that none of the republics could join until they had been admitted to the Conference on Security and Cooperation in Europe (CSCE).[7] The occasion for their admission to the CSCE was to be a CSCE ministerial scheduled for later that month in Prague. This was an obvious attempt by the French to make Open Skies subordinate to the CSCE. Although they were isolated in their stand, the French would not back down on what they saw as a matter of fundamental importance to the future of their conception of the European security architecture.[8] The French ambassador in Vienna was thus under pressure from home, and somewhat isolated in Vienna, but he gained the personal respect of many in his efforts to find workable compromises.[9]

By coincidence, Canada was in the chair of the plenary when the issue came to a head. After intensive consultations it was decided that Canada would act in that capacity to send a letter inviting the new countries to participate in the Open Skies conference. The French were somewhat suspicious, and made it clear that Canada was acting alone and without the formal sanction of the plenary, even though every other country supported the Canadian letter.[10]

In the event, only two former republics showed interest in joining the negotiation immediately: Belarus and Ukraine.[11] The fact that these countries already had representatives in Vienna as a result of their UN membership had a lot to do with this. The desire of these two countries to participate created two problems. First, what to do about the French objection to their participation in Open Skies before they had been admitted to the CSCE? Second, how to deal with the anger felt by many of the other CSCE states (such as Sweden and Finland) that had sought admission to the conference for several years and were being told that they would have to keep waiting, even though these brand new countries were being invited to join? Even though the latter question could be answered with the perfectly logical statement that the new countries were successors to a state that had already been a member of the conference, it looked awkward to admit the former Soviet republics but not to admit Sweden and Finland.

Interestingly, the Turks took a leading role in arguing that the new countries be admitted immediately. Ankara believed that many of the new countries in the Caucasus would be sympathetic to Turkish concerns, as she had historic relations and ethnic ties with many of them. This led to the singular situation of the Turkish ambassador lecturing his French counterpart about the necessity of incorporating as many countries as possible into the negotiation.[12] This was an irony not lost upon the audience, and led to another discussion of the participation question generally, and Cyprus in particular, which solved nothing and only raised tempers.

It was finally agreed not to have any more formal Open Skies plenaries until after the CSCE meeting in Prague,[13] but to seat the former Soviet republics as participants in the meantime. This let the former Soviet republics into the Open Skies process but delayed their acceptance (which could only be granted by an Open Skies plenary) until they were members of the CSCE. The French could live with this compromise. Unfortunately, it also meant that the other CSCE states would not be able to take the floor at plenaries, as they were not allowed to speak at informal plenaries. The work of the contact groups remained unchanged.[14]

Once again, rapidly evolving international events had forced the participation question to take a new twist, which had added to the political complexity of the negotiation. Once again, however, the issue had been ducked in the absence of the political will to forge a compromise. Although the main holdout was France this time, many of the questions were the same. The ability of the negotiators to constantly come up with new ways of avoiding an answer, while allowing the work to continue, indicates that differences over participation were not of sufficient gravity to prevent the technical work of the conference from proceeding. Of course, though it was regarded as politically important that these new countries join, none of them were crucial to the success of the Open Skies regime itself.

While it is true that the participation issue did not prevent the technical work of the Open Skies conference, however, it is also the case that no final decisions were in danger of being made up to this point. Both Greece and Turkey (and France as well) had reserved their positions on all final decisions pending the outcome of the participation debate. It was thus understood throughout the work of all of the informal groups that the potential existed for everything to be derailed unless an answer could be found.

Moreover, to the extent that progress was made up to this point, it was made in areas of the negotiation in which the questions were sufficiently technical that the participation issue was not directly relevant. Thus, while technical progress could be made in areas such as sensors, it was not possible in others. The section of the treaty dealing with the formula by which other states would accede to the regime, for example, was as blank as it had been when the North Atlantic Treaty Organization (NATO) states put forward their draft treaty in Ottawa in February of 1990.

The rapidly accelerating end-game meant that the linkages between the mechanical aspects of the discussion and the political question were becoming more difficult to avoid. The French response to the Canadian thoughts on the "joker" quota is a case in point. While the Canadians had put the idea forward as a purely technical suggestion to expand the quota formula to deal with a different political dynamic in the wake of the breakup of the Warsaw Treaty Organization (WTO), the French had linked it to their belief that the CSCE should play a daily role in the operations of the regime. These linkages would grow, both in number and in complexity, as the end-game evolved.

The Open Skies negotiators had shown that the dispute over participation in the negotiation could be side-stepped on the way to an eventual agreement. It was becoming increasingly apparent that an endless stream of tactical measures could be devised to prevent this dispute from completely derailing a negotiation, but only up to a point. Everyone knew that, once the relationship between the technical aspects of the matter under discussion and its political side had been exhausted, such tactical measures would grow increasingly complex and wear increasingly thin. Eventually, choices would have to be made.

## THE DAILY GRIND

In the midst of these various political disputes, the daily grind resumed. There was a different feel to the post-Christmas work, however. The dynamics of the end-game were accelerating rapidly. Most of the Vienna-based players were now sufficiently familiar with the issues to permit speedy work. The individuals representing bigger countries were also used to working with each other by now, and much progress was made behind closed doors. The ambassadors of the larger countries began to couch their discussion of the more difficult issues within the context of the expectation of their ministers that the treaty would be ready for signature by March. The German ambassador was particularly forceful in this regard.[15]

At the working level, the various chairmen began to emphasize the fact that texts which had been set aside could not be continually revisited, except for paragraphs that required amendment in the light of decisions elsewhere. Although most agreed with this, many found it difficult to refrain from suggesting improvements to texts that were already agreed, much to the annoyance of the chairs of various groups. In retrospect, the requirements of the deadline led to some cases of what was later called "sloppy" and "poor" drafting, which had to be corrected in subsequent negotiations.[16]

Aside from imposing limitations on the time available to make technical improvements to the texts, the beginning of the decision-making phase signaled a stepping-up of the pressure to address the outstanding political and technical issues. Those subjects that had been avoided in open discussion now arose, as did the few remaining problems in the many areas that had already been largely dealt with. As the U.S. head of delegation would later say, "The . . . Helsinki signing date was quite frankly . . . a negotiation device. It forced the Russians to make some decisions more quickly than they were probably ready to do."[17] This was quite true, but the deadline also put the rest of the delegations in the same position.

In the final analysis, it was the imposition of an agreed deadline that triggered the shift to the "decision-making crisis" so necessary for closure of the negotiations. Without the self-imposed pressure of a date, and the fact that a certain amount of political capital had been attached to that date, final compromises would not have been achieved.

The sensor discussions were strongly affected by this shift. By mid-February it was clear to the large countries that were working with the Russians on the sensor issue that they could not change the position of the Russian military on several outstanding issues. Basically, the Russians were agreeing to sensor capabilities that *looked* reasonable until one probed a little further. Then it became apparent that the details of the Russian position were such that the sensors would have been of significantly less capability than had been thought.[18]

Ironically, the Russian military was playing exactly the game, in reverse, the Americans had played in Ottawa and especially in Budapest. Instead of promising to make sensors available on the basis of some ill-defined concept of "comparability" as the United States had done in an attempt to maintain an advantage while accepting the notion of equivalence in principle, the Russians were agreeing to make equal sensors available to those using their aircraft on the basis of rather ill-defined measurements of calibration. It was obvious to those dealing with the issues at length that this tactic was being driven by the military side of the Russian delegation, over which the civilians did not seem to have much control.[19]

Simply put, the Russians used different techniques to measure the resolution of their sensors than the Western countries did. This was particularly the case with respect to synthetic aperture radar (SAR). It was thus possible for them to argue that they were prepared to accept the same resolution as the rest were, but then to propose methods of calibrating the sensors that called into question much of the capability of the sensor.[20] All attempts to persuade them to accept a different standard for the calibration of the sensors, or to work out a method that both sides could use, came to naught.

The Russians also attempted to make use of the fact that they would be supplying the aircraft for flights over themselves in order to cut down on the amount of territory that could be seen at any given time. This was done by arguing that "their present observation aircraft had a ceiling of about 15,000 feet, while ours had a ceiling of about 30,000 feet. Simple mathematics will tell you that you can view a much larger area at a higher altitude."[21]

In order to break the jam, a series of meetings involving technical experts from all of the delegations were held to discuss the state of the sensor articles and annexes. The hope of the large countries working on the issue was that a larger group would be able to pressure the Russians into a more flexible position. There was also a recognition of the fact that it was time to let those not involved in the smaller group on the sensor issues in on the talks, as they would have to accept any agreement. The mood on the eve of these meetings was not good. Many of the technical experts believed that the Russian military was determined to hold a tough line. Some of the more pessimistic felt that the Russian military was trying to scuttle the agreement by holding out for impossible sensor positions while giving public statements that seemed encouraging.[22]

Although the potential existed for the wider meetings to have complicated the discussions, in that they involved many new players, this was not the result. Two reasons may explain this. First, the technical issues were well developed at this stage. The larger countries continued their role of providing the remainder of the delegations with largely worked out texts for discussion and agreement. In the case of the sensor discussion, the text had two bracketed versions wherever disagreement existed. The version recommended by the Russians was so unacceptable to the remainder of the conference that the text put forward by the other, larger countries soon came to represent an acceptable alternative. Little discussion was required on a political level. Second, the issues, though inherently political in their ultimate effects, were basically technical in terms of their details. This led to a lack of political polemics in the actual discussions. It was simply a matter of technical experts trying to work out a technical compromise with the Russians. Once that was seen as unattainable, the next step was to see if a means could be found to prevent the difference from causing the delegations to miss the deadline.

After many late-night sessions, at which tempers got short, it was decided to embody as many areas of agreement in the treaty as possible. All those questions that could not be resolved were left for the first session of the Open Skies Consultative Commission (OSCC) to deal with. This was all that could be achieved in the time available. Interestingly, it was in the context of these sensor discussions that the idea of test targets resurfaced. The allies came to the conclusion that such targets would be useful if they were to use Russian aircraft with sensor calibration methods they did not entirely trust.[23]

## ISSUES DEFERRED

The sensor issue thus became the first candidate for what would be one of the methods of dealing with some of the most difficult questions of the end-game: deferring a decision until after the signature of the treaty. This tactic is a well-known one, as are its dangers. The danger is that pushing difficult questions off until later will lead to "counterfeit" agreements that do not command the respect of their adherents. By the same token, however, the perceived political need to complete the negotiation by a certain date, and the desire to avoid enshrining in the treaty unacceptable positions, often leads to a situation in which deferring certain issues is seen as the lesser evil. This was very much the line of reasoning in the negotiating room at the time.[24]

Interestingly, once tentative recognition had been achieved that some issues would be deferred, a mini-negotiation began as to which issues would be so treated, and what relationship would exist between them. In other words, trade-offs between the topics that could not be resolved in the end-game became themselves a part of the end-game negotiations. Before the questions of sensors and sensor calibration could be deferred, for example, several delegations demanded that its linkage to the dispute over costs be acknowledged.[25] Specifically, the Russians insisted that some of the costs associated with providing an aircraft for overflights of one's territory be defrayed by the user of the aircraft. This ran counter to the view of many NATO countries. The NATO countries discussed this question several times in their caucus, recognizing that it was to be a critical end-game concession to be held in reserve.

The United States remained adamant that it would not pay the costs of being forced to use a Russian aircraft. Although all supported the U.S. at first, an increasing number were prepared to examine alternatives in the end-game. First the French and the Germans, and then the British, signaled to the NATO caucus that they were prepared to agree to some formula whereby they would pay for those things they would have to buy in any case. In effect, these countries were prepared to reimburse the Russians for such things as fuel and lubricants.[26] This was widely debated by the NATO countries. Many were prepared to go along with it. Indeed, as part of their emerging coalition, the Western European Union (WEU) countries worked actively, under German chairmanship, to establish a compromise. Countries such as Canada and Turkey preferred to remain with the Americans in taking a hard line, however.[27] As the issue played itself out, it became apparent that the Americans were not going to give way on the cost question until the sensor calibration issue was resolved. On the other hand, the Russians claimed that they needed some sort of indication that their point of view would prevail before they could send the treaty home.[28]

With a compromise not possible before the deadline, the German ambassador took the lead in fashioning a statement in which a large number of countries subscribed to the cost-sharing formula, but mention was made of the fact that some did not like the idea. The statement concluded with an agreement to resolve the issue in the first meeting of the OSCC.[29] Significantly, the United States insisted that the language referring the cost issue to the OSCC be exactly the same as that which referred the sensor calibration question to that body. It was thus clear that a linkage between the eventual solution to the sensor calibration issues and that of the cost question had been established as part of the end-game.[30]

## QUOTAS

Not all questions were candidates for deferral, however. Some states argued that the allocation of active quotas, which was likely to be a difficult exercise, be deferred to the first session of the OSCC.[31] The United States refused to accept this logic, however, insisting that states should know how many overflights they would be allocated, and over which other parties, before they signed the treaty. The U.S. delegation argued that they would have difficulty sending the treaty to the Senate unless they could state how many overflights the United States would be entitled to perform over Russia.[32]

This set the stage for a quota de-confliction exercise. The French chaired the game, in deference to the fact that they had displayed an interest in it since the Ottawa round and had an expert on the subject in their delegation.[33] It had been agreed that only 75 percent of the total passive quota of each participant would count during the first three years of the regime's existence in order to provide a work-up for all. Accordingly, only 75 percent of the total active quota could be allotted against each state in the initial distribution.[34]

After each country had declared its total passive quota,[35] the chairman asked each country to declare its active intentions. To no one's surprise, this quickly resulted in the countries of what had been the Warsaw Pact being oversubscribed. Russia, Belarus, and Ukraine were particularly overbid as many of their former allies sought the right to overfly these new countries in addition to requests from all of the NATO countries. My own notes of March 6, 1992, on the result of the first set of requests, show that a total of thirty-four flights had been requested over Russia, as opposed to the twenty-seven that were on offer (Russia and Belarus had not officially declared their intention to become a combined party yet, after which twenty-eight flights were on offer); seven had been requested against Belarus, as opposed to the four on offer before they combined with Russia; and eighteen against Ukraine, as opposed to the nine on offer. All of the other former WTO states were similarly oversubscribed. None of the NATO states were oversubscribed.

The problem was made worse in that, by general agreement, three of Russia's passive quota were held in reserve for the eventual use of Sweden, which would get two, and Finland. This meant that the Russia-Belarus group had twenty-eight flights on offer instead of the thirty-one that strict application of the 75 percent rule would have achieved. As the U.S. head of delegation later said, "[T]he entire Russia-Belarus quota is fully taken, as is Ukraine's . . . . The initial flights to be taken as a result of the treaty are definitely focused more towards the Eastern European nations."[36]

The next few weeks witnessed a difficult negotiation, with the chairman trying to persuade, cajole, and embarrass various countries to surrender at least part of their active quota requests. Several techniques were used. The chairman, for example, circulated draft, deconflicted quota formulas that arbitrarily sliced some overflight requests off countries. Although he did not use any specific formula, the chairman did make an appeal to such factors as the need for neighbors to have at least some flights over each other, and the existence of certain historical relationships. Not surprisingly, those countries that benefited from the application of these factors were supportive of them, and those who did not refused to recognize their validity.

The countries that had been left out by the chair then had to request that their initial requests be put back in the matrix, with the chairman often asking them to explain why they should get a particular flight as opposed to someone else. Recognizing the extremely difficult job he had taken on, no one objected to this technique, though they often objected to the decisions. Efforts were also made to persuade the countries that had been oversubscribed to increase their passive quota. Although no one did this, Poland did agree to waive the 75 percent rule and accept its full complement of six passive quotas from the beginning of the regime in order to deconflict its portion of the matrix. The Poles did this in return for the United States agreeing to give them one of their flights over Russia.

Although these techniques did result in a few deconflictions, it was a slow process and they would not have resulted in deconfliction of the entire matrix. What did break the log-jam were two developments. Foremost of these was the fact that the WEU decided to approach the quota issue as a group, rather than as individual nations. Accordingly, they decided to carve up the number of flights they were requesting on an individual basis and spread them around the group as a whole. This resulted in fewer total requests to overfly Russia and its former allies. The fact that France was chairing the game had some impact upon the willingness of the other WEU countries to accept a diminution of their original active quota requests. There was a desire on the part of France and its partners that the WEU be seen as playing a role in solving the problem. The German chair of the WEU caucus was also quite active in promoting a compromise. Finally, the fact that these countries saw the Open Skies regime as their only means of independently monitoring events beyond the Urals stimulated them to search for ways to make the negotiations work. The second method of deconflicting the matrix lay in persuading certain countries to "share" overflights over the most heavily subscribed areas.[37] As might be expected, however, no one got exactly what they wanted at the end of the game.

## OPERATIONAL QUESTIONS

As the detailed questions relating to sensors and quotas were gradually resolved, the outstanding operational questions were tackled. One such question had to do with the timelines for such matters as the amount of preflight notification, including prearrival notification, to which the overflown state was entitled, and the amount of time that was to elapse before the flight could commence after the presentation of the flight plan.[38] The original NATO Basic Elements Paper had established a two-stage, short-notice timeline.[39] The observing country would notify the observed country of its intent to conduct an overflight sixteen hours before arrival. A flight plan would be filed within six hours of arrival. The flight would commence twenty-four hours after the flight plan had been handed over, with the aircraft inspection to occur in that twenty-four-hour period. As will be recalled, this timeline had been the subject of considerable discussion. The final figures were a compromise between the desire of some to make the overflights as short-notice as possible, and the concerns of others that an adequate period be provided to protect sensitive areas.

As with several of the original proposals for Open Skies, these figures were primarily advanced for political reasons and took little note of practical difficulties. Specifically, some concern existed that the proposed timelines would not work for those countries that had to perform lengthy transit flights to reach the point of entry in the country to be overflown. After such a lengthy transit flight, a period of crew rest could be required before the crew would be ready to escort the host country's inspectors in their inspection of the aircraft.

Moreover, if a lengthy inspection of the aircraft were allowed, another crew rest period might be required before the overflight could take place. Of course, the larger countries could avoid this problem by sending two groups of people, along with their aircraft, but many smaller countries did not envisage doing this. Simply put, then, many NATO countries would have had trouble meeting the very limitations they were proposing.

The deficiencies were understood, even as the original timeline proposals were being put forward. In response to the protestations made at the time by some of those who would actually have to fly the aircraft that the NATO timelines would be difficult to make work, a political decision was made to stick with the proposed timelines to demonstrate the desire of the NATO countries to develop a short-notice regime. As long as an actual treaty was not in the cards, the practical aspects of the timelines issue were not as important as the political point to be made by adopting this position, even if it was not technically realistic for several nations.

Once the treaty became a realistic possibility, NATO's timelines had to be revisited. This was initially resisted by the U.S. delegation. The United States would not have been adversely affected because it intended to send enough people to allow for adequate crew rest by their flight crew while others supervised the aircraft inspection. Many of the others were determined to see the timelines revisited, however, and began questioning aspects of the timeline sections of the treaty before the Christmas break. At the first meeting on aircraft inspection, for example, Canada, Germany, and the United Kingdom all pointed out that the proposed twenty hours for aircraft inspection was too long. They argued that such a lengthy period of time was unnecessary for two reasons. First, the political circumstances of the regime were now changed to the point that a much greater degree of trust could be extended. Second, the host now had the right to insist that its own aircraft be used if it suspected that illegal sensors might be hidden aboard the aircraft.

The initial pre-Christmas discussion of these points was inconclusive because several related operational questions had to be resolved before this one could be put to rest, but the point had been made. Once the various issues came together after Christmas, a concerted assault was made on the timelines question. It began with a paper prepared by the Canadian delegation and circulated on January 23.[40] The paper argued that the proposed timelines would not work in practice, and were unfair to both smaller countries and those that had to perform lengthy transit flights. These ideas were already under consideration within the conference, but the paper served to bring them out. It also served to include Canada in the group of five larger nations (France, Germany, Italy, the UK, and the U.S.), which were already working on the issue. After some initial discussion, in which the United States tried to preserve as many of the initial concepts as possible, an entirely new concept was outlined, largely by the U.S. delegation. Above all, the new concept emphasized flexibility.[41]

The new concept provided a series of periods within which each activity (be it notification, arrival, preflight inspection, and so on) had to be concluded, but did not say when these activities would have to be begun or concluded so long as it was within the overall period.[42] Exactly when things would be done within these periods was left to the two nations involved to work out, based on their needs. Accordingly, countries with shorter transit flights, which would not require crew rest upon arrival, could move to the next phase of the overflight process quickly, whereas those that had just come off a lengthy transit flight could opt for rest upon arrival. This basic concept gained rapid endorsement. After some discussion, the final sequence was adopted.[43]

The observing country will notify its intention to conduct a flight seventy-two hours before its intended arrival. The country to be observed will then acknowledge this notification within twenty-four hours of its receipt. The acknowledgment will also indicate whether the observed country intends to exercise its right to provide the aircraft. Once in country, the observing party will have ninety-six hours to complete the entire flight sequence. Within this ninety-six-hour period an eight-hour aircraft inspection may occur, but has to terminate four hours before the observation flight begins. When this inspection occurs is up to the two nations to decide based upon crew rest and other requirements. The mission plan is to be handed over as soon as possible after arrival, and the observed country will have four hours to approve it or propose changes to it, if required in the interests of flight safely. The flight will commence twenty-four hours after the mission plan's submission. Once the observation flight is completed, the observing party has to leave within twenty-four hours, unless safely reasons preclude departure within that time. Simultaneous flights are not permitted.[44]

The seventy-two-hour period caused some discussion, with the U.S. questioning whether that much advance notice was required. All of the other countries at the table supported the longer advance period, however, as they wanted the longer time to prepare to receive an aircraft. To U.S. protestations that the short-notice character of the regime was being compromised, it was replied that the observed country would not have the flight plan until after arrival. In other words:

> [T]he observed country will know three days in advance that an observing party will be arriving in-country, thereby allowing it to prepare to receive the aircraft or to offer one of its own, but will not know the route of the observation flight until 24 hours before the flight is scheduled to begin.[45]

The discussion over timelines was only one of several such discussions over the technical details of the treaty that occurred during the Vienna Conference. Other topics that received the same discussion, for example, were the requirements of meshing the various air traffic control procedures, the procedures for notification, emergency flight procedures, and so forth. Moreover, the timelines discussion was not particularly unique in terms of the way it unfolded.[46] The way in which the timelines issue was dealt with, then, demonstrated the manner in which positions that had been reached on a conceptual level during the preliminary posturing, and largely for political reasons, had to be substantially revised once the prospect of an agreement loomed large. Part of this was due, of course, to the enormous political changes that occurred since Open Skies had been resurrected in May of 1989.

But these changes also bore testimony to the fact that many of the decisions made earlier had been made with tactical negotiating considerations in mind, and without sufficient regard for how they would work when actually conducting overflights. This phenomenon was perhaps a natural result of the fact that complex issues were reduced to relatively simple concepts during the largely political phase of the negotiation in order to create a currency for eventual trade-offs. After the trade-offs were struck, the detailed negotiation began. However, when the detail had to be reconstructed during the end-game, this went on in the context of a number of other aspects of the package that were undergoing a similar process. Unforeseen complications arose in that the technical implications of the tentative compromises, both individually and collectively, were discovered for the first time during this period. Although the development of a series of large, easily manipulated concepts was necessary in order to lay the foundation of trade-offs upon which a successful negotiation depends, there was a price to be paid for this reliance on broad concepts once the issues, and their interrelationship, were discussed in detail. For it is here that a breakdown could occur when unexpected, or even anticipated, complications arose against the pressures of the looming deadline.

Two techniques and factors helped the Open Skies negotiators to overcome this problem, and the complexity that it introduced to the end-game. First, the fact that the text was in the hands of nations that made a degree of expertise available on the issue meant that the proposals which reached the large group had already benefited from a thorough examination. This creation of vertical working groups did not lead to solutions every time. But it did ensure that the first consideration of each issue was carried on in a smaller, more workable setting.

Of course, a danger existed that the proposals which reached the smaller nations would have reflected only the concerns of the bigger participants. Although perhaps a very real concern in other multilateral negotiations, this was not overwhelmingly troublesome in the Open Skies talks, as the approaches adopted by the leading countries were acceptable to the others, with minor modifications for exceptional circumstances. When the leading countries disagreed, as they did over sensor calibration, for example, the different viewpoints they held were a microcosm of the larger group.

Second, though many of the issues were quite complex, the broad range of trade-offs remained remarkably stable throughout the negotiation. Confusion may have existed over several technical details, but it was not so great as to cloud the overall objectives. This may have been a result of the relative simplicity of the regime under consideration, or of the intensive interim negotiation between the Budapest and Vienna rounds, which had clarified the issues. No doubt the changing political landscape had something to do with it, as there was little deliberate mischief-making except on such highly charged issues as the Greek-Turk dispute over Cyprus. Had any of the larger nations, or a collection of the smaller, been determined to prevent the treaty, it would have been a relatively simple matter to have manipulated a technical issue like timelines or sensors into an insoluble problem.

## THE PARTICIPATION COMPROMISE IS STRUCK

Without doubt, the most difficult issue of the end-game was the question of the expansion of the regime (which was the question of Cyprus) and the quasi-related question of the CSCE–Open Skies link. This was an area in which it did seem as though an insoluble impasse might exist. The Cyprus question was, of course, the linchpin of the regime expansion issue. All were agreed that some mechanism had to be found that would allow the other CSCE countries to join the regime. The Turks insisted that these countries come forward on a one-by-one basis, thereby permitting them to reject Cyprus. The Greeks insisted that all of the CSCE countries join in at the same time, thus bringing Cyprus in with the rest. Most favored the Greek idea but were not committed to either, so long as the problem was solved. The French threw their weight behind the Greeks, largely because it suited their own pro-CSCE agenda.[47]

The positions that the negotiators took into the end-game had thus not changed from the discussion on the subject during the Ottawa round.[48] Indeed, the extent of mistrust felt by the Greek and Turkish governments was such that Greece had earlier felt constrained to propose that the overflown state should have the right to object to the sale of data resulting from any overflight of itself to other specific parties. This proposal was widely criticized by all of the other delegations, and was quickly withdrawn by Greece.[49]

The French, meanwhile, added a new wrinkle to the formula by insisting that Open Skies become part of the broader CSCE process and that such organs as the OSCC meet within the framework of the Conflict Prevention Centre (CPC). This proposal was flatly rejected by the Americans, who remained adamant that a CSCE Confidence-building Measure (CBM) could not be applicable to U.S. territory. Washington's aversion to this idea was well known, and stemmed from its fear that such a link might be a slippery slope to such things as naval arms control.[50] As the end-game loomed, the French adopted the tactic of linking the questions of expansion and the CSCE–Open Skies relationship by insisting that all CSCE members sign the treaty as founding members. As noted above, this had the effect of supporting the Greek position on the Cyprus question, although that was not why the French did it.

On the eve of the end-game the major players had adopted firm positions on these issues. The French were especially adamant that their conception of the Open Skies–CSCE relationship be approved. The Americans were equally determined. As the intelligence utility of the regime faded, however, Washington became more of a spectator. It would not compromise on a first principle regarding the territorial application of the CSCE to achieve an Open Skies agreement. But, since the treaty could not be signed without them, the Americans sat back and let others persuade the French to modify their stance.

This was quickly taken up by the Germans and the British, who placed considerable significance on the treaty, and put some pressure on France to compromise.[51] Moreover, the French ambassador in Vienna demonstrated the ability to approach his instructions creatively and to impress upon his superiors at home the need for compromise, and was widely credited with finding a way through the minefield. Once France had modified its position, many others were active in helping to find a way to express the eventual compromise in a manner that helped the French ambassador sell it to Paris.[52]

After the French ambassador returned to Paris for instructions, a chink appeared in the French position on the accession issue. The French ambassador proposed that all CSCE countries be entitled to join the regime but that their requests for quotas (both passive and active) be approved by the OSCC. This would have meant that Cyprus could join the regime, but that its requests for quotas could have been continually vetoed by Turkey. In effect, Cyprus could be a member of the regime but not a functioning member.[53] This was not good enough for the Turks, who did not like the idea of Cyprus being admitted to the regime at all for reasons of political principle. Eventually (for reasons that will be discussed below), the French and the Greeks had to compromise further and accept the Turkish formula, which held that each CSCE country would have to come forward on an individual basis and be approved by the OSCC.[54]

In order to provide an appearance of a special place for the other CSCE countries, a three-stage expansion process was developed. The first stage recognized that the newly independent former Soviet republics could join at any time. The second created a six-month window after the treaty's entry into force during which only CSCE states would be entitled to apply for membership, but their applications would have to be approved by all other signatories on an individual basis. Finally, after six months, any other state "which . . . is able and willing to contribute to the objectives of the Treaty" could apply to join.[55]

The French made a similar retreat on the Open Skies–CSCE link question. This involved a number of compromises that removed all of their bracketed language concerning such things as the position of the OSCC with respect to the CPC. The French had insisted that the OSCC be an integral part of the CPC. The conference eventually settled on language that mandated the OSCC to request the use of the facilities of the CPC, but not to be a part of the CPC per se.[56]

Once the basic compromises had been made on a political level, all of the remaining brackets on the treaty fell away. Many of these brackets were to be found over technical issues, such as quotas, but were really the technical aspects of the larger disputes. The French had placed brackets around certain paragraphs while they held out for language that would have given the CPC the right to be involved in any emergency overflights conducted under the "joker" provisions of the quota mechanism. Once the broader question of the Open Skies–CSCE relationship was settled, the brackets vanished. The final provisions for emergency flights, for example, did mention that the CSCE, through its bodies, could request that the OSCC consider such flights. But it also mentioned that "other relevant international organizations" could also request such flights, as could individual parties to the regime.[57] The French had originally argued that only the CSCE should exercise this power.

The manner in which the Turks prevailed would seem to indicate that their ability to stand firm was greater than that of the Greeks. It also indicated that the French, despite their insistence upon the CSCE link, were prepared to compromise in the interests of obtaining the Open Skies agreement (and may well have been playing a longer game in terms of the evolution of the European security system). One may ask why this is so. Turkey, after all, was isolated, and was actively opposed by two states, one of which (France) was a leader in the negotiation. The answer may lie in the balance of interests during the end-game. France, though committed to its position on the CSCE question from a political standpoint, was also very interested in obtaining an Open Skies treaty as a means of acquiring an independent means of getting beyond the Urals. Moreover, France's major European allies (the Germans and the British) were similarly committed to the achievement of the Open Skies regime. Of course, Turkey was also interested in obtaining an Open Skies regime. But Cyprus was an issue of first principle for Ankara, and the Turkish delegation managed to convey the attitude that it was under instructions to allow the entire negotiation to fail rather than to compromise on the issue. Neither the French nor the Greeks were able to do the same.

In retrospect, it was apparent that the Open Skies–CSCE link was not absolutely crucial to the French, so long as the treaty contained language that did not preclude the idea of an eventual link at some point in the future. The French may thus have believed that they could pursue the link between the CSCE and all European security mechanisms, including Open Skies, at another time in much the same way as they had accepted the less than satisfactory reference to the CSCE–Open Skies link in the original NATO Basic Elements Paper (BEP) in December of 1989, and then repudiated it once the Ottawa Conference began in February of 1990. In other words, their retreat was not so much final as tactical.

Indeed, at the same time as they were abandoning their position in Vienna, the French delegation to the preparatory meeting of the upcoming CSCE ministerial in Helsinki was distributing a paper calling for all security mechanisms in Europe to fall within the purview of the CSCE. The ideas behind the paper had been under discussion within NATO for some time.[58] It would thus seem that the French were following the course noted by Hedrick Smith when he wrote: "One of the enduring lessons of the (negotiation) game is that agreement does not equal solution. It is merely a transition point to a new struggle, the winners trying to secure their gains, the losers trying to undo them."[59]

This left the battle to the Greeks and the Turks. In addition to the relative imbalance of power between these two, which favored Turkey, the recent changes in Europe also favored the Turks. Many of the new countries created from the remains of the USSR looked to Ankara in cultural and historical terms, and the Turks played this for all it was worth during the end-game. In the end, the Turks simply outlasted the Greeks by refusing to budge until Athens could be brought under sufficient pressure to impel it to do so first. Much of this pressure came from Greece's European Union partners, which wanted the regime more than they were prepared to support Athens, and who believed that Turkey would not give in. Once France had abandoned Greece over the CSCE issue, the Greek delegation was unable to resist the tide.

Obviously, this was followed by Sweden and Finland with great interest. The outcome of the dispute would determine whether they could join the regime as founders, as they desperately wanted, or whether they would have to continue to wait for a resolution of the Cyprus dispute. Once it became clear that they would not join the regime from the outset, a means of ensuring that they would be entitled to participate in the work of the OSCC was sought. This was important in that the first session would deal with many of the remaining issues, and would be a continuation of negotiations. As a part of the overall deal on the political aspects of the end-game, Turkey was persuaded that the first session of the OSCC would be run according to the same procedures and rules as had governed the conference. This meant that much of the work would be conducted within informal contact groups, to which all of the CSCE states who desired would be granted access.[60] This informal arrangement was given teeth by the adoption of a CSCE Ministerial Declaration on Open Skies, which called for the regime's membership to be opened as soon as possible, and noted that the CSCE countries would participate in the OSCC.[61]

The dispute over the CSCE link and the expansion formula was interesting in that the French chaired the discussions and were custodians of the relevant texts. This position should have given them great influence. That it did not is testimony to the fact that the chair is not necessarily a strong place from which to advance a position. But neither is it a hindrance. Although they could not ignore suggestions for a modification to the text in their role as chair, neither were the French compelled to abandon their view as a function of their duties. The chair allowed the French to keep the issue front and center. It could not be forgotten or ignored in any discussion, no matter how peripheral or technical, until the French were prepared to modify their stand. Though this did not win them the point, it allowed the French to manufacture a heightened sense of impending crisis in the end-game. Of course, their status as leaders would likely have allowed them to accomplish much the same effect had they not been in the chair.

## CONCLUSION

With the achievement of an agreement on the questions of regime expansion and the link to the CSCE, the Open Skies Treaty was completed. The treaty was initialed by the delegations on March 21 and conveyed to Helsinki for signature by the ministers on March 24, 1992.[62] The end-game had achieved a treaty by the deadline, but that treaty was far from complete. As they left Vienna, all of the delegates recognized that the first session of the OSCC would be little more than the continuation of the negotiations by another name. Indeed, informal consultations on the issues confronting the OSCC began the very next week. The conclusion of the Open Skies negotiation was not, then, a conclusion at all. It was an act of passage to the next phase of the development of the regime.[63]

# 8 Into Force and Into the Future

The Open Skies story did not, of course, end with the signing of the treaty. A lengthy period ensued that has seen the treaty enter into force (EOF) and become a significant, if largely unknown, feature of security relations in the Euro-Atlantic area. Many of the issues that dogged the negotiation have found resolution during this period, but others remain stubbornly resistant to compromise. Meanwhile, thought has been given to how the regime might evolve to keep pace with political and technological developments. Finally, a few analysts and officials have begun to think tentatively about whether the Open Skies idea, or some variant of it, might be extended to other troubled regions of the world, or to other purposes.

The European security situation has, of course, changed beyond recognition since the treaty was signed. The prospect of large-scale war between two alliances has disappeared, along, indeed, with one of those alliances, but regional crises and small wars have erupted in the Balkans and some of the former Soviet republics. Meanwhile, implementation of the Conventional Forces in Europe (CFE) Treaty, the arms control treaty that was to have been the bedrock of the European security architecture, has been suspended by Russia because of differences with the North Atlantic Treaty Organization (NATO)countries. Interestingly, given their suspicions of the regime during its negotiation, it is the Russians who have been the most active users of the Open Skies regime and who are among the small minority that have made the investments to introduce improved sensor capabilities.

## 1992–2002: THE "TRIAL IMPLEMENTATION" PERIOD

Although signed in March, 1992, the treaty did not come into force until January 1, 2002. The key reason for this was the lengthy time that Russia, Belarus, and Ukraine took to ratify the treaty. This ten-year period was not an inactive time, however. A process of preparing for the EOF was under way, and nearly four hundred "test flights" were undertaken; in reality, the Open Skies regime was operating, after a fashion, before the treaty came into force. It was particularly useful in helping to verify compliance with the initial stages of the CFE Treaty, and several trial overflights returned data for that purpose.

A critical development during this extended period of provisional application was the development of the Open Skies Consultative Commission (OSCC) into a fully functioning body capable of overseeing the work of the treaty. The treaty had created this body to be a mechanism whereby the parties to the treaty could meet regularly (up to four times a year, or more often, as necessary) to agree on modifications and also to resolve disputes, if they could not be resolved bilaterally. Significantly, it had been agreed that many implementation decisions pertaining to the treaty that had not been resolved in Vienna could be adopted by the OSCC, rather than having to be negotiated, re-signed, and reratified—a laborious process that everyone increasingly came to recognize would be cumbersome and would hinder the evolution of the regime as experience was gained and new sensors and flight procedures developed. Most decisions of the OSCC did not change the treaty, but rather provided operational guidance in such areas determining the resolution of different sensors permitted under the treaty. The OSCC was also mandated with approving applications for accession to the treaty by states that wished to join, though this did not happen until the treaty came into force in 2002.

When they concluded the treaty the delegations had agreed that certain articles would be provisionally brought into force, pending the EOF of the entire thing after the appropriate ratifications. Recognizing that the OSCC would have much work to do before EOF, they agreed that the article creating it should be among those provisionally in force.[1] The OSCC began its work on April 2, 1992—a mere nine days after the signing of the treaty. It established informal working groups around such issues as costs, sensor calibration, flight procedures and rules, and others. Between 1992 and 2000 the OSCC members agreed upon twenty-two legally binding "Decisions" (as well as several administrative decisions) that have the same effect as the treaty itself. The OSCC also issued a

"Sensor Guidance Document" as agreements were reached on the sensor calibration and certification process.[2]

It was during this critical phase that the "operators" got their hands firmly around the regime and were able to make modifications to some of the procedures agreed by the negotiators. This was useful in that it enabled those who would have to actually operate the flights to finally have their say in how they should be run. They soon found that many of the operational provisions of the treaty that had been negotiated in the somewhat adversarial mood of the conference rooms had to be modified to work in practice; overflight missions cannot be completed unless the operators from the overflown and the overflying state cooperate to achieve the objectives of the mission. It was, then, during this time that the true underlying objective of the treaty in promoting a cooperative approach to security began to be fully realized.

During this period, several countries established within their militaries small operational units that would take charge of the technical preparations for EOF. Many nations selected and prepared the aircraft and sensor package that they intended to use going forward, and work began to develop the means that would be used to certify the sensors, as called for in the treaty. This process required intensive scientific discussion and collaboration between the sensor experts and operators from the various countries to develop commonly understood meanings for the various agreements in principle that were contained in the treaty.[3]

For example, the treaty specified that thirty-centimeter resolution was permitted for optical cameras. In practice, however, the actual resolution returned from any given flight would vary depending on many factors, including the atmospheric conditions prevailing at the time. It was agreed that cameras should be certified if they consistently returned imagery with a resolution of between twenty-five and thirty-five centimeters in various atmospheric conditions during multiple certification tests. Working out how to achieve this consistently took time and much discussion over certification targets and methodologies. It was then necessary to devise a means whereby the overflown state would be able to make sure that only such cameras were present during its preflight inspection.[4]

This process then had to be repeated for the other sensors permitted under the treaty, such as synthetic aperture radar (SAR),[5] thermal, and electro-optical systems.[6] In the case of thermal systems, for example, it was necessary to devise a method involving targets with a suitable, reliable thermal contrast. The methodology eventually agreed in 2007 involves laying out a series of test targets made up of five-millimeter-thick aluminum strips that are painted with a special paint in different tones of gray. Under the sun, the strips absorb heat differently, but in predictable ways that can be measured. The overflying aircraft passes over the strips and the known heat, and contrast between the strips is recorded. Once the data is processed, it is possible to determine if the sensor meets the standards of the Open Skies Treaty.[7] With respect to electro-optical and video cameras, the Russians were concerned that the use of constantly rolling electro-optical and video cameras might be used to acquire information that could be useful in devising and perfecting possible flight paths for cruise missiles. Fixes had to be found that convinced the Russians this would not happen.[8]

As these various agreements for individual sensors were reached, and the technical and operational procedures for calibrating them were agreed, procedures had to be developed that would be used to actually certify individual Open Skies aircraft and their sensor packages.[9] This process involved several "mock" certification exercises, to which members of the treaty were invited to send experts. Usually held over several days, these certification exercises involved an intensive inspection of the aircraft and sensors, followed by a certification of a set of ground test targets. The aircraft then flew repeatedly over the targets over several days at various altitudes and in varying conditions with both host nation and invited experts on board. Finally, those observing the exercise were taken to the data processing facility to observe the raw data being processed and were allowed to inspect the data closely to verify that it was within the parameters outlined in the treaty and subsequently agreed to during the EOF period.[10] As they went through this process repeatedly in several countries and for several different aircraft and sensor packages, the experts from all of the treaty countries came to know each other well and developed significant professional respect and trust. Many Open Skies veterans of this period consider this to have been among the most important products of the entire process and one of the key benefits of the treaty.[11]

Given that such work was done, and that many of the participating countries found the treaty useful, the question must be asked as to why it took so long to come into force. As will be recalled, the treaty specified that its EOF required that all states with a quota of more than eight passive overflights were required to ratify it before it would enter into force (along with the two depository states, Canada and Hungary—and Canada was also a member of the group of states having a passive quota of more than eight overflights). By 1995 all of these countries had ratified the treaty except the Russia/Belarus joint party and Ukraine. There are several reasons why these two countries had not done so.[12]

First, Russian politics was in a state of considerable flux, with relations between President Yeltsin and the Duma (parliament) being marked by acrimonious disputes. It is therefore likely that President Yeltsin did not want to use political capital on the ratification of Open Skies, particularly when it was working, after a fashion, with trial overflights taking place. What capital President Yeltsin did have with the Duma in terms of ratifying arms control agreements was expended on ratification of the Strategic Arms Reduction Treaty of 1991, the Chemical Weapons Convention, the Comprehensive Test Ban Treaty, and the CFE Treaty itself.

Second, though it had agreed to the signing of the Open Skies Treaty, large elements of Russia's military and security community remained suspicious of the regime and of the West. There was also considerable dislike of NATO's expansion to include several former Russian allies during the 1990s. In all, there was a sense in many quarters in Moscow that Open Skies would expose Russian weaknesses with little to be gained in return, and that its EOF was primarily a benefit to the West.

Third, Russian officials were concerned at the cost implications. Since it was clear that all of Russia's passive quota would be used by the many states interested in overflying that country, and since Russia had made clear that it was going to insist on the "taxi option" (that is, that it would provide the aircraft for flights over its own territory, and therefore have to absorb most of the costs), the costs of full regime implementation were going to be considerably greater for Russia than for any other country. Russia's economy was suffering during these years of transition to a market economy, and its defense budget was under pressure. In the Ukrainian case, it seems that cost was the critical issue, along with the fact that its new and fledgling military had other priorities. It may also be that poor parliamentary practice caused the two attempts made to ratify the treaty (in 1996 and 1998) to fail. In any case, Ukraine did not ratify until it became clear that Russia's views were changing and that Moscow would do so.[13]

So what brought about a new perspective on the treaty in Moscow? The first signals that their views were evolving came in terms of increased participation in the trial overflights and other activities of the by now greatly extended provisional period of application. In 1995 Russia had participated in only two trial overflights. In the period 1997 to 2001, they participated in between fourteen and eighteen trial overflights each year.

Several factors contributed to this evolution. Perhaps most significant was the decline in the numbers and performance of Russian reconnaissance satellites during this period.[14] Suddenly, Russian military and security officials began to see that Open Skies could be a real benefit in that the regime would allow them to conserve dwindling satellite resources for other missions, while still acquiring much needed information. In a research note on Open Skies prepared for the Duma it was pointed out that the EOF would permit Russia to close the gap between itself and the United States (and NATO) in terms of information collection, and specifically would allow Russia to compensate for diminished Russian satellite resources. The document concluded: "[We] can conclude that the Treaty on Open Skies is advantageous to Russia, and allows for some compensation of Western superiority in obtaining information with minimal expenditures."[15] The same document went on to show that the costs of the regime were competitive with the cost of obtaining equivalent information by other available means. Beyond this, Russia's position toward engagement with the West changed as Vladimir Putin succeeded Yeltsin. Moreover, members of the Duma itself took part in trial overflights during this period, including a flight over the United States in 1997, and came to see the possible benefits of the treaty.

In addition to its work on sensors, the OSCC had to revise the quota system when several countries of the now-defunct Warsaw Pact joined NATO and were prohibited from overflying each other by the terms of the internal NATO agreement that states of the alliance would not overfly each other. This also had the effect of increasing the number of states wishing to overfly the Russia/Belarus joint party, which placed a further premium and stress on this quota. The OSCC also had to revise quotas and other legal matters when Czechoslovakia broke apart, though the new Czech and Slovakian republics joined right away in their own right. Finally, although new countries could not formally apply to join the regime until it had entered into force, it was agreed in 1994 that representatives of the other Organization for Security and Cooperation in Europe (OSCE) nations could participate as observers in various activities of the provisional application period, including trial overflights and aircraft/sensor certification exercises and observing the discussions of the OSCC. As expected, Sweden and Finland were most active in this regard, though Croatia, Slovenia, and the three Baltic states also participated in some events.[16]

By far the most politically complex questions considered by the OSCC during this period were those relating to the accession of new states to the treaty.

As expected, Sweden and Finland came forward immediately to indicate that they would request membership once the treaty came into force. So did many others, notably newer states that emerged from the breakup of the Soviet Union and also from the fighting in the Balkans in the 1990s. Many of these states were motivated as much by a desire to quickly join all of the structures and agreements of the Euro-Atlantic security system, as by their desire to overfly other countries. Some of these new countries did find Open Skies useful in terms of monitoring new neighbors, however. The treaty provisions on accession (Article 17) allowed for countries of the OSCE to be admitted as soon as possible, and these countries were to be given preference for application in the six months after EOF. These countries, such as Sweden and Finland, were encouraged to become active, informally, during the provisional application period, as the end-game of the treaty negotiation had envisaged. However, the perennial issue of Cyprus was never far from the surface. It had been hoped by many Open Skies members that all of the remaining countries of the CSCE (which subsequently became the OSCE in 1994) would be admitted as a group once the treaty came into force. But Turkey had forcefully served notice as the treaty was being negotiated that it would veto this idea and would insist that each country come forward and apply individually. The stage was thus set for the continuation of the Cyprus dispute into the future of the Open Skies regime.

## ENTRY INTO FORCE

As the foregoing indicates, when the Open Skies Treaty finally did enter into force, considerable work had been done, allowing the regime to be implemented quickly. The OSCC established new working groups on certification, sensors, and flight procedures on October 24, 2001. These groups, drawing on the previous work, were able to quickly develop procedures for aircraft and sensor certification. Thus the actual and formal certification of Open Skies aircraft took place between January 1 and July 31, 2002. An initial certification schedule was established:

- The certification of planes and sensors from Hungary, Ukraine, and the Russia/Belarus joint party took place at the Naval Air Station at Nordholz, Germany between April 15 and 29, 2002;
- Certification of the U.S. Open Skies aircraft and sensors took place at the Wright-Patterson Air Force Base in the United States between May 8 and 15, 2002;
- Certification of a unique arrangement between a group of ten countries to develop and use a common "sensor pod" containing all of the optical and electro-

optical sensors which can be attached to each country's C-130 "Hercules" aircraft when needed was carried out at Orleans Bercy airbase in France between June 19 and 26, 2002;[17] and

- The UK and Bulgarian aircraft and sensors were certified at RAF Brize Norton in the United Kingdom between July 8 and 16, 2002.[18]

As the treaty came into force, Russia announced that it would not require that its aircraft be used for overflights departing from its eastern point of entry (Ulan Ude, near Lake Baikal in Siberia). This relieved Russia of the cost and burden of keeping an aircraft on short notice to fly to Siberia to host overflights there. Moreover, Russia has not, to date, exercised its right to provide the aircraft for overflights of itself from its other point of entry near Moscow. As the taxi option had been a key Russian demand, and as the Russian military had been determined to prevent foreign aircraft overflying Russia, these moves signaled a considerable evolution in Moscow's attitudes toward the treaty. Russia has also been one of the more forward-looking treaty members in terms of installing new sensors up to the very top capabilities permitted by the treaty and subsequent OSCC decisions. While other countries, including the United States, have used older aircraft and not significantly upgraded their sensors since the treaty came into effect, Russia has recently procured two brand new aircraft (TU-214) and outfitted them with digital electro-optical video and infrared and SAR sensors, permitted under the treaty and subsequent decisions of the OSCC.[19] Russia is the first party to use digital, instead of film, sensors.

As expected, several countries applied to join Open Skies as soon as it was in force. Those that have been accepted, in the order in which they were accepted, are Finland, Sweden, Lithuania, Croatia, Bosnia and Herzegovina, Latvia, Slovenia, and Estonia. As expected, Turkey insisted that countries come forward individually, and promptly vetoed Cyprus when it did so in 2002, while welcoming all of the others. In addition, two of the former Soviet republics exercised their right to join the treaty as original signatories, being successor states to the USSR: Georgia and Kyrgyzstan, the latter of which has not yet ratified. The number of parties to the treaty now stands at thirty-four. Finally, Hungary and Romania terminated their bilateral Open Skies Treaty in 2004, having joined NATO and the Confidence-building Measure (CBM) value of their agreement having been fulfilled.

In 2005 the first Open Skies Review Conference was held from February 14 to 16, chaired by Germany. The conference was a low-key affair with virtually no public or media coverage. The states parties agreed that the treaty was working well and reviewed progress to date in implementing it and developing the sensor package. France, Germany, and Sweden made proposals to expand the application of Open Skies to include environmental monitoring, and also to the field of crisis prevention and management in the context of OSCE or other relevant international organizations. As had happened in the negotiation of the treaty itself, the majority rejected these ideas, preferring to let the regime continue to function as originally framed. Once again, the Cyprus issue reared its head, with Turkey objecting to the inclusion in the final document of the conference a statement that the application of Cyprus to join the treaty was still pending on the agenda of the OSCC. The dispute over this point meant that it was not possible to agree on a final document of the conference. Eventually the final document had to be read into the record as a chairman's statement rather than an agreed document. The statement ended with these words: "[T]he application of Cyprus remains on the agenda of the Open Skies Consultative Commission (OSCC)." Turkey objected to this statement.[20]

Although most regime members took the view that the treaty should not formally expand its scope or purpose to include environmental monitoring or crisis management, an interesting event had occurred just before the review conference relating to the fighting that erupted between Russia and Georgia in 2008 over the breakaway regions of Abkhazia and South Ossetia. In May 2010, the United States and Romania deliberately requested an Open Skies overflight of the area of Russia near the Georgian border. Russia vetoed the segment of the flight that was planned to fly within ten kilometers of the Russia-Georgia border. Russia stated that the flight came too near to a border with a state that was not a party to the treaty: "Abkhazia." Such flights near the border of a nonmember country can be restricted under Article VI, Section II, para. 2 of the treaty—a provision that Turkey and Finland had shown great interest in during the negotiations. The United States and Romania promptly protested that they had not requested an overflight near a nonmember's border, as Georgia was a member (Russia is the only Open Skies member to recognize Abkhazia as a separate country). The entire episode had, of course, been fashioned to make a point, and this was reflected in the OSCC.[21] In 2012, Georgia announced that it would not permit Russia to perform any overflights of Georgia until the matter is resolved.[22]

This dispute played out in an atmosphere of generally worsening relations over European arms control. Russia suspended its implementation of the

CFE Treaty in 2007. Russia's stated reasons for this extraordinary act had to do with disagreements over issues such as NATO's enlargement since the end of the Cold War, which had, Russia claimed, distorted what had been a balance between the two security alliances in Europe. Another issue was related to controversies over the disposition of forces between Russia and various newly independent former Soviet republics—particularly the continued presence of Russian forces in parts of Georgia, despite the Georgian government's request that they leave. Russia was particularly annoyed that the NATO states had not ratified the Adapted CFE Treaty of 1999 (largely in protest over Russia's actions in Georgia and Moldova), while she had. Not mentioned in Russia's announcement of suspension, though widely believed to be a key issue, was NATO's plan to establish a missile defense system in Europe, which Russia had vigorously protested for some time before 2007.[23] While the controversy over the CFE Treaty has not officially impacted Open Skies, and indeed has increased the importance of the overflights since CFE Treaty inspections have ceased, the soured mood has affected European security discussions.

In 2010 the second review conference was held under U.S. chairmanship from June 7 to 9. The treaty was well established and working smoothly in terms of its operational and technical aspects.[24] The working group on sensors, which had, as noted above, begun consideration of new sensors in 2006, had reached agreement on new sensors by 2010. The most politically contentious issue dealt with by the 2010 Review Conference was Cyprus. Whereas the issue had been dealt with relatively quietly at the 2005 Review Conference, it was more contentious in 2010 and has had an impact on the work of the OSCC going forward. Once again, most members of the conference wished to record that the question of Cyprus remains on the agenda of the OSCC. Turkey objected, stating that their veto of the Cypriot application had settled the matter and that it should be removed from the agenda. A final document was adopted that used less specific language; "States Parties . . . note that one application for accession is on the agenda of the Open Skies Consultative Commission."[25] Subsequently, all delegations, save Turkey and Bosnia-Herzegovina, issued a statement in which they stated, "We support Cyprus's application to the Treaty on Open Skies."[26] This caused the Turkish delegation to issue a strong statement: "It is a source of dismay that an issue that lies outside the scope, mandate and purview of the Open Skies bodies and of the Review Conference has been brought to the Closing Session . . . . [T]he presentation of Cyprus in Open Skies fora by the Greek Cypriot administration is neither legal nor legitimate."[27] It had been hoped that the matter would rest there, but the Turkish foreign minister ordered the Turkish delegation in Vienna to block any agenda of subsequent OSCC meetings that mentioned Cyprus, effective January 1, 2011. This has seriously impeded the ongoing work of the OSCC, although specific work-arounds have been found to allow some business to go forward, such as the annual allocation of quotas.[28]

While this episode has engaged much attention, there is a broader sense that the treaty is languishing and needs a high-level political push to re-energize it. As part of this, the United States needs to replace its aging aircraft and sensor suites and lead the discussion of new ways forward for the regime. In the final conference document of the 2010 Review Conference, the chair had drawn attention to this issue in noting that budget constraints, the impending retirement of several older aircraft, and the need to upgrade sensor packages were issues to be confronted going forward.[29] Although a recent Presidential Policy Directive of March 1, 2012, reportedly mandated the U.S. Department of Defense to upgrade U.S. Open Skies assets, there is concern that the costs of doing so will not be easy to fund in the current fiscal climate. DoD funding for arms control generally is not a priority, and, as Open Skies is an orphan within the U.S. Air Force, vulnerable to budget-cutting exercises.[30]

Even as these events play out, however, some are considering what other steps could be taken to enhance and extend the treaty.

## OPEN SKIES IN OTHER CONTEXTS

### New Regional Applications of Open Skies

Away from the official diplomacy around the treaty, the years since it was signed have featured a number of analysts considering the possibility of developing Open Skies–like regimes in other regions of the world. The reasoning is simple: if Open Skies can help to build confidence from Vancouver to Vladivostok, why can't the idea do the same in other regions? In the first few years after the treaty was signed, a number of papers and analyses were prepared proposing such developments in various regions.[31] More specifically, work has been done to develop detailed proposals on the application of the idea in the India-Pakistan context,[32] the Korean context,[33] and in the Middle East.[34] The United States also familiarized Latin American governments with Open Skies, as part of a broader effort to promote the consideration of CBMs in the region within the Organization of American States.[35] Thought has also been given to providing the United Nations with an aerial monitoring capability to support peacekeeping and other UN operations, rather than relying on member states to provide such capabilities on an ad hoc basis.[36]

All of this work argues that cooperative aerial monitoring is, in principle, applicable in other regions. But most analysts recognize that this will not be accomplished simply as a matter of promoting the expansion of the present regime to those regions, or the adoption of the present treaty with little, if any modification by nations in other regions. In each regional case, there are significant local issues and histories, which mean that different considerations and even different basic goals will be in play. In the India-Pakistan case, for example, any overflight regime that might be possible would likely be restricted to the disputed border area, and have capabilities sufficient only to permit monitoring of specific border issues.[37] Nothing in the history of many years of India-Pakistan attempts at confidence-building indicates that either country will allow the other to range freely over its entire national territory for broad purposes of collecting information. In the Middle East, there is already a substantial history of overflight regimes, but, once again, they have been very specific to two particular geographic areas: the Sinai and Iraq. In each case, they have been carried out by a third party.[38] Again, there is nothing in the present Middle East situation which leads one to believe that a broad regime aimed at allowing unrestricted overflights of the entire region will be acceptable to most of its countries for many years to come and until fundamental changes have taken place in the region's security structure.

These considerations lead to a broader issue in relation to the idea of applying the Open Skies model, or indeed other CBMs developed during the East/West confrontation, to other regions; the basic idea of wide-ranging, highly intrusive transparency for its own sake as a means to promote confidence and stability may, for the time being, at least, be unique to the Euro-Atlantic region. More recent work on whether transparency stimulates trust or suspicion in various contexts is questioning the underlying assumptions of the Open Skies Treaty that if "a little transparency is good, then a lot of transparency must be better." In fact, a desire for too much transparency in itself is sometimes a double-edged sword that can do more harm than good in the wrong circumstances.[39] Marquardt has taken this argument further and argues that the historical U.S. policy of promoting transparency in international relations is itself a somewhat cynical ploy to discipline rivals by challenging them to open up and expose their military inferiorities, and also to loosen their control over their publics—very much one of the main reasons why many in the Eisenhower administration were supportive of Open Skies in 1955. In Marquardt's view, American calls for "transparency" are therefore to be seen as part of a larger U.S. attempt to impose its own values on the international system, and to do so in a way which weakens states that do not share those values.[40]

Whatever one thinks of these arguments, the specifics of the present Open Skies Treaty are unique to the Euro-Atlantic area and the product of a particular approach to building confidence that may not travel well. Moreover, it must be recognized that, even in the Euro-Atlantic area, the Open Skies negotiations did not hit their stride until the Cold War was effectively over. In other words, the kind of wide-area, indiscriminately intrusive, free-ranging transparency allowed for under the Open Skies regime was possible in the context of solidifying relationships that were already improving, rather than in the context of a relationship marked by a sense that conflict was still possible.

This does not mean that cooperative aerial monitoring is not a concept applicable to other contexts. But the specific circumstances will vary greatly, and the nations involved in other regional negotiations will likely have very different answers to the basic question, What is this regime for? Perhaps, then, it would be better for advocates of the Open Skies idea not to promote the Open Skies Treaty itself as an example of the kind of regime that could be sought in other regions, but rather to consider what specific issues and concerns could be addressed by cooperative aerial monitoring generally, and how a regime of such monitoring could be devised that is consistent with the history, problems, and traditions of the region where it is being considered. In most other regional cases, cooperative aerial monitoring regimes will likely be far less invasive than Open Skies. The Open Skies Treaty does offer lessons to any other region considering embarking on the path of developing a cooperative aerial monitoring system, and these will be outlined and discussed in the concluding chapter of this book. But the Open Skies Treaty itself very likely does not offer a fully formed model for the use of other regions.

### The Environment Question

Since the beginning of the regime, it has been noted that cooperative environmental monitoring could be an area where the Open Skies regime could be extended.[41] The OSCC held two seminars on the subject before the entry into force in December 1992 and July 1994, and another in 2004. The efficacy of this was demonstrated when the United States used its Open Skies aircraft to overfly and assess the damage caused by Hurricane Mitch in Central America in 1998 and along the Gulf Coast after Hurricane Katrina in 2005. The German Open Skies aircraft was used to help monitor and assess flood damage in Europe in 1997. Each of these cases involved monitoring and assessing damage after a natural disaster, rather than ongoing environmental monitoring as such, but the point has been made that Open Skies can play a useful role.

While the use of Open Skies for environmental monitoring has an intuitive appeal, and is certainly technically feasible, there are arguments to be considered. First, there are a number of private companies that provide this service on contract at a fraction of the cost of mounting an Open Skies overflight for the purpose. These private companies have sensor suites optimized for the purpose, and it would be costly to adapt the current Open Skies sensor suites to this objective—particularly at a time when many states are reluctant even to upgrade the currently allowed sensors. Second, such flights may become a source of friction between countries, unless they are undertaken under the terms of a treaty on environmental issues, which mandates cooperative steps for verification and monitoring.[42]

At this time, there seems little chance that Open Skies states parties will achieve consensus within the OSCC to pursue work on the environmental issue. Of course, nothing prohibits individual regime members from using their overflights for this purpose on an individual or bilateral basis.

### Open Skies and the Elimination of WMD

Another subject that has been considered by those wishing to expand the capabilities and functions of the existing Open Skies regime has to do with using such overflights to complement and improve upon the verification techniques available for monitoring compliance with various international arms control and disarmament treaties, both present and the future. Once again, since the signing of the Open Skies Treaty, it has been argued that modifications to the Open Skies regime could enhance its role in terms of helping to verify several arms control and disarmament agreements.[43] More recently, an appeal has been made to adapt the Open Skies regime to serve as a mechanism for helping to verify deep nuclear weapons reductions on the way to a world free of such weapons.[44] This idea is based on much scientific research, which has shown that airborne sampling of the atmosphere can be an effective wide-area means of detecting evidence of nuclear activity. Such evidence could then serve as a cue for further inspections.[45]

This represents a new area of application for a cooperative aerial monitoring regime. Of course, the use of aerial monitoring to detect evidence of nuclear, biological, or chemical weapons activity is not new. The first evidence that the USSR had exploded an atomic bomb in 1949 came via aerial sampling of winds downrange by the U.S. Air Force.[46] Since then, an active program of aerial sampling has been carried out by several countries to keep tabs on each other's WMD and other activities. The UN Special Commission charged with verifying that Iraq has dismantled all WMD programs in the wake of the first Gulf War had an aerial component, provided by the United States, Germany, and Chile.[47] In both of these cases, however, the data was not gathered in a cooperative manner, but rather an adversarial one—a key difference from one of the fundamental tenets of Open Skies.

What would be new, then, would be the creation of a worldwide, cooperative program of aerial sampling dedicated to verifying deep cuts in, or even the elimination of, nuclear weapons and other kinds of WMD. This would require a fleet of aircraft with sensors optimized for this purpose and the ability to cover all states of potential concern globally. This could begin with an adaptation of the present Open Skies regime. As Drell and Stubbs point out in their article, for the purposes of helping to verify deep nuclear cuts, and other agreements that would be necessary to create a world without nuclear weapons (such as a Fissile Material Cut-off), four of the five nuclear weapons states as recognized under the Nuclear Non-proliferation Treaty (the NPT) are already members of Open Skies. Only China is not. The use of Open Skies aircraft, with additional sensors suited to this objective, and with permission granted to overfly China for this purpose, along with the other nuclear weapons states (the United States, Russia, the UK, and France), would allow the assets of Open Skies Treaty to be used for an entirely novel purpose.

Of course, if a worldwide agreement on nuclear disarmament were to be signed, it would have to cover other states of proliferation concern, such as India, Israel, Iran, North Korea, and Pakistan and others. In this case, a new cooperative aerial monitoring agreement would likely have to be reached as part of the provisions of agreements on deep cuts and eventual elimination of nuclear weapons and other WMD. The Open Skies platforms already in operation, if modified to permit airborne sampling, could serve as the basis for such a system, with others contributing additional aircraft to build up the truly global system.

All of this is ambitious and will take many years. But President Obama has officially committed the United States to the goal of a nuclear-weapons-free world, and the idea is being discussed with a seriousness that has been missing in past.[48] Its proponents recognize that the goal of a nuclear-free world will be a long-term one; as President Obama said, "We may not get there in my lifetime."[49] But thought can be given now to how this will work, and cooperative work can begin to explore different combinations of sensors and to gather data on how effective they might be. The lessons of other arms control negotiations show that lengthy periods of scientific research are required to develop the verification provisions. Such research has the effect of gradually convincing states that such undertakings can be verified. The recently signed Comprehensive Test Ban Treaty, for example, which bans all nuclear testing, was preceded by decades of cooperative international research to develop and perfect the worldwide seismic monitoring system that is now the foundation of that treaty's verification system.[50]

Indeed, research and cooperation into an international cooperative aerial monitoring system for eventual treaties to eliminate nuclear weapons and other WMD may represent a new lease on life for Open Skies. If the United States, Russia, and other leading Open Skies nations could agree to make use of their Open Skies experiences and assets as a foundation for research into the development of techniques for cooperative aerial monitoring of future agreements on the elimination of WMD, this would represent a future for the regime that would justify investments in new capabilities and also a revitalization of the treaty itself. It would also be thoroughly consistent with the basic objectives of Open Skies, going all the way back to the proposal first made by President Eisenhower in 1955.

The twenty years since Open Skies was signed, and the ten years since it came into force have seen the quiet implementation and development of the regime. But a malaise has settled on the process. There is a feeling that a high-level political impetus is required to keep the development of the regime on track and to open it up to new challenges and opportunities. This will be considered in the Conclusion of this book.

# Conclusion

The Open Skies negotiation took many twists and turns on the way to the treaty. The proposal was almost not launched, suffered a lack of both clear goals and bureaucratic interest, was regarded with grave suspicion by powerful interests in the bureaucracies of both superpowers, was regarded as less than a priority by the European allies for much of its life, and endured a largely disappointing first two rounds of talks before finally hitting its stride in the summer of 1991. Of course, by that point the world into which the initiative had been relaunched by President Bush had changed dramatically.

I am firmly convinced that among the main impediments to the negotiation's early success were the related facts that it was a "top-down" initiative, and that it lacked a clear statement of goals. As a top-down initiative, Open Skies was an orphan; it lacked a bureaucratic constituency in the powerful interagency process in Washington. It was also regarded by many in the national security and intelligence bureaucracy as being of little benefit to the United States. Furthermore, those who might have been expected to champion its merits within the U.S. government, such as the State Department or the Arms Control and Disarmament Agency, were either lukewarm to it or regarded Open Skies as a threat to other goals, such as the achievement of an aerial inspection protocol as part of the verification provisions of the Conventional Forces in Europe (CFE) Treaty.

Internally, the fact that Open Skies was imposed on a skeptical bureaucracy presented considerable difficulty when that bureaucracy was ordered to put flesh on the idea. Having rejected the idea when consulted before Blackwill, Zelikow and the Canadians performed a bureaucratic and political end-run; the security and intelligence bureaucracies in Washington were none too pleased to be confronted with a public statement by the president in his Texas A&M speech. Accordingly, they dug in their heels and used the fact that the president's statement was vague as to the specifics and goals of the proposal to stall throughout the period leading up to the Ottawa Conference. Moreover, they insisted that the initial alliance negotiating position be such that the United States would have realized significant intelligence advantages from the regime—something they knew the Soviets would not accept.

The lack of a clearly enunciated and agreed goal that could easily be translated into parameters for the regime further handicapped the initiative through the Ottawa and Budapest rounds. In the absence of any specific purpose for the overflights under discussion, those in the intelligence and military communities of both superpowers who viewed the entire enterprise with suspicion were able to manufacture problems. Furthermore, there was no way of holding these interests accountable in their own capitals for the failure of the negotiations. They were each able to point to their positions as being consistent with the requirements of "confidence-building" (in the absence of any definition of what that meant in the context of Open Skies), and to their adversaries' positions as being unreasonable.

Moreover, there was no opportunity to explore confidentially with Moscow whether or not the Soviet bureaucracy was prepared to accept the idea of negotiations over the subject. Such discussions are often conducted in private, when there is no stigma attached to failure and the issues can be tentatively explored. When the Soviets did agree to negotiate in September 1989 at Jackson Hole, they were doing so largely to avoid the stigma of being seen as unwilling to talk about Open Skies as they had been in 1955, but there had been no discussions aimed at identifying problems and bridging positions before the delegations turned up in Ottawa to begin the formal process.

Such consultations as did exist prior to the Ottawa round were largely between the nations of the North Atlantic Treaty Organization (NATO) alliance. These produced a basic concept of operations for the regime based upon the initial U.S. concept of operations, and a draft negotiating text. But they did not point the way to the resolution of the more thorny operational and political problems, such as regime expansion and the question of a link to the Conference on Security and Cooperation in Europe (CSCE), in a way that would ever be satisfactory to the NATO allies, much less the Soviets.

What little prenegotiation there was largely took the form of bilateral meetings with the Soviets, at which they asked questions but volunteered little. To the extent that any signals were sent by the Soviets in the autumn of 1989, they did point to differences in approach and outline some of the concerns that they would bring to the talks. But they were lost in the noise of the NATO nations attempting to get their own positions settled. They were also regarded by many as signs of a Soviet desire to enter the negotiation with a tough initial position, rather than as a fundamental dislike of Open Skies as such.

What then sustained the Open Skies initiative? Moreover, what changed such that it was eventually able to prosper? I believe that once again, two interrelated factors are the answers to these questions. First, the fact that it was a top-down initiative, which was identified above as a weakness, was also the only thing that allowed the proposal to see the light of day in the first place. The bureaucracy would not have championed the idea itself, and did not do so when working on President Bush's first request for new arms control ideas.

More important, however, the idea would not have survived in the absence of high-level political commitment to pursue it. In addition to its presidential launch, Open Skies benefited from the fact that high level political figures pursued it in spite of the desire of many in their bureaucracies. Presidents Bush and Gorbachev were not supposed to discuss Open Skies at their 1990 Summit in Washington. In fact, they discussed it at greater length than any other arms control issue, save START. This discussion led Bush to order the U.S. bureaucracy to keep working on the idea at a time when many hoped it would quietly go away.

Secretary of State Baker and Foreign Minister Shevardnadze pursued the wishes of their presidents later that summer at Irkutsk. Working directly with each other and only a few aides from both sides, Baker and Shevardnadze were able to work out the essential aspects of what would become the treaty. Although political events would intervene in the Soviet Union to prevent the quick pursuit of the ideas explored at Irkutsk, the discussion did serve to demonstrate that an agreement was possible, and that high-level figures were determined to pursue it. The "Irkutsk formula," and indeed the idea that Open Skies had even been discussed at any length, came as a shock to many in the security and intelligence bureaucracies of the superpowers, and as a shot in the arm to Open Skies.

Finally, high-level political impetus was given to the initiative by countries other than the superpowers at critical moments. Canada, Hungary, and, later, the powerful European allies (Germany, France, and the United Kingdom) brought pressure to bear to keep the idea alive and to search for compromise. The reasons for the growing European involvement will be discussed below, but in the cases of Canada and Hungary, Open Skies fulfilled a number of goals.

Open Skies served to reinforce Canada's security ties to Europe at a time when declining defense expenditures called this into question. It served to demonstrate North America's willingness to share the burden of openness being asked of the Europeans under such regimes as the Stockholm accords and the CFE verification provisions. For both Canada and Hungary, Open Skies served to give smaller countries, those without sophisticated National Technical Means, an independent ability to monitor events. This capability was of far greater direct importance to Hungary than Canada, which does benefit as an intelligence ally of the United States.

Coming at a time when the president was unsure whether to relaunch Open Skies, high-level Canadian involvement may have tipped the balance. Canada's constant pushing was also a factor in bringing the subject to the negotiating table in a short period. Although this may have robbed the negotiation of any chance for a suitable period of prenegotiation, the fact that Open Skies enjoyed very little support within the U.S. or Soviet bureaucracies could have meant that such a period of prenegotiation would have been unsuccessful anyway. Canada and Hungary then helped to keep Open Skies on the European security agenda in the immediate aftermath of the Ottawa and Budapest conferences.

High-level involvement by the most powerful European allies was crucial in pressuring the U.S. bureaucracy to move in new directions and in forging the final compromises. The growing interest of the Europeans was motivated by a realization that Open Skies would enable them to independently monitor events outside of the CFE verification zone. Their interest was also moved along by the fact that their other priorities, such as the conclusion of the CFE Treaty and German unification, had been realized. Although the Europeans did not take up the cause of Open Skies until after the CFE had been signed, their combined weight proved irresistible. This was particularly so as international events were moving in such a way as to open up the possibility that those opposed to Open Skies in the U.S. and Soviet bureaucracies were either losing their interest in opposing the idea in Washington, or losing their jobs in Moscow.

This, in turn, points to the second factor in the survival and eventual success of Open Skies. Open Skies was relaunched at a time of significant changes in the world. However, no one involved in this relaunching realized how far those changes would go or how quickly. When President Bush made his Texas A&M

speech, many of the key bureaucratic players in the two superpowers retained a view of the world that had yet to evolve to keep pace with the changes under way. For example, many of the factors that caused Canada to embrace the idea created suspicion in some quarters in Washington. The democratization of information gathering was not welcomed by many in the U.S. intelligence community who feared the loss of an advantage. The Soviet military and intelligence communities continued to harbor the same dim views of the idea of openness for its own sake as they had in 1955.

As the Berlin Wall fell, as communist regimes were toppled throughout Eastern Europe, as the Warsaw Treaty Organization disbanded, and as the Soviet Union imploded, many of those who had resisted Open Skies were either removed from their positions or lost interest in opposing it. Like a chameleon, Open Skies was able to adapt, transforming itself from an adversarial, intelligence-gathering exercise to a truly cooperative confidence-building regime. As Europe changed, the rationale for a confidence-building-oriented version of Open Skies became stronger and the number of countries that saw its benefits grew.

The Open Skies negotiation can be said to have been both the last major East-West multilateral security negotiation of the Cold War and the first major multilateral European security negotiation and agreement of the post–Cold War era. Beginning with President Bush's call upon states of NATO and the Warsaw Treaty Organization (WTO) to negotiate in May of 1989 and ending in an agreement signed by twenty-five states (including those that used to belong to the WTO and some new states created from the breakup of the USSR) in March of 1992, the Open Skies talks spanned one of the most tumultuous periods in history.

As such, it was inevitable that many of the political battles that underlay the negotiation would represent the extraordinary developments under way. Open Skies began for many as an idea aimed at achieving unilateral advantage in the gathering of intelligence. It ended as the first truly cooperative Confidence-building Measure (CBM) of the post–Cold War period. The disputes that characterized much of the negotiation, both within and between various delegations, were a microcosm of the broader changes taking place.

Anyone walking into the Ottawa Conference Centre in early February 1990 would have recognized the basic structure and problems of that conference had they attended any other East-West negotiation throughout the Cold War. Having no other model of negotiations to rely on, many delegations reverted to type throughout the Ottawa and Budapest rounds. But, as the changes in Europe caught up with Open Skies, its protagonists tried again, this time proving successful. That they were successful is testimony to their persistence, ingenuity, negotiating skill, and, perhaps most of all, the resilience and timeliness of the idea of Open Skies itself.

While the Open Skies Treaty as such may not be replicable in other regional contexts, cooperative aerial monitoring has much to contribute to reducing tension in a variety of regional situations around the world. Moreover, some version of the idea may make its greatest contribution as a means of helping to monitor and verify both present and future treaties designed to sharply reduce and even one day eliminate nuclear weapons and other Weapons of Mass Destruction (WMD). If ever serious negotiations begin on the creation of a cooperative aerial monitoring regime, either in other troubled regions, or to help verify the reduction and elimination of WMD, the Open Skies experience points to a series of lessons and conclusions as to how such negotiations should be entered into.

Lesson 1 is that *Cooperation* (in mission operations), *Equality* (in sensors), and *Sharing* (in sensor capabilities and overflight results) are what might be called the "Golden Rules" of Open Skies. Allowing another state to perform a surveillance overflight is one of the most dramatic concessions a state can make in terms of its sovereignty. No state will do so unless the flights are done in a cooperative manner; done on the basis of equality; and the results are shared. It was not until the NATO states fully embraced these concepts that the Open Skies Treaty took shape. In any future negotiation over the creation of a cooperative aerial monitoring regime, for whatever purpose, the situation is likely to be no different. Much time can be saved if future negotiators begin from positions based on these "Golden Rules," rather than attempting to create a regime based on a desire to achieve an advantage.

Lesson 2 is that "Form Follows Function." The shape and scope of a future cooperative aerial monitoring regime must be determined by the answer to a basic question: "What is the problem to which such a regime could be part of the solution?" Is the purpose confidence-building? If so, how is it agreed among the participating states that confidence is to be built?; what needs to be seen, and how often, in order to increase confidence? Is the purpose of a future regime the verification of a specific arms control or disarmament treaty? Again, what is it that needs to be seen on the overflights to achieve this aim, and what capabilities are required to do so? In short, once the political *goals* of the regime are identified and agreed, discussion of the technicalities can go forward. Absent this, various interests will compete over their conceptions of what the regime should be for, and will draw lines in the sand. It was not until both sides in the Open Skies talks had come to a basic agreement at the highest political level over the political and technical goals of the regime that the negotiations finally hit their stride in Vienna. It still wasn't easy to develop the regime after this breakthrough had been achieved, but it was impossible before it.

Lesson 3 is to get those who will actually operate the overflights into the negotiating room from the start and listen to their advice. The NATO Open Skies negotiators felt that demanding exceptionally short-notice, intrusive overflights sounded good as an opening position in the adversarial world of East-West arms control negotiations that they were used to when the Open Skies talk began. But they found eventually that such flights aren't so easy in practice. As the Open Skies negotiations went forward, and the initially competitive environment began to disappear with the end of the Cold War, the NATO countries found that many of their own operational demands of the Soviets wouldn't actually have worked, or would have been prohibitively expensive once attention turned away from scoring debating points to actually having to implement them. Most of the early NATO positions on issues such as prenotification schedules and flight plans had been worked out initially by diplomats and lawyers, without the operators present. The key objective at the beginning of the talks was to make a point to the Soviets, rather than to work with them to craft a regime that would actually work. Again, it wasn't until the delegations approached the negotiations over flight procedures in a cooperative and noncompetitive spirit that the real operational solutions to these questions, which the actual operators had been suggesting from the start, began to be found. Those solutions stressed the need for the flights to be undertaken in a cooperative spirit, rather than an adversarial one.

Lesson 4 concerns the relationship between cooperative aerial monitoring and arms control. A flexible approach to designing a future regime can produce an agreement that fulfills the requirements of confidence-building, while also promoting other purposes. Open Skies has shown that a cooperative aerial monitoring regime does not have to be a formal part of an arms control regime to be of benefit to it. Indeed, some separation can be useful, provided the technical aspects of the Open Skies regime are complementary to the needs of arms control regimes. In the case of the Open Skies Treaty, had the discussion over cooperative aerial monitoring in the East-West context linked the idea formally to the CFE Treaty (as negotiators of the verification provisions of the CFE Treaty had wished to do at the time), such overflights would have been restricted to the CFE zone—from the Atlantic to the Urals. The Open Skies Treaty allows states to go far beyond that zone and monitor military equipment outside the area of application of the CFE—this is a critical benefit of the Open Skies Treaty, especially since implementation of the CFE Treaty has since been suspended by Russia. The key to success is to design the sensor package and flight operations to be relevant and complementary to arms control regimes, but not necessarily to follow slavishly any specific arms control treaty. This is a lesson that should be borne in mind as consideration is given in the coming years to more ambitious agreements aimed at reducing and eventually eliminating nuclear and other WMD.

Finally, lesson 5 is that the United States must lead the process, but it must define its interests in an expansive and flexible manner. A well-developed cooperative aerial monitoring regime will benefit the U.S. but is of disproportionate benefit to countries without their own National Technical Means. Narrowly defined, this may mean that such a regime is of more limited interest to the United States, though even aerial inspections can return data not available to satellites. But such a situation can be very much in the U.S. national interest, if that interest is defined in wider terms to include increasing the comfort level of small and medium-size countries and persuading them to join in a process of embracing cooperation with each other as a means of reducing regional tensions. This is a critical benefit to the United States.

* * *

As this book is finished, the Open Skies Treaty has once again hit something of a low period. The treaty is working well from a technical standpoint, but political questions, such as how to expand the present regime, have arisen that call into question its ability to develop further. Meanwhile, some are questioning whether it returns data that is worth the cost. Despite a presidential policy directive, there are concerns that the United States may not, for example, find the funds to upgrade the sensor package on its Open Skies aircraft, and may not even replace these aircraft when they retire.

This would be a short-sighted move. Cooperative aerial monitoring is a proven means of increasing confidence and promoting transparency. Although perhaps intangible when measured in dollars and cents, confidence and transparency are commodities in short supply in many troubled regions of the world, including some areas covered by the present treaty. While the present

Open Skies Treaty may not be something that can be simply transferred to other regions, its lessons and ideas can be modified to make them useful, and this would be a great benefit to the United States and the international community more generally.

Moreover, if President Obama's call for the creation of a nuclear free world is ever to be realized, cooperative aerial monitoring can and must be a significant part of verifying steps toward this goal and the broader goal of eliminating other kinds of WMD. Like the process that eventually led to the Open Skies Treaty itself, and has led to other significant arms control and disarmament agreements, the development of these ambitious objectives will require leadership and vision. To allow the present Open Skies to atrophy from neglect or disuse would both be a loss for Euro-Atlantic stability and also cast a negative pall over future attempts to realize the benefits of cooperative aerial monitoring in other parts of the world and for broader purposes.

Open Skies, and cooperative aerial monitoring generally, is one of the oldest CBM ideas in history. It has surfaced and resurfaced in many contexts and many guises over many decades. It is not finished yet. Indeed, with the same kind of leadership and vision that led to the achievement of the treaty itself, Open Skies most exciting and important contributions may yet lie ahead of it.

# Notes

## PREFACE

1. Drell, S., and C. Stubbs, "Realizing the Full Potential of the Open Skies Treaty," *Arms Control Today*, July/August, 2011. The Hoover workshop resulted in an op-ed by George P. Shultz, Sidney Drell, and Christopher Stubbs, "Modernize the Open Skies Treaty," *New York Times*, March 25, 2012.

## INTRODUCTION

1. For a comparison of the benefits of satellite versus aerial imagery, see Drell, S., and C. Stubbs, "Realizing the Full Potential of the Open Skies Treaty," *Arms Control Today*, July/August, 2011; and Spitzer, H., "The Improvement of Satellite Capabilities and Its Implications for the Open Skies Regime," in *Open Skies: A Cooperative Approach to Military Transparency and Confidence-building*, ed. Dunay, P., M. Krasznai, H. Spitzer, R. Wiemker, and W. Wynne (Geneva: UN Institute for Disarmament Research, 2004).

## CHAPTER 1

1. Not surprisingly, Eisenhower's own thoughts on this question attribute benign motives to the proposal. See Eisenhower, D. D., *Mandate for Change: The White House Years, 1953–6* (New York: Doubleday and Company, 1963), ch. 11. For the thoughts of those who largely believe that Open Skies was a serious attempt to reduce tension and lay the foundations for possible disarmament agreements, though they are not immune to the idea that Open Skies was in part a propaganda ploy, see Bundy, M., *Danger and Survival: Choices about the Bomb in the First Fifty Years* (New York: Random House, 1988), 296–305; Rostow, W., *Open Skies: Eisenhower's Proposal of July 21, 1955* (Austin: University of Austin Texas Press, 1982); Boulden, J., "Open Skies: The 1955 Proposal and Its Current Revival," *Dalhousie Law Journal* 13, no. 2 (1990): 611–49; Florini, A., "The Open Skies Negotiations," in *The Encyclopedia of Arms Control and Disarmament*, vol. 11,

ed. Burns, R. D. (Charles Scribner's Sons, 1993), and Bury, H., *Eisenhower and the Cold War Arms Race: 'Open Skies' and the Military Industrial Complex* (London: I.B. Tauris & Co., 2014). For more cynical interpretations of the 1955 proposal's intent, though not uniformly so, see Evangelista, M., "Cooperation Theory and Disarmament Negotiations in the 1950s," *World Politics* 42, no. 4 (July 1990); Prados, J., "Open Skies and Closed Minds," in Bischof, G., and S. Dockrill, eds., *Cold War Respite: The Geneva Summit of 1955* (Baton Rouge: Louisiana State University Press, 2000); Tal, D., "Eisenhower's Disarmament Dilemma: From Chance for Peace to Open Skies Proposal," *Diplomacy and Statecraft* 12, no. 2 (June 2001); Marquardt, J. J., "Transparency and Security Competition: Open Skies and America's Cold War Statecraft, 1948–1960," *Journal of Cold War Studies* 9, no. 1 (Winter 2007); and Marquardt, J. J., "Open Skies and American Primacy," *Diplomacy and Statecraft* 18 3 (September 2007). One of the Cold War's preeminent historians believes that Eisenhower's fear that concerns on both sides over the possibility of a surprise attack might lead to inadvertent nuclear war was genuine, and his desire to do something tangible to reduce them was also—but that he probably never expected Open Skies to be accepted by the Soviets and therefore saw it as largely a useful propaganda ploy. See Gaddis, J. L., *Strategies of Containment: A Critical Appraisal of Post-war American National Security Policy* (New York: Oxford University Press, 1982), 156–57. Osgood generally agrees with this thesis in his Osgood, K., *Total Cold War: Eisenhower's Secret Proposal Battle at Home and Abroad* (Lawrence: University of Kansas Press, 2006), ch. 6, as does Thomas in Thomas, E., *Ike's Bluff: President Eisenhower's Secret Battle to Save the World* (New York: Little Brown and Co., 2012), ch. 11.

2. Prados, "Open Skies and Closed Minds," 220. Prados reports that Rockefeller's position was an outgrowth of Eisenhower's interest in psychological warfare and the use of propaganda to unbalance an enemy and undermine his positions.

3. Eleven men were at the Quantico session. Most participants were academics who had substantial government experience. The names are found in Rostow, *Open Skies*, 27. Rostow was a participant and chaired the session.

4. Ibid., 30; Boulden, "Open Skies."

5. Gaddis, *Strategies of Containment*, 156–57. In a broader sense, the United States was interested in portraying itself as a more benign actor on the world stage than the USSR, as part of a campaign to "win over" opinion in postwar Western Europe toward a U.S.-led block that would oppose Soviet expansion and adhere to liberal economic practices. For more on the broader effort by the United States to "create" the idea of the "West," see Hitchcock, W. I., "The Marshall Plan and the Creation of the West," in Leffler, M. P., and O. A. Westad, eds., *The Cambridge History of the Cold War*, vol. 1 (Cambridge: Cambridge University Press, 2010), esp. 156–57.

6. "Letter from the Chairman of the Quantico Vulnerabilities Panel (Rostow) to the President's Special Assistant (Rockefeller). Summary of Recommendations: Quantico Vulnerabilities Panel," U.S. Department of State, *Foreign Relations of the United States*,

*1955–57*, vol. 5 (Washington, DC: U.S. Government Printing Office, 1988), 216–20. See also Rostow, *Open Skies*, 30; Boulden, "Open Skies"; Florini, "The Open Skies Negotiations."

7. Rockefeller's memo of July 6 to the president on the benefits of Open Skies is reprinted in Rostow, *Open Skies*, 134.

8. Rostow, *Open Skies*, 34–56; Boulden, "Open Skies"; Bundy, *Danger and Survival*, 296–97.

9. For the involvement of Stassen in the development of Open Skies, his thoughts on a revised U.S. approach to disarmament, and the reactions of Dulles, see Tal, D., "From the Open Skies Proposal of 1955 to the Norstad Plan of 1960: A Plan Too Far," *Journal of Cold War Studies* 10, no. 4 (Fall 2008). According to Tal, Dulles would later come to see the value of "playing the game" of disarmament, but only after Stassen had left the administration.

10. For a summation of U.S. views on the eve of the 1955 summit, see Bischof, G., "Eisenhower, the Summit and the Austrian Treaty," in Bischof, G., and S. Dockrill, eds., *Cold War Respite: The Geneva Summit of 1955* (Baton Rouge: Louisiana State University Press, 2000).

11. In fact, Rockefeller's staff was not in Geneva, as it had not been able to find sufficient hotel space. They were in Paris awaiting, as one of them later put it, "the moment when the US delegation in Geneva ran out of ammunition" (Rostow, *Open Skies*, 54).

12. Boulden, "Open Skies."

13. "Statement by President Eisenhower," in *The Geneva Conference of Heads of Government, July 18–23, 1955* (Washington, DC: Department of State Publication 6046, October 1955), 21.

14. Memorandum of Conversation (memcon), DDE and Zhukov, July 20, 1955, *Foreign Relations of the United States*, 1955–57, vol. 5, Austrian State Treaty: Summit and Foreign Ministers Meetings, 1955, ed. W.Z. Slaney (Washington DC: US Government Printing Office, 1987), 409. See also Fursenko, A., and T. Naftali, *Khrushchev's Cold War: The Inside Story of an American Adversary* (New York: W. W. Norton, 2006), 45–46.

15. "Soviet Proposal Introduced in the Disarmament Subcommittee: Reduction of Armaments, the Prohibition of Atomic Weapons, and the Elimination of the Threat of New War, 10 May, 1955," in U.S. Arms Control and Disarmament Agency, *Documents on Disarmament, 1945–1959*, vol. 1 (Washington, DC: U.S. Government Printing Office, 1991), 456–67.

16. "Statement by President Eisenhower," in *The Geneva Conference of Heads of Government, July 18–23, 1955*, 57–58.

17. Eisenhower, *Mandate for Change*, 521.

18. Ibid. See also Gaddis, J. L., *We Now Know: Rethinking Cold War History* (Oxford: Oxford University Press, 1997), 245, for more on Eisenhower's proposal and Khrushchev's reaction.

19. Krass, A. S., *Verification: How Much Is Enough?* (London and Philadelphia: Tay-

lor and Francis, 1985), 118. Quoted in Dunay, P., and H. Spitzer, "The Open Skies Negotiations and the Open Skies Treaty," in *Open Skies: A Cooperative Approach to Military Transparency and Confidence-building*, ed. Dunay, P., M. Krasznai, H. Spitzer, R. Wiemker, and W. Wynne (Geneva: UN Institute for Disarmament Research, 2004), 18. For more on the Soviet reaction, see Prados, "Open Skies and Closed Minds."

20. Zubok, V. M., "Soviet Policy Aims at the Geneva Conference, 1955," in *Cold War Respite: The Geneva Summit of 1955*, ed. Bischof, G., and S. Dockrill (Baton Rouge: Louisiana State University Press, 2000), 73–74.

21. See, for example, Abel, E., "Eisenhower Calls upon Soviets to Exchange Arms Blueprints; Asks Mutual Aerial Inspection," *New York Times*, July 22, 1955. The positive reaction of the U.S. Congress is reported in a July 22 story in the *New York Herald Tribune*; see Rostow, *Open Skies*, 57–59, for other reactions.

22. For the U.S. and Soviet proposals and counterproposals, see U.S. Department of State, *Documents on Disarmament, 1945–59* (Washington, DC: Government Printing Office, 1960), vol. 2, Documents 213 and 215, and Maps 1 and 2.

23. For a discussion of the proposals during the 1950s and 60s for aerial inspections in certain geographic zones, see Marquardt, "Transparency and Security Competition"; and Tal, "From the Open Skies Proposal of 1955 to the Norstad Plan of 1960." See also Boulden, "Open Skies"; Florini, "The Open Skies Negotiations"; and Fursenko and Naftali, *Khrushchev's Cold War*, 143–44, 284–86.

24. For an early example of a statement by a Soviet official on these points, see the August 1955 *Pravda* interview with Premier Bulganin, cited in Dunay and Spitzer, "The Open Skies Negotiations and the Open Skies Treaty," 19–20.

25. Dobrynin, A., *In Confidence: Moscow's Ambassador to America's Six Cold War Presidents, 1962–1986* (New York: Crown, 1995), 38–39.

26. Prados, "Open Skies and Closed Minds," 222–24, discusses the interplay between the U2 program and Open Skies. In a review of another paper on Open Skies, Prados advances the notion that Eisenhower had been duplicitous in not telling the Soviets that the U2 was under development when he made his Open Skies proposal. He argues that this knowledge might have led Moscow to view Open Skies differently: "Eisenhower did not do what he could have to induce Soviet leaders to retreat from their suspicions of Open Skies as a spy program—tell Moscow that the United States would peer over the Iron Curtain whatever happened and that its real choice lay between freedom to surveille the United States or no coverage at all. Had Khrushchev known this, his own calculations might have been different . . . . But absent knowledge that the Americans were coming anyway, Moscow never had the choice." See Prados, J., *H-diplo Article Review of Marqardt's "Transparency and Security Competition: Open Skies and America's Cold War Statecraft, 1948–1960,"* July 4, 2007. Available at www.h-net.org/~diplo/reviews/PDF/Prados-Marquardt.pdf. I view this as a naive argument. Given the mood of the times, it is likely that Khrushchev's reaction to being told in advance of the U2 would have been

to try to score a propaganda point about American "spying" and to order the Soviet military to embark on a crash program to shoot it down the moment it appeared over the USSR.

27. See Fursenko and Naftali, *Khrushchev's Cold War*, 281, 285.

28. Clark, J., "Foreword," in *Open Skies: Technical; Organizational; Operational; Legal and Political Aspects*, ed. Chestnutt, H., and M. Slack (Toronto: York University Press, 1990), v.

29. Major General V. Kuklev, deputy chief of the USSR Armed Forces Directorate, in an interview with M. Ponomarev entitled "Kuklev Elaborates on Military Openness, Security," *Krasnaya Zvezda*, November 5, 1989 (translation in FBIS-SOV-89–214, November 7, 1989).

30. Although the two did take steps toward a measure of cooperation when they enshrined provisions banning measures to deceive satellites in several of their future arms control agreements.

31. Borawski, J., "NATO, Europe and Open Skies," in *Open Skies*, ed. Chestnutt and Slack, 21.

32. Dunay and Spitzer, "The Open Skies Negotiations and the Open Skies Treaty," 21.

33. Borawski, "NATO, Europe and Open Skies," 98; Dunay and Spitzer, "The Open Skies Negotiations and the Open Skies Treaty," 22.

34. *Document of the Stockholm Conference on Confidence- and Security-Building Measures and Disarmament in Europe Convened in Accordance with the relevant Provisions of the Concluding Document of the Madrid Meeting of the Conference on Security and Co-operation in Europe*. Available at *www.state.gov/t/isn/4725.htm*, para. 89.

35. Ibid., para. 90.

## CHAPTER 2

1. The importance that the NATO allies attached to these two developments as indicators of the new Soviet attitude to transparency is made clear in the opening paragraphs of their Basic Elements Paper, which outlined their initial view of the Open Skies regime. See North Atlantic Treaty Organization, Press Service (NATO-PS), *Open Skies Basic Elements*, NATO Press Service, Annex to M-2(89) 46, December 15, 1989.

2. For more on President Bush's views during this period, see Bush, George H. W., and B. Scowcroft, *A World Transformed* (New York: Random House, 1998), 37–54.

3. Tucker, J., "Negotiating Open Skies: A Diplomatic History," in *Open Skies, Open Control and Cooperative Security*, ed. Krepon, M., and A. Smithson (New York: St. Martin's Press, 1992), 3. Tucker was deeply involved in the U.S. Open Skies negotiation. His account is an authoritative guide to internal U.S. policy-making.

4. See, for example, the views of two senior officials of the Bush administration on this point: Zelikow, P., and C. Rice, *Germany Unified and Europe Transformed: A Study in Statecraft* (Cambridge: Harvard University Press, 1997), 20–21.

5. Evans, M., "West Sees Offer as a Ploy to Exploit Its Differences," *The Times*, January 20, 1989, in which a Soviet offer to reduce its short-range nuclear weapons if the West does not modernize its Lance missiles is discussed. See also Brodie, I., "Russia Exploits West German Fears of Limited Nuclear War," *Daily Telegraph*, February 6, 1989.

6. Bush and Scowcroft, *A World Transformed*, 46–47.

7. Ibid., 39.

8. Congressional Research Service, Senior Specialists Section, *Soviet Diplomacy and Negotiating Behavior—1989–1990: Gorbachev-Reagan-Bush Meetings at the Summit*, Committee on Foreign Affairs, Special Studies Series on Foreign Affairs Issues, vol. 3 (Washington, DC: U.S. Government Printing Office, April 1991), 202–3.

9. Tucker, "Negotiating Open Skies," 4.

10. U.S. government official, interviews with Noble and Lysyshyn, and personal knowledge.

11. Evans, M., "Moscow Keeps up Pressure over Lance Row," *The Times*, May 9, 1989; Schmemann, S., "Kremlin Move Adds to NATO Split," *New York Times*, May 13, 1989, 1, 6.

12. These two are specifically named in Tucker, "Negotiating Open Skies," 4.

13. Ibid.

14. All of these points are made in Tucker, "Negotiating Open Skies." See also Tucker, J., "Back to the Future: The Open Skies Talks," *Arms Control Today* 20, no. 8 (October 1990); and Florini, A., "The United States and Open Skies," in *Open Skies: Technical; Organizational; Operational: Legal and Political Aspects*, ed. Chestnutt, H., and M. Slack (Toronto: York University Press, 1990), 113–18.

15. Tucker, "Negotiating Open Skies," 6.

16. Ibid.

17. Bush and Scowcroft, *A World Transformed*, 54.

18. For more on Canada's role at this point, see Clark, M., "Opening the Skies," *Maclean's*, February 12, 1990; Boulden, "Canada and Open Skies," in *Open Skies*, ed. Chestnutt and Slack; Clark, J., "Foreword," in *Open Skies*, ed. Chestnutt and Slack; and Jones, P. L., "Open Skies: Opportunity for the 1990's," in *Open Skies*, ed. Chestnutt and Slack.

19. Clark, "Opening the Skies." Interviews with Noble and Lysyshyn. I was working for Lysyshyn at this time.

20. Jones, "Open Skies," 156, from which the following quotations are taken.

21. Ibid.

22. Ibid.

23. Ibid.

24. Interviews with Noble and Lysyshyn.

25. Ibid. See also Clark, "Opening the Skies."

26. Interviews with Noble and Lysyshyn.

27. point made in Boulden, "Canada and Open Skies."

28. The existence of the letter is publicly referred to in Clark, "Opening the Skies";

and Noble, J., "The Open Skies Treaty Initiative: Prospects for an Agreement and Precedents," Paper presented at a Canada-USSR Conference entitled *Ending the Cold War: International Law and Global Co-operation in the Era of Perestroika and Disarmament*, Simon Fraser University, Vancouver, B.C., June 20–22, 1990, 11. The contents of the letter have never been publicly discussed. I am drawing on my personal knowledge of the letter's contents and on interviews with Noble and Lysyshyn for the specific points I am about to make.

29. Interview with Noble.

30. Events at the meeting are discussed in Clark, "Foreword."

31. In addition to ibid., see also Tucker, "Back to the Future," 20, for the president's reaction to the Canadian demarche.

32. Bush and Scowcroft, *A World Transformed*, 54.

33. Clark, "Opening the Skies," 19–20.

34. Bush and Scowcroft, *A World Transformed*, 54. Borawski reports that the Canadians gave Open Skies the "critical push" in his "NATO Europe and Open Skies," in *Open Skies*, ed. Chestnutt and Slack, 120.

35. Smith, R. J, "Bush Openness Plan a Bow of Symbolism," *Washington Post*, May 13, 1989. The same story went on to point out that the proposal was a "top-down" one, and had generated "little enthusiasm at the State Department or elsewhere in the government."

36. See Boulden, "Canada and Open Skies," 109, for more on this idea.

37. For a full transcript of the speech, see "Change and the Soviet Union," *Current Policy* 1175 (Washington, DC: U.S. Department of State, Bureau of Public Affairs, 1989). Text also available at *www.presidency.ucsb.edu/ws/index.php?pid=17022.*

38. Ibid.

39. Tucker, "Negotiating Open Skies," 8.

40. See, for example, Smith, "Bush Openness Plan a Bow of Symbolism"; Hoffman, D., "Bush Urges Soviets to Broaden Reforms; Arms Offers Sidestepped in Major Speech," *Washington Post*, May 13, 1989, A1; Gordon, M. R., "2 Suitors for Europe; Bush, Gorbachev Try to Impress NATO Allies with Offerings of Peace," *New York Times*, May 13, 1989, sec. 1, p. 7; "Soviet Deeds, American Words" (editorial), *New York Times*, May 14, 1989; MacKenzie, C., "Few Salute as Bush Unfurls His Foreign Policy," *Globe and Mail*, May 20, 1989.

41. See comments by Raymond Garthoff and Stanley Sloan in Gordon, "2 Suitors for Europe." Spurgeon Keeney's skepticism may be found in MacKenzie, C., "Bush Backs Gorbachev's Reform Bid," *Globe and Mail*, May 13, 1989, A1.

42. Administration official quoted in Morrison, D.C., "Opening the Skies," *National Journal*, December 9, 1989, 3020.

43. See "Bush's Speech Repeats Offers from Past," *Pravda*, May 16, 1989 (translated in Foreign Broadcast Information Service, *Soviet Union Daily Report*, May 17, 1989, 13.

44. See Remnick, D. "Moscow Media Criticize Bush Policy Statement," *Washington Post*, May 17, 1989, A30, for a round-up of Soviet commentary on the Bush speech.

45. It will be recalled that the president had said that the initiative was "one which I *hope* would include allies from both sides" ("Change and the Soviet Union," 1989, emphasis added). See also Borawski, "NATO Europe and Open Skies," 120.

46. Interviews with Noble and Lysyshyn. See also Clark, "Opening the Skies," 20.

47. Interviews with Noble and Lysyshyn. Also personal knowledge.

48. North Atlantic Treaty Organization (NATO), "Declaration of the Heads of State and Government Participating in the Meeting of the North Atlantic Council in Brussels in Brussels," May 29–30, 1989.

49. Talbott, S., *Deadly Gambits* (London: Pan Books, 1984), 74.

50. Jones, P. L., "CFE Aerial Inspections and Open Skies: A Comparison," in *Verifying Conventional Force Reductions in Europe: CFE I and Beyond*, ed. Chestnutt, H., and M. Slack (Toronto: York University Press, 1991), 88; and Jones, P. L., "Open Skies: A Review of Events at Ottawa and Budapest," *Verification Report 1991: Yearbook on Arms Control and Environmental Agreements*, ed. Poole, J. B. (London: Apex Press and VERTIC, 1991).

51. My point that the Open Skies proposal suffered from the lack of clear and agreed purpose is supported by Tucker, "Negotiating Open Skies," 10, and by the U.S. Congress, Office of Technology Assessment, *Cooperative Aerial Surveillance in International Agreements, OTA-ISC-480* (Washington, DC: U.S. Government Printing Office, July 1991), 24.

52. Newhouse, J., *Cold Down: The Inside Story of SALT* (London: Pergamon-Brassey's, 1989), 114.

53. Tucker, "Negotiating Open Skies," 9.

54. Ibid. The text of NSD 15 has been declassified and is available on the website of the George H. W. Bush Presidential Library. See *National Security Directive 15: Open Skies*, Secret, June 22, 1989. Available at *http://bushlibrary.tamu.edu/research/pdfs/nsd/nsd15.pdf*. See also Tucker, "Back to the Future," 21. Tucker agrees with my analysis that the directive was so broad that it did not provide a coherent set of criteria upon which to design the regime.

55. Tucker, "Negotiating Open Skies," 10. The bulk of this discussion on the internal U.S. policy-making process is drawn from Tucker, who was a participant in it. I am also drawing on my knowledge as a former Canadian official who was working on the issue and receiving regular briefings from U.S. bureaucratic players. Also Hawes interview.

56. Tucker, "Negotiating Open Skies," 10. Interestingly, the Verification Research Unit in Ottawa had come to exactly the same conclusions, for the same reasons. For more on the relationship between CFE Aerial Inspections and Open Skies, see Jones, "CFE Aerial Inspections and Open Skies."

57. Richelson, J. T., *The US Intelligence Community* (Cambridge: Ballinger, 1985), 12; Freedman, L., *US Intelligence and the Soviet Strategic Threat*, 2nd ed. (London: Macmil-

lan, 1986), 8–29. The official history of the NRO be found at *www.nro.gov/history/csnr/programs/NRO_Brief_History.pdf.*

58. Tucker, "Negotiating Open Skies," 65.

59. For more on the relative strengths and weaknesses of satellites versus aircraft as observation platforms, see Stibrany, P., "Airborne and Space-Based Sensors: A Comparison," in *Open Skies,* ed. Chestnutt and Slack, 35–40. See also U.S. Congress, Office of Technology Assessment, *Cooperative Aerial Surveillance in International Agreements.*

60. Stibrany, "Airborne and Space-Based Sensors"; U.S. Congress, Office of Technology Assessment, *Cooperative Aerial Surveillance in International Agreements.* See also Tucker, "Negotiating Open Skies," 12.

61. For more on this question, see Florini, A., and Y. Dehqanzada, *Secrets for Sale: How Commercial Satellite Imagery Will Change the World* (Washington, DC: Carnegie Endowment for International Peace, 2000).

62. Tucker, "Negotiating Open Skies," 12.

63. Ibid., 12–13.

64. Strobel, P., "White House Favors Not-Too-Wide Open Skies Proposal," *Washington Post,* July 18, 1989, A10.

65. Tucker, "Negotiating Open Skies," 13.

66. Ibid.

67. As Zelikow would later say, "Our military authorities very carefully examined the implications of an Open Skies regime for their operation very early on. And we're satisfied that we can take the operational measures necessary to preserve the security of our operations." In Tucker, "Back to the Future," 21.

68. All of these points were subsequently incorporated into the eventual NATO position, which was made public in what became known as the Basic Elements Paper. See NATO-PS, *Open Skies Basic Elements.*

69. Correspondence between the author and a former U.S. government official, June 4, 1991.

70. Interviews with Noble and Lysyshyn. Also personal recollection.

71. Noble, "The Open Skies Treaty Initiative," 11.

72. Clark, J., "Don't Dismiss Open Skies," *New York Times,* July 5, 1989. (The article was written by Lysyshyn).

73. Interviews with Noble and Lysyshyn. Also personal knowledge.

74. Shalnev, A., "Interview with Viktor Karpov," *Isvestia,* October 6, 1989 (emphasis added).

75. Cox, D., "Are Canada's Skies Open to Soviet Overflights?" *Toronto Star,* July 20, 1989, A23.

76. Interviews with Noble and Lysyshyn. Also personal recollection.

77. Ibid.

78. See, for example, Strobe Talbott's description of the bureaucratic infighting that

resulted from an attempt by Paul Nitze to go beyond his rigid instructions in the search for a compromise in the INF talks. This is the famous "walk in the woods" episode. See Talbott, *Deadly Gambits,* 116–51.

79. See, for example, Bunn, G., "Negotiating Arms Control and Disarmament Agreements," in *The Encyclopedia of Arms Control and Disarmament,* vol. 1, ed. Burns, R. D. (New York: Charles Scribner's Sons, 1993). Although the title is quite broad, this article is devoted to the U.S. way of negotiating, though it is no less useful for that.

80. Bunn, "Negotiating Arms Control and Disarmament Agreements," 400.

81. Garthoff, R., "Negotiating with the Russians: Some Lessons from SALT," *International Security* 1, no. 4 (Spring 1977): 19.

82. Tucker, "Negotiating Open Skies," 12. Also interviews with Noble and Lysyshyn, and personal recollection.

83. Shalnev, "Interview with Viktor Karpov"; Cox, "Are Canada's Skies Open to Soviet Overflights?"

84. Clark, "Opening the Skies."

85. As one Hungarian told a Canadian official in November 1989: "[In] ten years, we don't expect to be part of the Warsaw Pact." Quoted in Clark, "Opening the Skies," 20. The Canadian official was myself, and the Hungarian was off by eight years.

86. Ibid. Also interviews with Marton Krasznai, Noble, and Lysyshyn.

87. These questions were asked in public as well. See Cox, "Are Canada's Skies Open to Soviet Overflights?"

88. These points were made public in a letter of August 24, 1989, from the Canadian foreign minister's press secretary to the *Toronto Star*, in response to a *Star* editorial of August 5, 1989, asking whether Canada intended to offer these facilities to the Soviets. A copy of the letter is in my possession.

89. Personal knowledge; confirmed by Marton Krasznai.

90. Tucker, "Negotiating Open Skies," 16.

91. The arms control section of the press release that resulted from the meeting stated, in part, that an Open Skies regime "could make a genuine contribution to openness and confidence-building." The text of the arms control section is reprinted in *Arms Control Today* 19, no. 8 (October 1989): 22.

92. Personal knowledge of the letter's contents. See also Tucker, "Back to the Future," 21.

93. Personal knowledge. See also Tucker, "Back to the Future," 21

94. Clark, "Opening the Skies," 20.

95. Canadian Department of External Affairs, "An Open Skies Chronicle" (1989), *Disarmament Bulletin*, no. 12 (Winter 1989/90): 4.

96. See the transcript of the Canadian Broadcasting Corporation radio news program "The World at Six," September 27, 1989. At one point Shevardnadze told Clark that the USSR was "150%" behind Open Skies.

97. Correspondence with a former U.S. government official, June 4, 1991.

## CHAPTER 3

1. Interviews with Noble and Lysyshyn. Personal recollection. The completed paper was released as North Atlantic Council, *Open Skies Basic Elements*, NATO Press Service. Annex to M-2 (89) 46, December 15, 1989.

2. Tucker, J., "Negotiating Open Skies: A Diplomatic History," in *Open Skies, Open Control and Cooperative Security*, ed. Krepon, M., and A. Smithson (New York: St. Martin's Press, 1992), 17, refers to the straw man that was shared with allied governments. It has never been released to the public, but I am relying on a copy in my possession for the following points.

3. See the *Arms Control Reporter*, Institute for Defense and Disarmament Studies, Cambridge, MA, 1990, 409.B.4, B.5

4. See the October 24, 1989, entry of the *Reporter*, ibid., 409.B.4.

5. The following arguments were made publicly by the U.S. head of delegation to the Open Skies conference, Ambassador John Hawes, in an interview. See Hawes, J. H., "Transcript of a WorldNet Interview," *Wireless File* 27, February 9, 1990, 2. See also Florini, A., "The United States and Open Skies," in *Open Skies: Technical; Organizational; Operational: Legal and Political Aspects*, ed. Chestnutt, H., and M. Slack (Toronto: York University Press, 1990), 115.

6. *Reporter, 1990*, 409.B.4.

7. Hawes, "Transcript of a WorldNet Interview," 5.

8. Personal recollection. The fact that differences had existed over the timelines question is confirmed in the December 14–15, 1989, entry of the *Reporter, 1990*, 409.B.5.

9. Interviews with Hawes, Noble, and Lysyshyn. Also personal recollection.

10. See Borawski, "NATO Europe and Open Skies," in *Open Skies*, ed. Chestnutt and Slack, 125.

11. Interview with Hawes.

12. Ibid.

13. In an address to Open Skies workshop held in Ottawa in November of 1989, an official of the International Civil Aviation Organization (ICAO) stated that the twenty-four-hour period would not cause a problem, though some modifications to existing procedures might be necessary. See the remarks of Francisco Castro-Rodrigues in Chestnutt, H., and M. Slack, eds., *Open Skies: Workshop Report* (Toronto: York University Press, 1989), 52–53.

14. Interviews with Noble and Lysyshyn and personal recollection.

15. North Atlantic Council, *Open Skies Basic Elements*.

16. Ibid.

17. Ibid. For a discussion of flight safely rules, and military restricted airspace as it existed in one NATO country on the eve of Open Skies negotiation, see Clark, Lt. Col. R. H., "Canadian Overflight and Landing Clearances," in *Open Skies*, ed. Chestnutt and Slack, 77–81.

18. North Atlantic Council, *Open Skies Basic Elements.*

19. See Borawski, "NATO Europe and Open Skies," 128.

20. Interviews with Hawes, Noble, and Lysyshyn. Also personal recollection.

21. Hawes, "Transcript of WorldNet Interview," 5.

22. Interviews with Hawes, Noble, and Lysyshyn. Also personal recollection.

23. Florini, "The United States and Open Skies," 116.

24. Ibid.

25. Hawes, "Transcript of WorldNet Interview," 5.

26. Borawski, "NATO Europe and Open Skies," 128, discusses the reticence of Europe's neutrals to consider dramatic measures to increase transparency in Europe. See also Huldt, B., "Neutrality and the Nordic Security Pattern: A Swedish Perspective," in *The European Neutrals in the 1990s: The Challenges and Opportunities*, ed. Neuhold, H. (Boulder, CO: Westview Press, 1992), 34–35. As will be seen in Chapters 6 and 7, when they were able to take part in the Open Skies negotiations, some of the neutrals attempted to introduce restrictions to the evolving regime beyond those that, at the time, the Russians were asking for.

27. See Ponomarev, M., "Kuklev Elaborates on Military Openness, Security," interview with Major General V. Kuklev, deputy chief of the USSR General Staff, Armed Force Directorate, *Krasnaya Zvezda*, November 5, 1989 (translation in FBIS-SOV-89–214, November 7, 1989), 3.

28. See the comments by a French government official in Chestnutt and Slack, *Open Skies Workshop Report*, 96–97.

29. Borawski, "NATO Europe and Open Skies," 121.

30. Bertram, C., *Mutual Force Reductions in Europe: The Political Aspects,* Adelphi Papers no. 84 (London: International Institute for Strategic Studies, January, 1972), 3.

31. For more on French policy generally, see Yost, D. S., "France," in *The Allies and Arms Control*, ed. Hampson, F., H. von Reikhoff, and J. Roper (Baltimore, MD: Johns Hopkins University Press, 1992), 162–88; and Dunay, P., and H. Spitzer, "The Open Skies Negotiations and the Open Skies Treaty," in *Open Skies: A Cooperative Approach to Military Transparency and Confidence-Building*, ed. Dunay, P., M. Krasznai, H. Spitzer, R. Wiemker, and W. Wynne (Geneva: UN Institute for Disarmament Research, 2004), 26.

32. Tucker, "Negotiating Open Skies," 18.

33. See the comments by a French government official in Chestnutt and Slack, *Open Skies Workshop Report*, 96–97. See also Swales, N., "Note to the Parliamentary Centre for Foreign Affairs and International Trade," undated [early December 1989], 6.

34. Borawski, "NATO Europe and Open Skies," 122.

35. Personal recollection.

36. Borawski, "NATO Europe and Open Skies," 123.

37. See Yost, "France."

38. Florini, "The United States and Open Skies," 116.

39. Hawes, "Transcript of WorldNet Interview," 2.

40. Much of the following is drawn from the results of interviews and from Jones, P. L., "The Determination of Overflight Quotas for an Open Skies Regime," in *Open Skies*, ed. Chestnutt and Slack, 63–76.

41. Personal recollection.

42. Hawes, "Transcript of WorldNet Interview," 6.

43. These points are made in Jones, P. L., "CFE Aerial Inspections and Open Skies: A Comparison," in *Verifying Conventional Force Reductions in Europe: CFE I and Beyond*, ed. Chestnutt, H., and M. Slack (Toronto: York University Press, 1991), 100.

44. *Reporter, 1990*, 409.B.5.

45. Jones, "The Determination of Overflight Quotas for an Open Skies Regime," 70.

46. discussion on active and passive quotas may be found in ibid., 63–64.

47. Ibid., 70–73.

48. Ibid., and personal recollection.

49. See Borawski, "NATO Europe and Open Skies," 121–22. See also *Reporter, 1990*, 409.B.5.

50. See the comments by a French government official in Chestnutt and Slack, *Open Skies Workshop Report*.

51. In addition to ibid., see Borawski, "NATO Europe and Open Skies," 122.

52. Included in Jones, "The Determination of Overflight Quotas for an Open Skies Regime," 65.

53. Clark, M., "Opening the Skies," *Maclean's*, February 12, 1990; Boulden, "Canada and Open Skies," in *Open Skies*, ed. Chestnutt and Slack, 20.

54. Personal recollection; point confirmed by Hawes, Noble, and Lysyshyn.

55. Interviews with Hawes, Noble, and Lysyshyn. Also personal recollection.

56. Ibid.

57. North Atlantic Council, *Open Skies Basic Elements*.

58. Interview with Krasznai.

59. See *Reporter, 1990*, 409.B.5.

60. See, for example, Ponomarev "Kuklev Elaborates on Military Openness, Security"; Zhukov, Y., "Open Skies: New Confidence-Building Factors," *Pravda*, November 1, 1989 (translation in FBIS-SOV089–212, November 3, 1989), 4; Handelman, S., "Shevardnadze Ready to Visit Canada to Discuss Open Skies, Kremlin Says," *Toronto Star*, November 18, 1989.

61. summary of the Soviet response to the NATO BEP may be found in Pinchukov, Y., "Open Skies: A Source of Confidence or Suspicion?" unpublished paper, 1990.

62. Noble, J., "The Open Skies Treaty Initiative: Prospects for an Agreement and Precedents," paper presented at a Canada-USSR conference entitled *Ending the Cold War: International Law and Global Co-operation in the Era of Perestroika and Disarmament*, Simon Fraser University, Vancouver, B.C., June 20–22, 1990, 11.

63. Ponomarev, "Kuklev Elaborates on Military Openness, Security," 2.

64. In addition to the sources cited in Note 50, see the remarks attributed to a Soviet official in the November 1 entry of the *Reporter, 1990*, 409.B.4-B.5.

65. Krasznai interview.

66. Personal recollection of a discussion in Vienna with a Russian diplomat after the August 1992 coup attempt.

67. Ibid.

68. Noble, "The Open Skies Treaty Initiative," 16–17.

69. For a discussion of this aspect of organizing a multilateral conference, see Aurisch, K. L., "The Art of Preparing a Multilateral Conference," *Negotiation Journal* 5, no. 3 (July 1989): 279–88.

70. Personal recollections, confirmed by Mr. Ross Francis, interviewed on June 12, 1992. Mr. Francis was placed in charge of establishing the conference secretariat and developing the procedures.

71. Francis interview.

72. Ibid.

73. See *Reporter, 1990*, 409.B.8. There was also a three-day academic conference on Open Skies in Ottawa in November of 1989 that some government officials attended in their own capacities. This was not a prenegotiation, and there were no Soviet representatives present from Moscow. The papers of the conference were published as Chesnutt and Slack, eds., *Open Skies*.

74. Francis interview.

75. *Reporter, 1990*, 409.B.8.

76. Noble, "The Open Skies Treaty Initiative," 16–17.

77. *Reporter, 1990*, 409.B.8.

78. Interviews with Noble and Lysyshyn. Also personal recollection.

79. As a Canadian backgrounder paper put it: "Open Skies negotiations will not be without their difficulties, but the idea is about as straightforward as these things get." Canadian Department of External Affairs, *Open Skies: Challenge for the 1990s, Backgrounder Number 1* (Ottawa: External Affairs and International Trade, 1989).

80. *Reporter, 1990*, 409.B.14.

81. Clark, "Opening the Skies." The workshop resulted in Chesnutt and Slack, eds., *Open Skies*. As has been discussed, the seminar was not a prenegotiation exercise.

82. As the Canadian-Hungarian publication arising from the flight stated, "[T]he purpose of the overflight was to test the flight planning and safety procedures which will be crucial when an open skies regime is established." See Canadian Department of External Affairs, *Backgrounder Number 3*.

83. Ibid.

84. Noble, "The Open Skies Treaty Initiative," 13.

85. Canadian Department of External Affairs, *Backgrounder Number 3*.

86. See, for example, Brady, A., "Canadian Flight Tests Open Skies," *Associated Press*, January 6, 1990; Almond, P., "Canadians' Flight over Hungary Is First Test of Open Skies Plan," *Washington Times*, January 8, 1990; *Reporter, 1990*, 409.B.6.

87. *Reporter, 1990*, 409.B.8. Of course, these were the very aspects of the regime that were not tested during the trial overflight.

88. The process that led to the draft treaty is outlined in Noble, "The Open Skies Treaty Initiative," 14–15.

89. Point confirmed in an interview with Mr. Jason Reiskind, a lawyer with the Department of External Affairs who worked on the draft treaty project. Mr. Reiskind was interviewed on October 13, 1992.

90. Ibid.

91. Interviews with Hawes and Lysyshyn. Also personal recollection.

92. Ibid.

93. The process by which the two developed the joint draft is discussed in Noble, "The Open Skies Treaty Initiative," 14–15.

94. Personal recollection; point confirmed in Reiskind interview.

95. Ibid. Also Hawes and Lysyshyn interviews.

96. Ibid. Also personal correspondence with Ambassador James Goodby, who had led the U.S. delegation to several arms control negotiations with the Soviets over many years.

97. Reiskind interview.

98. The following discussions are drawn from personal recollection; confirmed during the Reiskind interview.

99. Ibid.

100. Newhouse, J., *Cold Dawn: The Inside Story of Salt* (London: Pergamon-Brassey's, 1989), 125. This idea was endorsed by Ambassador (ret.) Jim Goodby, himself a veteran of many U.S.-Soviet arms control negotiations, in private conversation with the author.

101. Point confirmed by Hawes.

## CHAPTER 4

1. See Bush, George H. W., and B. Scowcroft, *A World Transformed* (New York: Random House, 1998), 230–44. For their account of how the "2+4" formula announced in Ottawa was developed see Zelikow, P., and C. Rice, *Germany Unified and Europe Transformed: A Study in Statecraft* (Cambridge: Harvard University Press, 1997), 191–95. See also Sarotte, M. E., *1989: The Struggle to Create Post-Cold War Europe* (Princeton: Princeton University Press, 2009), 121–24.

2. The texts of the ministers' statements may be found in Open Skies Conference Secretariat (OSCS), *Record of Proceedings, ICO-CS-029* (Ottawa: Open Skies Conference Secretariat, February 26, 1990). The acronym "ICO-CS" was the name of the organization created within the Department of External Affairs to be the Open Skies Confer-

ence Secretariat, and all of the conference documents were numbered according to their sequence of release. Both the Hungarians and the Austrians retained the same lettering and numbering scheme for the sake of continuity. Documents of the secretariat shall henceforth be cited as OSCS—Open Skies Conference Secretariat.

3. OSCS, *ICO-CS-029*, 9.

4. Ibid.

5. Ibid., 21–22.

6. Ibid., 22. For more on the French position, see Smith, R. J., and D. Oberdorfer, "Two Alliances Differ on Germany's Future: Open Skies Meeting Was Planned to Deal with Monitoring East-West Military Activities," *Washington Post*, February 12, 1990, A25.

7. OSCS, *ICO-CS-029*, 59.

8. Ibid., 14–15.

9. For a more detailed description of the Soviet position, see Pinchukov, Y., "Open Skies: A Source of Confidence or Suspicion?" unpublished paper, 1990.

10. OSCS, *ICO-CS-029*. For the Polish view, see p. 29. For the Bulgarian, which was somewhat closer to that of the USSR than the rest, see p. 39. For Czechoslovakia's, which was especially opposed to the concept of blocs, see pp. 54–55, 57. For Romania's, see p. 65. For the GDR's, see p. 79. For Hungary's, see p. 92.

11. OSCS, OSCS, *Record Warsaw Treaty Organization; Basic Elements Paper on Open Skies, ICO-CS-011* (Ottawa: Open Skies Conference Secretariat, February 12, 1990).

12. Noble, J., "The Open Skies Treaty Initiative: Prospects for an Agreement and Precedents," paper presented at a Canada-USSR conference entitled *Ending the Cold War: International Law and Global Co-operation in the Era of Perestroika and Disarmament*, Simon Fraser University, Vancouver, B.C., June 20–22, 1990, 16.

13. OSCS, *ICO-CS-011*, 2.

14. Krasznai interview. Remarkably, Krasznai reports that some Warsaw Pact members insisted that English be used in Warsaw Pact caucus meetings at the Ottawa Conference.

15. Personal knowledge; point confirmed by Noble.

16. Ibid.

17. Noble, "The Open Skies Treaty Initiative," 16.

18. For more on the extraordinary events of this period, and on Gorbachev's decision that he would not use force to protect communist regimes in Eastern Europe or keep the Warsaw Pact together, see Brown, A., "The Gorbachev Revolution and the End of the Cold War," in *The Cambridge History of the Cold War*, vol. III, ed. Leffler, M. P., and O. A. Westad (Cambridge: Cambridge University Press, 2010); Cherniaev, A., "Gorbachev's Foreign Policy: The Concept," in *Turning Points in Ending the Cold War*, ed. Skinner, K. K. (Stanford, CA: Hoover Press, 2008); Sebestyen, V., *Revolution 1989: The Fall of the Soviet Empire* (New York: Vintage Books, 2009).

19. Personal knowledge of NATO tactics; points confirmed by Noble and Lysyshyn.

20. Ibid.

21. The discussions were chaired by Lysyshyn. I was his assistant and was present throughout. The following is based on my notes of the meeting, and has been read by Lysyshyn for accuracy.

22. Noble, "The Open Skies Treaty Initiative," 16.

23. Ibid., 19–21; points confirmed by Lysyshyn and by my own notes.

24. Ibid. The draft of the communique that resulted from this meeting was entirely made up of bracketed text. I have a copy, though it is undated and does not have any official status, as it was a working paper.

25. Ibid., 18.

26. Ibid.

27. Confirmed by Lysyshyn and Francis (interviewed July 12, 1992), by Krasznai, and by my notes of the meeting.

28. Ibid.

29. Noble, "The Open Skies Treaty Initiative." Also my own notes as verified by Lysyshyn and Krasznai.

30. My own notes, as verified by Lysyshyn and Krasznai.

31. Ibid.

32. This position had been publicly announced by the Turkish foreign minister earlier that day. See OSCS, *ICO-CS-029*, 59.

33. My notes, as verified by Lysyshyn and Krasznai.

34. have a copy of the working draft in my possession. It was never made public.

35. My notes, as verified by Lysyshyn and Krasznai.

36. Noble, "The Open Skies Treaty Initiative," 19.

37. Ibid.

38. Tucker, J., "Negotiating Open Skies: A Diplomatic History," in *Open Skies, Open Control and Cooperative Security*, ed. Krepon, M., and A. Smithson (New York: St. Martin's Press, 1992), 21–22.

39. See the comments by Hawes, J. H., in his "Open Skies: From Idea to Negotiation," *NATO Review* 38, no. 3 (April 1990): 7.

40. The communique text was issued as *Open Skies Communiqué, ICO-CS-038* (Ottawa: Open Skies Conference Secretariat, February 13, 1990).

41. Ibid.

42. Point confirmed by Krasznai, Noble, and Lysyshyn.

43. OSCS, *ICO-CS-038*.

44. Ibid.

45. Noble, "The Open Skies Treaty Initiative," 19.

46. OSCS, *ICO-CS-038*.

47. Personal recollection; confirmed by Krasznai, Noble, and Lysyshyn.

48. See, for example, Lewis, P., "Dispute Between US and Soviets Persists on Intelligence Overflights," *New York Times*, February 17, 1990, sec. 1, 9, in which he quotes "sources" as claiming that "the Soviet stand reflects differences between Kremlin political leaders, who say they favor an Open Skies agreement, and military chiefs, who fear close aerial inspection." See also Lewis, P., "Soviet Position at Open Skies Talks Puzzles West," *New York Times*, February 25, 1990; and Howard, R., "Soviet Stance on Open Skies Linked to Struggles inside Kremlin," *Globe and Mail*, February 26, 1990.

49. Howard, "Soviet Stance on Open Skies."

50. See *Arms Control Reporter*, Institute for Defense and Disarmament Studies, Cambridge, MA, 1990, 409.B.9; Howard, "Soviet Stance on Open Skies."

51. Howard, "Soviet Stance on Open Skies."

52. Howard, R., "Talks on Open Skies Adjourn amid Impasses," *Globe and Mail*, February 28, 1990.

53. This list is taken from paragraph 1 of the Working Group A's *Report to Plenary*, which was tabled at the final Plenary of the Ottawa Conference. See OSCS, *Report of Subsidiary Working Group A to the Open Skies Conference, ICO-CS-068* (Ottawa: Open Skies Conference Secretariat, February 27, 1990). It was subsequently decided "to transfer responsibility for the issue of the role and status of observers to Working Group C," as this group's expertise was seen as more relevant to the question. See paragraph 2 of ICO-CS-069.

54. OSCS, *Report of Subsidiary Working Group B to the Open Skies Conference, ICO-CS-069* (Ottawa: Open Skies Conference Secretariat, February 27, 1990), para. 1.

55. OSCS, *Report of Subsidiary Working Group C to the Open Skies Conference, ICO-CS-066* (Ottawa: Open Skies Conference Secretariat, February 27, 1990), para. 1

56. OSCS, *Report of Subsidiary Working Group D to the Open Skies Conference, ICO-CS-070* (Ottawa: Open Skies Conference Secretariat, February 27, 1990). These reports were never made public, and I am relying on copies in my possession. An overview of the groups and their functions can also be found in the *Reporter, 1990*, 409.B.9–409.B.10.

57. Telephone interview with Mr. Ross Francis, June 12, 1992.

58. Mr. Francis later said that he had not expected all of the groups to meet in formal session every day when he had established the schedule. The desire to cover as much of the treaty text as possible in the available time made it necessary to do so, however. Francis interview, June 12, 1992.

59. The draft treaty was tabled as OSCS, *Open Skies Draft Treaty Text, ICO-CS-043* (Ottawa: Open Skies Conference Secretariat, February 16, 1990).

60. As Noble reports it, this had taken until 3 o'clock in the morning. Noble, "The Open Skies Treaty Initiative," 15. Noble chaired the alliance discussions over the draft treaty. I was present as his assistant.

61. Point confirmed by Krasznai, who was involved. See also ibid., 22.

62. OSCS, *Amendments to the Open Skies Draft Treaty Text, ICO-CS-063* (Ottawa: Open Skies Conference Secretariat, February 27, 1990).

63. Personal recollection; confirmed by Noble.

64. Ibid.

65. Personal recollection; confirmed in Reiskind interview.

66. Noble, "The Open Skies Treaty Initiative," 21–22. See also the reports of these two groups, OSCS, *ICO-CS-066*, and OSCS, *ICO-CS-070*.

67. Personal knowledge. I acted as assistant to the chairman of Group D throughout the Ottawa Conference; point confirmed in Reiskind interview.

68. Noble, "The Open Skies Treaty Initiative," 22. See also the reports of these two groups, OSCS, *ICO-CS-068*, and OSCS, *ICO-CS-069*.

69. Personal recollection; points confirmed by Francis.

70. These five issues are identified and discussed in various summations of the negotiations. They remained the same throughout the negotiation. See Hawes, "Open Skies," 7–8; Jones, P. L., "CFE Aerial Inspections and Open Skies: A Comparison," in *Verifying Conventional Force Reductions in Europe: CFE I and Beyond*, ed. Chestnutt, H., and M. Slack (Toronto: York University Press, 1991), 91–104; Jones, P. L., "Open Skies: A Review of Events at Ottawa and Budapest," in *Verification Report 1991: Yearbook on Arms Control and Environmental Agreements*, ed. Poole, J. B. (London: Apex Press and VERTIC, 1991), 75–80; Jones, P. L., "Open Skies: A New Era of Transparency," *Arms Control Today* 22, no. 4 (1992): 12–15; Jones, P. L., and M. Krasznai, "Open Skies: Achievements and Prospects," in *Verification Report 1992: Yearbook on Arms Control and Environmental Agreements*, ed. Poole, J. B. (London: VERTIC, 1992), 47–52; Noble, "The Open Skies Treaty Initiative," 23–25; Tucker, J., "Back to the Future: The Open Skies Talks," *Arms Control Today* 20, no. 8 (1990): 22–24; and Tucker, "Negotiating Open Skies," 25–28. The *Reporter, 1990*, 409.B.10–409.B.12, also gives a surprisingly complete round-up of the positions, considering this was supposed to have been a closed conference at the time. Unless otherwise cited, all of the material for the subsequent overview of the issues is drawn from these sources and personal recollections.

71. OCSC, *ICO-CS-069* lists the passive quotas each country had indicated it was willing to receive by the end of the Ottawa Conference.

72. Ibid.

73. See Jones, "CFE Aerial Inspections and Open Skies," 88–90; Jones, "Open Skies: A Review of Events at Ottawa and Budapest," 73–74; and Tucker, "Negotiating Open Skies," 28–30. See also *Reporter, 1990*, 409.B.10.

74. OSCS, *ICO-CS-069*.

75. Ibid.

76. *Reporter*, 409.B.10.

77. See Lewis, P., "Soviet Position at Open Skies Talks Puzzles West," *New York Times*, February 25, 1990; Guk, S., "Does the USSR Advocate Open Skies with Exclusion Zones?

The Soviet Position Has Been Distorted Says Deputy Minister of Foreign Affairs of the USSR Viktor Karpov," *Isvestia*, March 3, 1990 (translated in FBIS-SOV-90–043, March 5, 1990); OSCS, *ICO-CS-069*, paras. 6 and 7.

78. Personal recollection; point confirmed by Krasznai, Hawes, Noble, and Lysyshyn.

79. Confirmed by Krasznai.

80. Jones, "Open Skies: A Review of Events at Ottawa and Budapest."

81. Guk, "Does the USSR Advocate Open Skies with Exclusion Zones?"

82. Personal recollection; point confirmed by Hawes, Noble, and Lysyshyn.

83. This point is made in Pinchukov, "Open Skies."

84. Tucker, "Negotiating Open Skies," 26, 30; Hughes, D., "US, Soviet Differences Could Prevent Planned Signing of Open Skies Treaty," *Aviation Week and Space Technology*, April 2, 1990, 42.

85. Tucker, "Negotiating Open Skies"; Hughes, "US, Soviet Differences Could Prevent Planned Signing of Open Skies Treaty."

86. OSCS, *ICO-CS-068*, para. 10.

87. Tucker, "Negotiating Open Skies," 30.

88. Shelkov, V., "Interview with Soviet Deputy Foreign Minister V. P. Karpov at the Ottawa Open Skies conference," *Pravda*, March 4, 1990 (translated in Foreign Broadcast Information Service, *Soviet Union Daily Report*, 90, 043, March 5, 1990).

89. "Legitimizing Overflights by Spy Planes? An Interview with Major General Kuklev, First Deputy Chief of the General Staff," *Trud*, March 27, 1990 (translated in FBIS-SOV-90–063, April 2, 1990). Also quoted in Tucker, "Negotiating Open Skies."

90. Interviews with Noble and Lysyshyn. This was my strong feeling, both at the time and to this day.

91. Karpov alluded to the fact that the U.S. and UK intelligence communities were quite close in their positions in his *Isvestia* interview, March 3, 1990. "Question: How many states backed up the USA? Answer: Those who want to be members of the American information pool, specifically Great Britain."

92. Interview with Alex Garroch, an RAF officer who was a sensor expert on the UK delegation to the Open Skies process and who was opposed to the emphasis his own delegation took in the early rounds on intelligence collection, as opposed to cooperative aerial monitoring. Various email and telephone interviews, July/August 2012. Some members of the Canadian intelligence community were supportive of the U.S./UK position at the time.

93. The fact that the U.S. position had come to differ from that of its allies is discussed in Jones, "CFE Aerial Inspections and Open Skies," 91–92. That they sought to prevent discussion is a personal recollection confirmed by Noble, Lysyshyn, and anonymous former U.S. former government official.

94. This description of these discussions is confirmed in interviews with Noble and Lysyshyn.

95. Ibid.

96. Jones, "CFE Aerial Inspections and Open Skies," 96–98; Tucker, "Negotiating Open Skies," 27–28; OSCS, *ICO-CS-068*, para. 12; *Reporter, 1990*, 409.B.11.

97. In addition to Tucker, "Negotiating Open Skies"; and Hughes, "US, Soviet Differences Could Prevent Planned Signing of Open Skies Treaty"; see Guk, "Does the USSR Advocate Open Skies with Exclusion Zones?"

98. Jones, "CFE Aerial Inspections and Open Skies."

99. See Hawes's comments on the eve of the Ottawa Conference in Hawes, J. H., "Transcript of a WorldNet Interview," *Wireless File* 27, February 9, 1990.

100. Personal recollection of U.S. delegation arguments to the NATO Caucus at the Ottawa Conference. For confirmation, see Tucker, "Negotiating Open Skies," 27.

101. Point confirmed by Noble.

102. Jones, "CFE Aerial Inspections and Open Skies."

103. Ibid.

104. Ibid.; *Reporter, 1990*, 409.B.11; point confirmed by Krasznai.

105. Jones, "CFE Aerial Inspections and Open Skies"; OSCS, *ICO-CS-063*, para. 12.

106. Jones, "CFE Aerial Inspections and Open Skies"; OSCS, *ICO-CS-063*, para. 12.

107. was present at both meetings. There is no public record of them. The following summary of events at the meetings is taken from my own notes. It has been confirmed by Krasznai, Noble, and Francis, who were present for the first meeting, and by those three plus Lysyshyn, who was present for the second.

108. It must also be said that a member of the legal staff of the Polish delegation had an academic fixation on the question of the legal immunities to be accorded to observation flight crews and wanted to spend the entire day discussing this rather esoteric topic. Personal notes; confirmed by Noble and Francis.

109. Personal notes; points confirmed by Noble, Francis, and Krasznai.

110. Ibid.

111. Ibid.

112. The following is based upon my notes; confirmed by Krasznai, Hawes, Noble, Lysyshyn, and Francis.

113. In a press story reference is made to "a member of the Czechoslovak delegation [who] gave a carefully reasoned overview of the concessions each side would have to make in order to get a treaty." See Mooney, P., "Open Skies: Press Analysis," *Canadian Press Wire Service*, March 1, 1990. No specifics of the package were leaked to the press. The specifics are from my notes; confirmed by Krasznai, Hawes, Noble, Lysyshyn, and Francis.

114. Personal notes; confirmed by Krasznai, Hawes, Noble, Francis, and Lysyshyn.

115. As quoted in Mooney, "Open Skies: Press Analysis."

116. Personal notes; confirmed by Krasznai, Hawes, Noble, Francis, and Lysyshyn.

117. See, for example, the comments of one Western delegate: "The Soviets were just spinning their wheels. The talks are in a holding pattern now." Quoted in Howard, "Soviet Stance on Open Skies." See also the Canadian Press story "Soviet 'Stonewalling' Could Threaten Open Skies Outcome," *Ottawa Citizen*, February 22, 1990, for the following comment from another unnamed Western delegate: "It's a complete filibuster by the Soviets at the table—they are just stonewalling."

118. *Reporter, 1990*, 409.B.10; point confirmed by Francis.

119. Personal recollection; points confirmed by Francis.

120. Howard, "Talks on Open Skies Adjourn."

121. *Reporter*, 409.B.11.

122. Personal recollection. Also interviews with Noble and Lysyshyn.

123. Noble, "The Open Skies Treaty Initiative," 29, alludes to this problem.

124. Ibid. This crucial difference will be discussed in detail in the section on the Budapest Conference.

125. The exhibit, to be known as "Hungexpo," was to be held May 8–10 at Ferihegy Airport, Budapest. It was based on a similar exhibit that had been staged in Ottawa during the Open Skies conference. More on Hungexpo may be found in Hughes, "US, Soviet Differences Could Prevent Planned Signing of Open Skies Treaty."

126. Personal knowledge; points confirmed by Lysyshyn and Hawes.

127. The following account of these meetings is drawn from personal knowledge; confirmed by Noble and Hawes.

128. See, for example, the Karpov *Isvestia* interview: Guk, "Does the USSR Advocate Open Skies with Exclusion Zones?"; the Kuklev *Trud* interview: "Legitimizing Overflights by Spy Planes?"; Hawes, "Open Skies"; and Hawes's testimony before the U.S. Senate Foreign Relations Committee: "Testimony to the Committee on Foreign Relations," *U.S. Senate, Committee on Foreign Relations*, Washington, DC, January 30, 1990.

129. Krepon, M., "Open Skies: Testimony to Committee on Foreign Relations," *U.S. Senate, Committee on Foreign Relations*, Washington, DC, March 29, 1990.

130. Ibid.

131. Personal knowledge; point confirmed by Noble.

132. See "Statement in the Sensor Working Group: USA," April 24, 1990, in OSCS, *Report of Working Group A to Plenary, ICO-CS-107* (Budapest: Open Skies Conference Secretariat, May 10, 1990), para. 2 (revised) (emphasis added). Again, these documents were not made public, and I am relying on copies in my possession.

133. Ibid.

134. Ibid.

135. See Noble, "The Open Skies Treaty Initiative," 29, for the following; "Canada was of the view that it [comparability] meant exactly what it sounded like: whatever technologies we used would be available to the other participants."

136. See ibid. See also Jones, "CFE Aerial Inspections and Open Skies," 91; point confirmed by Garroch.

137. Personal knowledge; point confirmed by Noble and Garroch.

138. All of these documents may be found in OSCS, *Working Papers Distributed in Subsidiary Working Group A, Not Numbered* (Budapest: Open Skies Conference Secretariat, May 9, 1990).

139. See "Prepared Statement on Behalf of the Sixteen Nations by [the] Representatives of the United Kingdom," contained in ibid. The statement was read in early May.

140. Point confirmed by Krasznai.

141. Personal recollection; point confirmed by Noble.

142. OSCS, *IC-CS-107*, para. 4 (emphasis added).

143. For the technical aspects of the proposal, see *Working Paper on the Soviet Delegation in Group A: Permitted Observation Equipment*, in OSCS, *Working Papers Distributed in Subsidiary Working Group A, Not Numbered*, May 1, 1990.

144. Noble, "The Open Skies Treaty Initiative," 30.

145. OSCS, *IC-CS-107*, para. 16. See also Annex M, submitted by the USSR on May 4, 1990, and contained in OSCS, *Working Papers Distributed in Subsidiary Working Group A, Not Numbered.*

146. OSCS, *IC-CS-107*, para. 16. See also Annex M, submitted by the USSR on May 4, 1990.

147. Canada, Germany, Belgium, Norway, Denmark, and France were among these. Personal knowledge; confirmed by Noble and Garroch.

148. "DOD Official Says Open Skies Stalled: Budapest Treaty Unlikely," *Aerospace Daily* 154, no. 28 (May 9, 1990): 227.

149. Noble, cited in *Reporter, 1990*, 409.B.16; Tucker, "Negotiating Open Skies," 34.

150. OSCS, *Report of Working Group B to Plenary, ICO-CS-108* (Budapest: Open Skies Conference Secretariat, May 10, 1990), para. 4.

151. Anonymous U.S. official, quoted in "DOD Official Says Open Skies Stalled."

152. See OSCS, *ICO-CS-108*, para. 5.

153. OSCS, *Report of Working Group C to Plenary, ICO-CS-109* (Budapest: Open Skies Conference Secretariat, May 10, 1990); OSCS, *Report of Working Group D to Plenary, ICO-CS-110* (Budapest: Open Skies Conference Secretariat, May 10, 1990). See also Reiskind interview.

154. OSCS, *ICO-CS-110*.

155. I was the Canadian with whom he spoke. The following is taken from notes; confirmed by Noble.

156. The following is based upon my own notes of these discussions; points confirmed by Noble.

157. Ibid.

158. I was present. The following summary of the Lake Balaton session is taken from my notes of the meeting; points confirmed by Noble and Krasznai.

159. *Reporter, 1990*, 409.B.14. For further commentary on the fact that the treaty would not be signed on schedule, see Fairhall, D., "NATO Gives up Hope on Open Skies Signing," *Guardian*, May 5, 1990; Reuters, "Open Skies Parties Drop Deadline for a Deal," *New York Times*, May 5, 1990.

160. Personal notes confirmed by Noble and Krasznai.

161. Ibid.

162. For a similar assessment of Gorbachev's move to the right and its impact on Open Skies, see Tucker, "Negotiating Open Skies," 29.

163. Reuters, "Open Skies Parties Drop Deadline for a Deal."

164. Ground, J., "Open Skies Open and Reclose," *Trust and Verify* 10 (May 1990).

165. Ibid.

## CHAPTER 5

1. Strobel, W., "Open Lands, Open Skies, Closed Issues," *Washington Times*, May 31, 1990, A10.

2. Personal knowledge; confirmed by Noble and a U.S. government official who has requested anonymity.

3. See Strobel, "Open Lands, Open Skies, Closed Issues"; *Arms Control Reporter*, Institute for Defense and Disarmament Studies, Cambridge, MA, 1990, 409.B.16.

4. *Reporter, 1990*, 409.B.16.

5. Tucker, J., "Negotiating Open Skies: A Diplomatic History," in *Open Skies, Open Control and Cooperative Security*, ed. Krepon, M., and A. Smithson (New York: St. Martin's Press, 1992), 35. The list of arms control issues up for discussion at the meeting included five topics. In addition to START and Open Skies, CFE, Chemical Weapons and Nuclear Testing were expected to be raised. See "Arms Control Sticking Points," *Los Angeles Times*, May 16, 1990, p. A9.

6. *Reporter, 1990*, 409.B.17.

7. Tucker, "Negotiating Open Skies," 35.

8. "Summit in Washington: Key Sections from the Bush-Gorbachev News Conference," *New York Times*, June 4, 1990. See also Tucker, "Negotiating Open Skies," 35.

9. NATO-PS, *Message from Turnberry*, press communique M-1 (90) 29, June 8, 1990.

10. The paper was written by myself. References to it have been made in open sources, but its contents have never been discussed openly. For references to the paper's existence, see Jones, P. L., and M. Krasznai, "Open Skies: Achievements and Prospects," in

*Verification Report 1992: Yearbook on Arms Control and Environmental Agreements*, ed. Poole, J. B. (London: VERTIC, 1992), 48; *Reporter, 1990*, 409.B.17; and Lawson, R., "Soviets Reviewing Proposal That May Close Loop on Open Skies Treaty," *Inside Defense Electronics Weekly Report* 5, no. 22 (May 31, 1991). The following discussion about the paper's contents is drawn from my notes; confirmed by Lysyshyn.

11. Personal knowledge; confirmed by Hawes.

12. These fears are discussed in Jones and Krasznai, "Open Skies," 47–49; Jones, P. L., "Open Skies: A New Era of Transparency," *Arms Control Today* 22, no. 4 (1992): 10–11; *Reporter, 1990*, 409.B.17; Tucker, "Negotiating Open Skies," 35–36.

13. The most comprehensive outline of the differences and similarities between the two may be found in Jones, P. L., "CFE Aerial Inspections and Open Skies: A Comparison," in *Verifying Conventional Force Reductions in Europe: CFE I and Beyond*, ed. Chestnutt, H., and M. Slack (Toronto: York University Press, 1991).

14. See ibid; Hughes, D., "US, Soviet Impasse on Open Skies Reveals Key Differences on Overflights," *Aviation Week and Space Technology*, August 1990; *Reporter, 1990*, 409.B.17–18; Dunay, P., and H. Spitzer, "The Open Skies Negotiations and the Open Skies Treaty," in *Open Skies: A Cooperative Approach to Military Transparency and Confidence-Building*, ed. Dunay, P., M. Krasznai, H. Spitzer, R Wiemker, and W. Wynne (Geneva: UN Institute for Disarmament Research, 2004), 30–31.

15. The important agreements achieved by the U.S. CFE delegation are discussed in Jones and Krasznai, "Open Skies," 48; Jones, "Open Skies," 11; and Dunay and Spitzer, "The Open Skies Negotiations and the Open Skies Treaty," 30–32.

16. Jones, "Open Skies," 11.

17. Jones, "CFE Aerial Inspections and Open Skies," 90.

18. Ibid. The point that the two negotiations had different goals is also made in Dunn, L. A., and B. A. Henry, eds., "Open Skies and CFE Aerial Inspection," report of a workshop sponsored by the Arms Control Program of Los Alamos National Laboratory, August 30, 1990.

19. TASS, July 19, 1990 (translated in FBIS-SOV, July 20, 1990). See also *Reporter, 1990*, 409.B.17.

20. The Irkutsk discussion of Open Skies has not been widely reported in open sources. The following discussion is taken from Tucker, "Negotiating Open Skies," 36–38; and personal knowledge confirmed by Hawes.

21. Ibid. In their "Open Skies and CFE Aerial Inspection," Dunn and Henry refer to comments by U.S. government officials: "Sensors could be palletized and . . . made to operate in third party aircraft."

22. Tucker, "Negotiating Open Skies"; confirmed by Hawes.

23. In an interview in December of 1990, a Canadian official mentioned studies into the feasibility of "an all-purpose sensor pod that can be fitted on a host of aircraft. It

would have to be tamper-proof and acceptable to all involved." See Duffy, T., in the December 14, 1990, *Inside Defense Electronics*. See also Dunn and Henry, "Open Skies and CFE Aerial Inspection."

24. This problem was to become the basis of extensive negotiations; confirmed by Garroch.

25. See, for example, Hughes, D., "US, Soviet Impasse on Open Skies Reveals Key Differences on Overflights," note 14; Beech, E., "No Treaty to End Open Skies Talks," *Flight International*, May 16–22, 1990.

26. Mrazek, R., "Commentary: Open Skies Benefit All Countries," *Defense News*, May 28, 1990; Editorial, "Setback for Open Skies," *Winnipeg Free Press*, May 22, 1990; Editorial, "In Verification, Trust," *New York Times*, August 6, 1990.

27. "CFE to Be Signed Despite Disagreement," *Flight International*, September 26–October 2, 1990.

28. *Reporter, 1990*, 409.B.18.

29. See FBIS-SOV, November 20, 1990.

30. Peel, D., "CFE and Open Skies," *Disarmament Bulletin*, Ottawa, Department of External Affairs, no. 15 (Winter 1990/91): 10–11. See also *Reporter, 1990*, 409.B.18.

31. See, for example, Foxwell, D., "CFE Should Re-open Open Skies," editorial, *International Defense Review*, November 1990, 1205; and Krepon, M., "Bureaucrats Slow Open Skies," *Arms Control Today*, December 1990, 29 (in which Krepon calls for renewed discussions and a more flexible attitude from the U.S. bureaucracy).

32. Canada submitted a revised version of the paper to the allies in late November. Jones and Krasznai, "Open Skies," 48.

33. Tucker, "Negotiating Open Skies," 38; confirmed by Hawes.

34. These difficulties are described in Feinstein, L., "CFE Treaty Hits Potholes in Road to Ratification," *Arms Control Today* 12, no. 2 (March 1992); Dunay and Spitzer, "The Open Skies Negotiations and the Open Skies Treaty," 30–32.

35. Jones, "Open Skies," 11.

36. See Leopold, G., "US Begins Effort to Revive Open Skies Talks with Soviet Union," *Defense News* 5, no. 50 (December 10, 1990): 27.

37. Tucker, "Negotiating Open Skies," 42.

38. For their reaction to this development, which they called "startling," see Bush, George H. W., and B. Scowcroft, *A World Transformed* (New York: Random House, 1998), 430–32.

39. Tucker, "Negotiating Open Skies," 42.

40. See *Reporter, 1990*, 409.B.19, for a statement by an unnamed U.S. official that the United States was "not ready to commit to a meeting until we have sat down with the Soviets to see what flexibility they are willing to show."

41. Personal knowledge; point confirmed by Tucker, "Negotiating Open Skies," 44–45.

42. See also the February 15, 1991, comments of a Canadian official in the *Arms Control Reporter, 1991 (Reporter, 1991)*, Institute for Defense and Disarmament Studies, Cambridge, MA, 1991, 409.B.22.

43. See ibid., 409.B.21, for the statement, by an unnamed source, that NATO was working on a "package which would elicit a favorable response from the Soviet Union"; confirmed by Lysyshyn.

44. Tucker, "Negotiating Open Skies," 47.

45. Personal knowledge; confirmed by Lysyshyn and Hawes.

46. Ibid. See *Reporter, 1991*, 409.B.22, which states that a Canadian official, "[c]ontrary to [an] American official," previously interviewed by the *Reporter*, "believed that NATO needed to offer something to the USSR which would attract attention and interest." The same entry that quoted the Canadian official gave a summary of the compromises under consideration within the SPC.

47. Personal knowledge; confirmed by Lysyshyn and Hawes.

48. Ibid.

49. NATO-PS, "Council Discusses Open Skies and Lessons of the Gulf War," in *Atlantic News*, no. 2317, April 26, 1991. The new NATO plan is also discussed in Lawson, "Soviets Reviewing Proposal That May Close Loop on Open Skies Treaty"; "NATO Offers Soviets New Open Skies Plan," *Aviation Week and Space Technology*, June 10, 1991, 27; and Doughty, N., "NATO in New Push for Almost Forgotten Open Skies Treaty," *Reuters News Agency*, June 7, 1991. See also *Reporter, 1991*, 409.B.23.

50. Lawson, "Soviets Reviewing Proposal That May Close Loop on Open Skies Treaty." The official was myself.

51. This and subsequent quotations are taken from a copy of the compromise paper in the author's possession; confirmed by Hawes and Lysyshyn.

52. An outline of the Soviet response to the Canadian officials who handed over the NATO paper may be found in *Reporter, 1991*, 409.B.24–25.

53. Jones, "Open Skies," 12. This assessment of the initial Soviet response to the NATO paper was confirmed by Lysyshyn in an interview.

54. Tucker, "Negotiating Open Skies," 49. Tucker believes that Open Skies did not receive the required high-level attention from Russia's political decision-makers at this difficult moment.

55. Point confirmed by Lysyshyn.

56. Sharp, J., "Conventional Arms Control in Europe: Developments and Prospects in 1991," in *SIPRI Yearbook 1992: World Armaments and Disarmaments* (Oxford: SIPRI and the Oxford University Press, 1992), 461–63.

57. See *Reporter, 1991*, 409.B.25. An in-depth discussion of the negotiations leading to the agreement, and the reasons why Hungary and Romania decided to establish their own regime, may be found in Jones and Krasznai, "Open Skies," 53–55; and Kraznai, M., H. Spitzer, and W. Wynne, "Regional Applications of the Open Skies

Approach," in *Open Skies*, ed. Dunay and Spitzer, 149–56. The Hungarian-Romanian Open Skies Treaty was registered with the secretary general of the United Nations on May 21, 1991, and subsequently published as Document A/46/188 A/22638, May 24, 1991.

58. Points made in a private email from Marton Krasznai on July 27, 2013.

59. Doughty, N., "Soviets Dampen NATO Hopes on Key Open Skies Treaty," *Reuters News Agency*, June 6, 1991.

60. Ibid.

61. August 2 entry in the *Reporter, 1991*, 409.B.26; Dunay and Spitzer, "The Open Skies Negotiations and the Open Skies Treaty," 32–33.

62. The proposal was never disclosed to the public. The following is taken from personal knowledge and has been confirmed by Lysyshyn and Hawes.

63. This description of the proposal is taken from personal knowledge; confirmed by Hawes.

64. Ibid.

65. Personal knowledge; confirmed by Lysyshyn and Hawes.

66. *Reporter, 1991*, 409.B.26; Jones, "Open Skies,"12.

67. See the dismayed comments by an unnamed U.S. official in Leopold, G., "NATO to Re-Open Negotiations on Open Skies," *Defense News* 6, no. 33 (August 19, 1991): 1, 20.

68. Personal knowledge; confirmed by Lysyshyn.

69. Canadian Department of External Affairs, *Press Release no. 179, 1991*, Ottawa, August 9, 1991.

70. On the fact that the Soviets showed up in Vienna without instructions, see *Reporter, 1991*, 409.B.26. See also Jones, "Open Skies,"12.

71. For more on this theme, see Tucker, "Negotiating Open Skies," 51. See also Bunn, M., "Soviet Coup Fails: What Impact on Arms Control?" *Arms Control Today* 21, no. 7 (September 1991).

72. I was the Canadian representative to this process, and the following is based upon personal recollections.

73. The British and Americans were especially vocal in this regard, but the view was widely shared.

74. For a summation of this problem, see the April 24 entry in the *Reporter, 1991*, 409.B.23.

75. Ibid.

76. These concerns were shared by the USSR's former allies in Eastern Europe; confirmed by Krasznai.

77. See "Reopening of Open Sky Conference—Baltic Countries as Observers," *Atlantic News*, no. 2349, September 11, 1991. In the end, not one of the Baltic countries sent a representative to Vienna for the one-week session.

78. Point confirmed by Lysyshyn and Commander (then Lieutenant Commander)

F. W. (Ted) Parkinson, a Canadian naval officer responsible for overseeing the Canadian Defence Department's involvement in the Open Skies negotiations.

79. In reporting the fact that the Soviets had no new instructions, the *Arms Control Reporter* quoted an American official as saying: "That was no surprise," because of the coup attempt. See *Reporter, 1991*, 409.B.26.

80. Confusion exists over whether these individuals had served on previous Soviet Open Skies delegations. The *Reporter, 1991*, 409.B.26, states that Golovko had been on an earlier Open Skies delegation, while Romanov had not. Tucker, "Negotiating Open Skies," 52, states that both were new. In fact, Romanov was an Open Skies veteran, while Golovko was new.

81. Jones, "Open Skies," 12.

82. Personal recollection; confirmed by Lysyshyn Krasznai and Hawes.

83. Ibid.

84. *Reporter, 1991*, 409.B.26.

85. Ibid.

## CHAPTER 6

1. This was one of the first arms control statements by a Soviet official after the August coup, and was subjected to intense scrutiny by the Western media in an effort to see if the coup would have a tangible impact upon Soviet arms control policy. The media reaction to Golovko's statement was uniformly positive. See "Open Skies," *Associated Press*, November 5, 1991; Wise, M., "Soviets Back Open Skies Pact," *Washington Post*, November 6, 1991, A20; Wise, M., "Moscow Moves to Open Skies," *Independent*, November 6, 1991, 10; Wise, M., "Moscow Agrees to Aerial Inspection Treaty," *New York Times*, November 6, 1991, A11; "Re-opening of Open Skies Negotiations—USSR More Flexible," *Atlantic News*, November 8, 1991; "Change in Soviet Stance Clears Way for Open Skies Treaty," *Aviation Week and Space Technology*, November 11, 1991, 29; "Forecast Improves for Open Skies Negotiations," *International Defense Review*, December 1991, 1308.

2. Remarks attributed to Golovko in the November 6 stories by Wise in the *Independent* and *Washington Post.*

3. "Open Skies," *Associated Press*. This same story made the mistake of saying that the Open Skies negotiations were under the sponsorship of the CSCE.

4. See the November 6 stories by M. Wise in both the *Independent* and the *Washington Post.*

5. Personal recollection; confirmed by Lysyshyn, Parkinson Hawes, and Krasznai.

6. Tucker, J., "Negotiating Open Skies: A Diplomatic History," in *Open Skies, Open Control and Cooperative Security*, ed. Krepon, M., and A. Smithson (New York: St. Martin's Press, 1992), 55.

7. Jones, P. L., "Open Skies: A New Era of Transparency," *Arms Control Today* 22, no. 4 (1992): 12.

8. Canada, Hungary, Denmark, the Netherlands, and Norway, among others, were moved to occasionally comment on the manner in which events seemed to be moving.

9. Jones, "Open Skies," 12.

10. *Arms Control Reporter, 1991 (Reporter, 1991)*, 409.B.28.

11. Point confirmed by Lysyshyn, Parkinson, Hawes, and Krasznai.

12. Ibid.

13. For a description of the MBFR negotiation in this respect, see Dean, J., "East-West Arms Control Negotiations: The Multilateral Dimension," in *A Game for High Stakes: Lessons Learned in Negotiating with the Soviets*, ed. Sloss, L., and M. Scott Davies (Cambridge: Harvard Press, 1986), 1986, 94–95.

14. Personal recollection; confirmed by Lysyshyn, Parkinson, Krasznai, and Hawes.

15. Conforming is a process whereby the finished text is gone through in detail to ensure that all of the cross-references match.

16. Personal recollection; point confirmed by Parkinson.

17. Ibid. Open Skies was not the first time this tactic had been used in a multilateral negotiation in Vienna. During the MBFR talks, the U.S., UK, and Germany met regularly to develop proposals that were then presented to the other allies. See Dean, "East-West Arms Control Negotiations"; and Brady, L. P., *The Politics of Negotiation: America's Dealings with Allies, Adversaries and Friends* (Chapel Hill: University of North Carolina Press, 1991), 98.

18. Personal recollection; confirmed by Krasznai and Parkinson. This feeling was probably inevitable, but the personalities of some of the individuals involved in preparing and presenting the texts on behalf of the leaders sometimes made the degree of displeasure greater than it might otherwise have been.

19. Point confirmed by Krasznai.

20. Personal recollection; confirmed by Hawes and Parkinson.

21. See the transcript by Hawes made at the Henry L. Stimson Center, Washington, DC, March 31, 1992, 4.

22. Personal recollections; confirmed by Lysyshyn, Parkinson, Krasznai, Hawes, and Garroch.

23. In Borawski, J., "NATO, Europe and Open Skies," in *Open Skies: Technical; Organizational; Operational: Legal and Political Aspects*, ed. Chestnutt, H., and M. Slack (Toronto: York University Press, 1990), the author makes the point that these countries had, at this time, a "disappointingly modest" approach to transparency in previous CBM negotiations. Sweden's continued suspicion of Russia at this time is discussed in Huldt, B., "Neutrality and the Nordic Security Pattern: A Swedish Perspective," in *The European Neutrals in the 1990s: The Challenges and Opportunities*, ed. Neuhold, H. (Boulder, CO: Westview Press, 1992).

24. Personal recollections; confirmed by Lysyshyn, Parkinson, and Garroch.

25. Ibid.

26. This traditional concern is explained in Visuri, P., "Neutral Military Security in a Changing Europe: The Finnish Value," in *The European Neutrals in the 1990s: New Challenges and Opportunities*, ed. Neuhold, H. (Boulder, CO: Westview Press, 1992), 48–49.

27. This idea went back to the NATO Basic Element Paper of December 1989, and was expressed as: "The operation of the Open Skies regime will be without prejudice to states not participating in it." This exact phrase found its way into the Preamble of the final treaty.

28. Personal recollections; confirmed by Lysyshyn, Garroch, Parkinson, and Krasznai.

29. Correspondence with Hawes, November 18, 1992; point confirmed by Parkinson.

30. *Treaty on Open Skies*, "Preamble" (hereinafter referred to as *Treaty*) (emphasis added). Article VI, Section II, para. 2 also carries the admonition: "The flight path of an observation aircraft shall not be closer than, but shall be allowed up to, ten kilometers from the state border with an adjacent State that is *not* a State Party" (emphasis added). Overspill into the territory of an adjacent party is thus allowed, although the Preamble implores states to avoid it to the extent possible.

31. Conversations between myself and a Swedish diplomat during the Vienna Conference.

32. Huldt, "Neutrality and the Nordic Security Pattern."

33. Personal recollections; confirmed by Lysyshyn, Parkinson, Krasznai, and Hawes.

34. Ibid.

35. Personal recollection; confirmed by Parkinson and Garroch.

36. Personal recollection; confirmed by Lysyshyn and Parkinson.

37. Ibid.

38. The following was substantiated by a European diplomat who has requested anonymity, who was involved in the discussions within the WEU caucus in Vienna. I am also drawing upon person recollections and Parkinson.

39. Ibid.

40. Quotation from interview with a Dutch diplomat, involved in the discussions, who has requested anonymity.

41. Ibid.

42. Ibid. Also confirmed by a European sensor expert who sat in on many of these discussions.

43. Ibid. See also *Reporter, 1992*, 409.B.29.

44. The WEU officially declared itself defunct on June 30, 2011. However, the coalition of these states continues to cooperate on Open Skies.

45. Personal recollection; Point confirmed by Lysyshyn, Parkinson, Hawes, Krasznai, and Garroch.

46. Ibid.

47. Ibid.

48. Ibid.

49. The desire of the Soviet, and later Russian, military to accomplish this is referred to in Jones, "Open Skies," 12; Tucker, "Negotiating Open Skies," 61; and Hawes, "Statement." The point has been confirmed in the Garroch interview.

50. Jones, "Open Skies," 12; Tucker, "Negotiating Open Skies," 61; and Hawes, "Statement."

51. Personal recollections; confirmed by Lysyshyn, Krasznai, and Parkinson.

52. See the summation of the NATO position in Jones, "Open Skies," 11.

53. Personal recollections; confirmed by Lysyshyn, Hawes, and Parkinson.

54. "Quotas and Good Neighbors: Food for Thought," a nonpaper released by the Canadian delegation just prior to the November 22 break. The paper was never released publicly, and the subsequent discussion is based on a copy in the author's possession. The paper was written by myself and Ralph Lysyshyn.

55. Ibid.; also confirmed by Lysyshyn and Parkinson.

56. Ibid.

57. The Canadian paper firmly made the point, however, that it was not up to the Open Skies Treaty to assign this duty to the CPC, since Open Skies was a separate regime from the CSCE. What the treaty should do, the paper argued, was to ensure that nothing *prevented* the CPC from conducting such an overflight.

58. The following is taken from notes and interviews with U.S. and Dutch diplomats, who have requested anonymity.

59. Personal notes; confirmed by Lysyshyn.

60. Ibid.

61. Personal recollections; confirmed by Krasznai and Parkinson. Krasznai would later go on to work at the CPC and form the view that giving that institution a role in Open Skies crisis management flights would not have worked, as the CPC does not have "a strong enough mandate to play a pro-active (or independent) role in any conflict-prevention, crisis management activity." Krasznai email to the author, July 27, 2013.

62. See *Reporter, 1992*, 409.B.29, for more on the U.S./French dispute over the issue.

63. Personal recollection; confirmed by Lysyshyn, Parkinson, and Krasznai.

64. The following is drawn from personal knowledge and has been confirmed by Lysyshyn, Parkinson, and Krasznai.

65. Canada paid the costs of the overflight. The results of the flight were presented to the conference shortly after its resumption in January. See Canadian Department of External Affairs, *Open Skies: Second Trial Overflight—January 1992, Backgrounder Number 5* (Ottawa: External Affairs and International Trade, 1992).

## CHAPTER 7

1. *Arms Control Reporter, 1991 (Reporter, 1991)*, 409.B.28.

2. Lysyshyn, R. J., "Open Skies Ahead," *NATO Review* 40, no. 1 (February 1992): 24.

3. See speculations of a Western official in the January 13 entry in *Reporter*, 1992, 409.B.29.

4. See Hawes, J., "Statement," Henry L. Stimson Center, Washington, DC, March 31, 1990, 8, for the following comment: "The Russian military is still the old Soviet military."

5. *Reporter, 1992*, 409.B.29–30.

6. Ibid.

7. Ibid.

8. Personal recollection; confirmed by Lysyshyn, Parkinson, Hawes, and Krasznai.

9. Point made by Hawes.

10. Personal recollection; confirmed by Lysyshyn, Parkinson, Hawes, and Krasznai.

11. *Reporter, 1992*, 409.B.29–30.

12. Personal recollection; confirmed by Parkinson, and Hawes.

13. All of the former republics, except Georgia, joined the CSCE at the Prague meeting. See Reuters, "Ex-Soviet States Join European Security Forum," *Washington Post*, January 31, 1992, A14. Georgia's entry was delayed pending the resolution of concerns about human rights abuses.

14. Point confirmed by Lysyshyn, Parkinson, Krasznai, and Hawes.

15. Personal recollection; confirmed by Parkinson and Krasznai.

16. Point confirmed by Krasznai. This was particularly true for the operational questions presented in Article VI.

17. See Hawes's comments to the Stimson Center for this comment. Hawes, "Statement," 8.

18. The Russian tactic is mentioned in Jones, P. L., "Open Skies: A New Era of Transparency," *Arms Control Today* 22, no. 4 (1992): 12; Tucker, J., "Negotiating Open Skies: A Diplomatic History," in *Open Skies, Open Control and Cooperative Security*, ed. Krepon, M., and A. Smithson (New York: St. Martin's Press, 1992); and Hawes, "Statement," 5.

19. Personal knowledge; confirmed by Parkinson and Garroch. See also Hawes, "Statement," 8.

20. Tucker, "Negotiating Open Skies," 61.

21. Hawes, "Statement," 6.

22. Personal recollection; confirmed by Garroch and Parkinson.

23. Personal recollection; confirmed by Parkinson and Garroch (who recalled that the Swedes had played a particularly constructive role in developing this compromise).

24. Mention is made of this pressure in Jones, "Open Skies," 12–13.

25. Personal recollection; confirmed by Krasznai and Parkinson.

26. Ibid.

27. Personal recollection; confirmed by Parkinson and Lysyshyn.

28. Ibid., also confirmed by Krasznai, Garroch, and Hawes.

29. This statement was not made public. I am relying on personal knowledge of the statement's contents.

30. This idea is publicly suggested in Jones, "Open Skies," 13.

31. Personal recollection; confirmed by Parkinson, Krasznai, and Hawes.

32. Ibid.

33. See Hawes, "Statement," 5, for a comment on a "French mathematician [who] was wrapped up in this kind of thing for years."

34. This understanding is reflected in Annex A, Section II, para. 1 of the final treaty.

35. The annual passive quotas agreed in Vienna were: United States and Russia-Belarus (these two opted to act as a combined party)—42; Germany, Canada, France, the UK, Italy, Turkey, and Ukraine—12; Norway—7; Benelux (Belgium, the Netherlands, and Luxembourg opted to act as a combined party), Denmark, Poland, and Romania—6; Bulgaria, Spain, Greece, Hungary, Iceland, and Czechoslovakia—4; and Portugal—2. See Annex A, Section 1, para. 1 of the final treaty.

36. Hawes, "Statement," 4. See also U.S. Department of State, *Dispatch*, March 30, 1992, 258.

37. Canada and the United States share a flight over the Ukraine, as do Italy and Turkey; Annex A, Section II, para. 1 of the treaty.

38. The term "flight plan" is something of a misnomer, in that the overflying country cannot present a "flight plan" to the overflown country, but only "mission plan," outlining where it would like to go, at which altitudes, and when. The overflown country will then convert this document into a flight plan in accordance with its own national regulations, and file it with its own aviation authorities on behalf of the overflying country. For the sake of brevity, the term "flight plan" will be used to cover both concepts. The differences between the two are outlined in Article Two (Definitions), paras. 24 and 25 of the treaty.

39. See NATO-PS, *Open Skies Basic Elements*, NATO Press Service, Annex to M-2 (89), 46, December 15, 1989, Section VIII (Mission Operations), paras. 3–5.

40. The paper was never published outside of the conference. I am using my own copy for this discussion.

41. This account of the discussion is from my notes; confirmed by Lysyshyn, Hawes, Krasznai, and Parkinson.

42. See Article VI, Section I, paras. 5, 6, 9, 11, and 20, and Section II, paras. 4(E) and 6 of the treaty. See also Annex F, para. 4. Simultaneous flights can take place, if the host agrees.

43. Ibid.

44. In addition to the above, the timelines are discussed in Jones, "Open Skies," 15.

45. Ibid.

46. Point confirmed by Lysyshyn and Parkinson.

47. Point confirmed by Parkinson, Krasznai, Hawes, and Lysyshyn.

48. Ibid.; confirmed by Lysyshyn and Krasznai.

49. Hawes, "Statement," 7.

50. This issue is discussed in Jones, "Open Skies," 13, though not in the detail that follows.

51. Personal recollection; confirmed by Parkinson, Krasznai, and Hawes.

52. Ibid.

53. Ibid.

54. Ibid.

55. Article XVII, paras. 3–5.

56. See Article X, para. 6, of the treaty.

57. See Annex L, Section III, paras. 1–4, of the treaty.

58. Kivinen, O., and G. Brock, "French Alarm NATO by Pressing for New Defence Alliance," *The Times*, March 25, 1992.

59. Smith, H., *The Power Game* (New York: Random House, 1988), 545.

60. I believe that the Turks had always been willing to accept this, but they made it appear a major concession in the end. When the OSCC did convene, the Turks "maintained a close watch on their [the CSCE neutrals] status and challenged any attempt to increase their right of participation and observation." See Jones, P. L., "Open Skies: Events in 1992," in *Verification 1993: Peacekeeping, Arms Control and the Environment*, ed. Poole, J. B., and R. Guthrie (London: Brassey's and VERTIC, 1993).

61. See Conference of Security and Cooperation in Europe, "The CSCE Declaration on Open Skies," Helsinki, March 24, 1992. See, esp.,, operative para. 2.

62. For press coverage of these events, see Wise, M., "24 Countries Agree on Open Skies Pact," *Washington Post*, March 21, 1992; White, "Old Enemies Agree to Surveillance Flights," *Financial Times*, March 21, 1992; Tyler, P., "Agreement Will Open Skies to Reconnaissance Flights," *New York Times*, March 21, 1992; "Former Cold War Foes Sign Open Skies Treaty," *Reuters News Agency*, March 24, 1992; Pick, H., "Pact Legalises Aerial Spies," *Guardian*, March 24, 1992; and Grier, P., "Treaty Precludes Military Surprises Worldwide," *Christian Science Monitor*, March 26, 1992.

63. Jones, "Open Skies: Events in 1992," 159.

## CHAPTER 8

1. Article X of the treaty.

2. The full text of all Decisions taken by the OSCC, both during the period of provisional implementation and since entry into force (up to February 2012), have been placed online by the U.S. State Department and may be found at http://www.state.gov/t/avc/cca/os/c26158.htm.

3. See Spitzer, H. and R. Wiemker, "Technical Preparations for Treaty Implementation," in Dunay, P., and H. Spitzer, "The Open Skies Negotiations and the Open Skies Treaty," in *Open Skies: A Cooperative Approach to Military Transparency and Confidence-Building*, ed. Dunay, P., M. Krasznai, H. Spitzer, R. Wiemker, and W. Wynne (Geneva: UN Institute for Disarmament Research, 2004), for more on the work done in this pe-

riod. A list of the individual aircraft types selected by the various treaty signatories during this period appears on p. 72.

4. See "Decision Number Three to the Treaty on Open Skies Methodology for Calculating the Minimum Height above Ground Level at which Each Optical Camera Installed on an Observation Aircraft May Be Operated during an Observation Flight," OSCC 1/December 3, June 29, 1992, at http://www.state.gov/documents/organization/106719.pdf. See also Armstrong, D. G., "Technical Challenges under Open Skies," *Proceedings of the Second International Airborne Remote Sensing Conference and Exhibition, Strasbourg*, Environmental Research Institute of Michigan, Ann Arbor, vol. 1, 1994, 49–60.

5. See "Decision Number Seven to the Treaty on Open Skies Methodology for Determining the Ground Resolution of a Synthetic Aperture Radar (SAR)," OSCC/II/December 7, December 10, 1992, at http://www.state.gov/documents/organization/106723.pdf.

6. See "Decision Number Thirteen to the Treaty on Open Skies Methodology for Calculating the Minimum Permissible Flight Altitude When Using Optical and Video Cameras," OSCC/V/December 13, April 18, 1994, at http://www.state.gov/documents/organization/106731.pdf.

7. See Spitzer, H., "News from Open Skies: A Cooperative Treaty Maintaining Military Transparency," in *VERTIC Brief*, no. 8 (London: VERTIC, February, 2009), 7.

8. I am grateful to Alex Garroch, who was very much involved as a UK sensor expert and who discussed the experience with me at length in various email and telephone interviews in the summer of 2012.

9. The technical and operational procedures were established within the OSCC's informal working group on sensors, in cooperation with various national verification units. The work of the informal group was interrupted in 1997 because of the missing ratifications from Russia, Belarus, and Ukraine, and resumed in 2005. The group profited from strong support from the United States, which provided the chair and numerous experts, as well as from Germany, which hosted trial exercises and workshops. Private communication with Dr. H. Spitzer of Germany, who was involved in this work, January 2013.

10. For an outline of one such process, the certification of the German Open Skies aircraft in June of 1997, see Spitzer and Wiemker, "Technical Preparations for Treaty Implementation," 88–89. Tragically, this aircraft and its crew were lost in a midair collision a short while later during a transit flight unrelated to the treaty. The Germans also hosted two "mock" multilateral test certifications in August of 2000 and 2001 that allowed states to practice before the treaty came into effect.

11. Garroch interviews, see Note 8, above. Also, correspondence with Diana Marvin over the summer of 2012.

12. See Britting, E., and H. Spitzer, "The Open Skies Treaty," in *Verification Yearbook*,

*2002*, ed. Findlay, T., and O. Meier (London: VERTIC, 2002), 226–27; and Marquardt, J. J., "Open Skies: Not a Moment Too Soon," *Bulletin of the Atomic Scientists*, January/February 2002, 19. It should be noted that Russia and Belarus declared themselves to be a "Group of States Parties" under Article III of the treaty, and Belarus waited for Russia to ratify.

13. See "Ukraine Ratifies Open Skies Treaty," *Arms Control Reporter*, April 2000, at http://www.armscontrol.org/node/2928. See also Dunay, P., and H. Spitzer, "The Open Skies Treaty Post Signature," in *Open Skies*, ed. Dunay et al. Krasznai reports that cost questions had been a significant concern for all of the Warsaw Pact countries since the beginning of the negotiation. Krasznai email, July 27, 2013.

14. See Ladygin, S., "Russia and Open Skies," *Military Parade, Armed Forces MIC and Politics*, November 2001, at http://www.milparade.com. Point also made in 2002 in Britting and Spitzer, "The Open Skies Treaty," 226; and Dunay and Spitzer, "The Open Skies Treaty Post Signature." See also Podwig, P., "History and the Current Status of the Russian Early Warning System," *Science and Global Security* 10 (2002): esp. 48–50, for a discussion of the deterioration of the Russian reconnaissance and early warning satellite fleet in the 1990s.

15. See *Council Meeting of the State Duma with Attachments*, excerpts from the Minutes no. 5, Federal Assembly of the Russian Federation, February 10, 2001, as cited in Dunay and Spitzer, "The Open Skies Treaty Post Signature," 62.

16. The methods by which the OSCC considered all of these questions is laid out in "Decision Number Six to the Treaty on Open Skies Rules of Procedure and Working Methods of the Open Skies Consultative Commission," at http://www.state.gov/documents/organization/106722.pdf.

17. The so-called pod group contains Belgium, Canada, France, Greece, Italy, Luxembourg, Netherlands, Norway, Portugal, and Spain. The pod is commonly owned and is stored in Belgium between use. A trial certification of the pod had been carried out in Germany in the summer of 2001.

18. See Krasznai, K., "Post Ratification Phase and Entry into Force," in *Open Skies*, ed. Dunay et al., 97. As of 2013, Germany, Great Britain, and the Czech Republic no longer operate Open Skies aircraft for cost reasons. These countries lease other nations' Open Skies aircraft for their missions. Upon joining the treaty after its entry into force, Sweden certified an aircraft and sensor package. Romania certified its aircraft in 2008.

19. In 2010, for example, the OSCC decided after four years of discussion that modern commercially available digital aerial cameras could be used, with up to four color channels and well as panchromatic imaging capabilities. See OSCC Decision 9/10, Digital Imagery Processing, OSCC 4th Meeting, 52nd Session, OSCC (52), Journal Number 167, Agenda item 4, July 12, 2010. Available at http://www.state.gov/documents/organization/194721.pdf.

20. See "Statement by the Chairman of the First Review Conference on the Imple-

mentation of the Treaty on Open Skies at the Closing Plenary," OSCC.RC/45/05, Vienna, February 16, 2005. Available at http://2001–2009.state.gov/t/vci/cca/os/106901.htm.

21. See, for example, OSCC, "Statement by the Delegation of Romania (also on Behalf of the United States of America) to the Open Skies Consultative Commission," 2nd Meeting of the 52nd Session, OSCC (52), Journal no. 165, Agenda item 8, May 17, 2010; OSCC, "Statement by the Delegation of the Russian Federation to the Open Skies Consultative Commission," 2nd Meeting of the 52nd Session, OSCC (52), Journal no. 165, Agenda item 8, May 17, 2010; and OSCC, "Statement by the Delegation of Georgia to the Open Skies Consultative Commission," 2nd Meeting of the 52nd Session, OSCC (52), Journal no. 165, Agenda item 8, May 17, 2010.

22. Communication with Diana Marvin, July 6, 2012. See also Ministry of Foreign Affairs of Georgia, "Statement of the Ministry of Foreign Affairs of Georgia on a Decision to Cease Performing Its Obligations vis-a-vis the Russian Federation under the Open Skies Treaty," April 5, 2012, on the website of the Georgian embassy to the UK, at http://uk.mfa.gov.ge/index.php?lang_id=ENG&sec_id=193&info_id=14626.

23. For Russia's statement, see "Statement by Russia's Ministry of Foreign Affairs Regarding Suspension by Russian Federation of Treaty on Conventional Armed Forces in Europe," Ministry of Foreign Affairs, Russian Federation, December 12, 2007, at http://www.mid.ru/Brp_4.nsf/arh/10DA6DD509E4D164C32573AF004CC4BE?OpenDocument. For analysis and comment on the decision, see BBC News, "Russia Suspends Arms Control Pact," July 14, 2007. Available at http://news.bbc.co.uk/2/hi/europe/6898690.stm; and Kramer A. E., and T. Shanker, "Russia Steps Back from Key Arms Treaty," *New York Times*, July 14, 2007. By 2011, high-level talks aimed at revising the CFE Treaty had failed, and the Obama administration announced that the United States was suspending treaty implementation. See Collina, T. Z., "CFE Treaty Talks Stall," *Arms Control Today*, September 2011; and Kimball, D.G., "US Suspends CFE Treaty Implementation," *Arms Control Today*, December 2011.

24. See Open Skies Review Conference, "Final Document of the Second Review Conference on the Implementation of the Treaty on Open Skies," OSRC(2) Journal, Agenda item 4(b), Vienna, June 9, 2010.

25. Ibid.

26. "Interpretative Statement on the Final Document of the Second Review Conference," Journal of the Second Review Conference, OSRC(2).JOUR, 7–9 June 2010, Annex 14. Bosnia-Herzegovina later joined the statement.

27. Statement by the Delegation of Turkey, OSRC(2).JOUR, June 7–9, 2010, Annex 15.

28. Communication with Diana Marvin, July 6, 2012; and Spitzer, H., "Open Skies in Turbulence; A Well-functioning Treaty Is Endangered by Outside Developments," *Security and Human Rights* 22, no. 4 (Winter 2011).

29. See Open Skies Review Conference, "Final Document of the Second Review

Conference on the Implementation of the Treaty on Open Skies," OSRC(2) Journal, Agenda item 4(b), Vienna, June 9, 2010.

30. These points were made by various participants at a workshop on the future of Open Skies at the Hoover Institution at Stanford University, March 2012. The existence of the Presidential Policy Directive (PPD 15—"Implementation of the Open Skies Treaty") is noted on the website of the Federation of American Scientists, but its contents have not been made public. See http://www.fas.org/irp/offdocs/ppd/index.html. Recently, the secretary of the U.S. Air Force issued an instruction to all commands updating its guidance on the implementation of Open Skies. No mention is made of PPD 15 or impending upgrades to the aircraft or sensors. See U.S. Air Force Instruction 16–604; *Implementation of, and Compliance with, the Treaty on Open Skies*, March 28, 2012, at http://www.fas.org/irp/doddir/usaf/afi16–604.pdf.

31. See, for example, Hawes, J. H., "Open Skies: Beyond Vancouver to Vladivostok," Stimson Center Occasional Paper no. 10 (December 1992); Jones, P., "Open Skies in Other Regional Contexts" in *Verification 1994: Arms Control, Peacekeeping and the Environment,* ed. Poole, J. B., and R. Guthrie (London: VERTIC and Brassey's, 1994); and Krasznai, M., H. Spitzer, and W. Wynne, "Regional Applications of the Open Skies Approach," in *Open Skies,* ed. Dunay et al., 166–82.

32. See, for example, Chaudry, Air Marshal M. A. (Pakistan Air Force, ret.), and Air Marshal K. C. Cariappa (Indian Air Force, ret.), "How Cooperative Aerial Monitoring Can Help in Reducing Tensions between India and Pakistan," Cooperative Monitoring Center Occasional Paper/22, SAND-98–0505/22 (Albuquerque, NM: Sandia National Laboratories, December 2001).

33. Olson, J., "Confidence-building Measures to Support the Sunshine Policy," SAND2001–2159P (Albuquerque, NM: Sandia National Laboratories, July 2001).

34. Krepon, M., and P. D. Constable, "Confidence-building, Peace-making and Aerial Inspections in the Middle East," Occasional Paper no. 6 (Washington, DC: Henry L. Stimson Center, 1992).

35. Krasznai, Spitzer, and Wynne, "Regional Applications of the Open Skies Approach," 175–78.

36. Krepon, M., and J. P. Tracey, "'Open Skies' and UN Peace-keeping," *Survival* 32, no. 3 (May/June 1990); Smithson, A. E., "Multilateral Aerial Inspections: An Abbreviated History," in *Open Skies, Arms Control and Cooperative Security,* ed. Krepon, M., and A. E. Smithson (New York: St. Martin's Press, 1992); and Dorn, A. W., "Blue Sensors: Technology and Cooperative Monitoring in UN Peacekeeping," Cooperative Monitoring Center Occasional Paper 36, SAND 2004–1380 (Albuquerque, NM: Sandia National Laboratories, April 2004).

37. At a Track Two meeting in Lahore, Pakistan, in September 2012, a group of senior retired officers from India and Pakistan developed a proposal for the demilitarization of the disputed Siachen region. The proposal includes a provision for cooperative aerial

overflights of the region so that each side can assure itself that it remains demilitarized. The proposal may be found at http://www.uottawa.ca/media/media-release-2663.html.

38. See Krepon and Constable, "Confidence-building, Peace-making and Aerial Inspections in the Middle East."

39. For more on this argument, see Lindley, D., *Promoting Peace with Information: Transparency as a Tool of Security Regimes* (Princeton: Princeton University Press, 2007).

40. For the application of this thesis specifically to the Open Skies idea, see Marquardt, J. J., "Open Skies and American Primacy," *Diplomacy and Statecraft* 18 (2007). For a more general application of it to U.S. foreign policy, see Marquardt, J. J., *Transparency and American Primacy in World Politics* (Farnham, Surrey: Ashgate, 2011), which includes a section on Open Skies between pages 98 and 111.

41. See, for example, the discussion of the idea in Hawes, "Open Skies." For more on the idea, see Lindley, D., "Cooperative Airborne Monitoring: Opening the Skies to Promote Peace, Protect the Environment, and Cope with Natural Disasters," *Contemporary Security Policy* 27, no. 2 (2006).

42. These points were discussed at the Open Skies workshop at the Hoover Institution, March 2012.

43. See, for example, U.S. Congress, Office of Technology Assessment, *Verification Technologies: Cooperative Aerial Surveillance in International Agreements, OTA-ISC-480* (Washington, DC: U.S. Government Printing Office, 1991); and Gabriele, M. D., "The Treaty on Open Skies and Its Practical Applications and Implications for the United States," RAND Graduate School Dissertation, 1997, esp. ch. 3, "Use of the Open Skies Treaty as a Tool for Verification."

44. Drell, S., and C. Stubbs, "Realizing the Full Potential of the Open Skies Treaty," *Arms Control Today*, July/August, 2011. See also the op-ed by George P. Shultz, Sidney Drell, and Christopher Stubbs, "Modernize the Open Skies Treaty," *New York Times*, March 25, 2012. Both of these articles, in addition to calling for an Open Skies regime capable of assisting in the verification of disarmament treaties, also call for the existing regime to be enhanced through the adoption of more sophisticated sensors for the CBM mission itself.

45. A number of scientific papers have been written on this. For example, see Saey, P. R. J., "Ultra-Low-Level Measurements of Argon, Krypton and Radioxenon for Treaty Verification Purposes," *ESARDA Bulletin*, no. 36 (2007); Kalinowski, M. B., et al., "Conclusions on Plutonium Separation from Atmospheric Krypton-85 Measured at Various Distances from the Karlsruhe Reprocessing Plant," *Journal of Environmental Radioactivity* 73, no. 2 (2004): 203; Kalinowski, M. B., H. Daerr, and M. Kohler, "Measurements of Krypton-85 to Detect Clandestine Plutonium Production," *INESAP Bulletin*, no. 27 (December 2006); and Bowyer, S. M., et al., "Automated Particulate Sampler for Comprehensive Test Ban Treaty Verification (the DOE Radionuclide Aerosol Sampler/Analyzer)," *IEEE Transactions on Nuclear Science* 44, no. 3 (June 1997): 551. On uranium-

conversion facilities, see Kemp, R. S., "Initial Analysis of the Detectability of UO2F2 Aerosols Produced by UF6 Released From Uranium Conversion Plants," *Science and Global Security*, Vol. 16, No. 3 (2008): 115–125. On uranium-enrichment and spent fuel reprocessing facilities, see Krey, P. W., and K. W. Nicholson, "Atmospheric Sampling and Analysis for the Detection of Nuclear Proliferation," *Journal of Radioanalytical and Nuclear Chemistry* 248, no. 3 (2001): 605–10. All of these sources are also cited in Drell and Stubbs, "Realizing the Full Potential of the Open Skies Treaty."

46. For a document, classified Top Secret at the time, that outlines the process whereby the United States detected large amounts of radiation and traced them back to the first Soviet atomic bomb test, see U.S. Air Force Deputy Chief of Staff for Operations, Atomic Energy Office, Section 1, "U.S. Weather Bureau Report on Alert Number 112 of the Atomic Detection System," September 29, 1949, Top Secret, Source: Harry S. Truman Library, President's Secretary's Files, box 199, NSC-Atomic. Declassified version available at http://www.gwu.edu/~nsarchiv/nukevault/ebb286/doc08.PDF.

47. See Molander, J., "Mandated Aerial Inspections: The Iraqi Case," in *Open Skies, Arms Control and Cooperative Security*, ed. Krepon and Smithson. The United States provided high-altitude, wide-area coverage overflights using U2 aircraft, while Germany and later Chile provided helicopters for low-altitude, spot-area coverage capabilities. For a broader discussion of the Iraqi experience, which places aerial inspections in the wider framework of the verification regime, see Findlay, T., "Lessons of UNSCOM and UNMOVIC for WMD Non-Proliferation, Disarmament and Arms Control," in *Arms Control after Iraq: Normative and Operational Challenges*, ed. Sidhu, W. P. S., and R. Thakur (Tokyo: United Nations University, 2006).

48. George Shultz, Henry Kissinger, William Perry, and Sam Nunn have penned a series of op-eds calling for the complete elimination of nuclear weapons: "A World Free of Nuclear Weapons," *Wall Street Journal*, January 4, 2007; "Toward a Nuclear Free World," *Wall Street Journal*, January 15, 2008; "How to Protect Our Nuclear Deterrent," *Wall Street Journal*, January 20, 2010; and "Deterrence in the Age of Nuclear Proliferation," *Wall Street Journal*, March 7, 2011. The op-eds are all available at http://www.nuclearsecurityproject.org/publications/wall-street-journal-op-eds.

49. See "Remarks by President Barak Obama, Hradcany Square, Prague, Czech Republic, April 5, 2009." Available at http://www.whitehouse.gov/the_press_office/Remarks-By-President-Barack-Obama-In-Prague-As-Delivered.

50. For an overview of the global system, see the "Verification Regime" page on the CTBTO (Comprehensive Test Ban Treaty Organisation) Available at http://www.ctbto.org/verification-regime/.

# Bibliography


Abel, E., "Eisenhower Calls upon Soviets to Exchange Arms Blueprints; Asks Mutual Aerial Inspection," *New York Times*, July 22, 1955.

Aerospace Daily, "DOD Official Says Open Skies Stalled: Budapest Treaty Unlikely," *Aerospace Daily* 154, no. 28 (May 9, 1990).

Almond, P., "Canadians' Flight over Hungary Is First Test of Open Skies Plan," *Washington Times*, January 8, 1990.

*Arms Control Reporter*, various.

"Arms Control Sticking Points," *Los Angeles Times*, May 16, 1990.

Armstrong, D. G., "Technical Challenges under Open Skies," *Proceedings of the Second International Airborne Remote Sensing Conference and Exhibition, Strasbourg*, Environmental Research Institute of Michigan, Ann Arbor, vol. 1, 1994.

Aurisch, K. L., "The Art of Preparing a Multilateral Conference," *Negotiating Journal* 5, no. 3 (July 1989): 279–88.

BBC News, "Russia Suspends Arms Control Pact," July 14, 2007, at http://news.bbc.co.uk/2/hi/europe/6898690.stm.

Beech, E., "No Treaty to End Open Skies Talks," *Flight International*, May 16–22, 1990.

Bertman, C., *Mutual Force Reductions in Europe: The Political Aspects, Adelphi Papers, no. 84* (London: International Institute for Strategic Studies, 1972).

Bischof, G., "Eisenhower, the Summit and the Austrian Treaty," in *Cold War Respite: The Geneva Summit of 1955*, ed. Bischof, G., and S. Dockrill (Baton Rouge: Louisiana State University Press, 2000).

Boulden, J., "Canada and Open Skies," in *Open Skies: Technical; Organizational; Operational: Legal and Political Aspects*, ed. Chestnutt, H., and M. Slack (Toronto: York University Press, 1990).

Borawski, J., "NATO, Europe and Open Skies," in *Open Skies: Technical; Organizational;*

*Operational: Legal and Political Aspects*, ed. Chestnutt, H., and M. Slack (Toronto: York University Press, 1990).

Boulden, J., "Open Skies: The 1955 Proposal and Its Current Revival," *Dalhousie Law Journal* 13, no. 2 (1990): 611–49.

Bowyer, S. M., et al., "Automated Particulate Sampler for Comprehensive Test Ban Treaty Verification (The DOE Radionuclide Aerosol Sampler/Analyzer)," *IEEE Transactions on Nuclear Science* 44, no. 3 (June 1997).

Brady, A., "Canadian Flight Tests Open Skies," *Associated Press*, January 6, 1990.

Brady, L. P., *The Politics of Negotiation: America's Dealings with Allies, Adversaries and Friends* (Chapel Hill: University of North Carolina Press, 1991).

Britting, E., and H. Spitzer, "The Open Skies Treaty," in *Verification Yearbook, 2002*, ed. Findlay, T., and O. Meier (London: VERTIC, 2002).

Brodie, I., "Russia Exploits West German Fears of Limited Nuclear War," *Daily Telegraph*, February 6, 1989.

Bundy, M., *Danger and Survival: Choices about the Bomb in the First Fifty Years* (New York: Random House, 1988).

Bunn, G., "Negotiating Arms Control and Disarmament Agreements," in *The Encyclopedia of Arms Control and Disarmament, vol. 1*, ed. Burns, R. D. (New York: Charles Scribner's Sons, 1993).

Bunn, M., "Soviet Coup Fails: What Impact on Arms Control?" *Arms Control Today* 21, no. 7 (September 1991).

Bury, H., *Eisenhower and the Cold War Arms Race: 'Open Skies' and the Military Industrial Complex* (London: I.B. Tauris & Co., 2014)

Bush, George H. W., and B. Scowcroft, *A World Transformed* (New York: Random House, 1998).

Canadian Broadcasting Corporation (CBC), "The World at Six," *Canadian Broadcasting Corporation Radio News Program*, September 27, 1989.

Canadian Department of External Affairs, *Open Skies: Challenge for the 1990s, Backgrounder no. 1* (Ottawa: External Affairs and International Trade, 1989).

Canadian Department of External Affairs, *Open Skies: Opportunity for the 1990s, Backgrounder no. 2* (Ottawa: External Affairs and International Trade, 1989).

Canadian Department of External Affairs, *Open Skies: Report of the Canada-Hungary Trial Overflight, Backgrounder no. 3* (Ottawa: External Affairs and International Trade, 1990).

Canadian Department of External Affairs, *Open Skies Backgrounder no. 4* (Ottawa: External Affairs and International Trade, 1991).

Canadian Department of External Affairs, *Press Release no. 179, 1991*, Ottawa, August 9, 1991.

Canadian Department of External Affairs, *Open Skies: Second Trial Overflight—January 1992, Backgrounder no. 5* (Ottawa: External Affairs and International Trade, 1992).

Canadian Open Skies Delegation, Vienna, Austria, "Quotas and Good Neighbours: Food for Thought," presented at the Vienna Open Skies Conference, November 1991.

Canadian Press, "Soviet 'Stonewalling' Could Threaten Open Skies Outcome," *Ottawa Citizen*, February 22, 1990.

"CFE to Be Signed Despite Disagreement," *Flight International*, September 26–October 2, 1990.

"Change in Soviet Stance Clears Way for Open Skies Treaty," *Aviation Week and Space Technology*, November 11, 1991.

Chaudry, M. A., Air Marshal (Pakistan Air Force, ret.) and Air Marshal K. C. Cariappa (Indian Air Force, ret.), "How Cooperative Aerial Monitoring Can Help in Reducing Tensions between India and Pakistan," Cooperative Monitoring Center Occasional Paper/22, SAND-98–0505/22 (Albuquerque, NM: Sandia National Laboratories, December 2001).

Cherniaev, A., "Gorbachev's Foreign Policy: The Concept," in *Turning Points in Ending the Cold War*, ed. Skinner, K. K. (Stanford, CA: Hoover Press, 2008)

Chestnutt, H., and M. Slack, *Open Skies: Workshop Report* (Toronto: York University Press, 1989).

Chestnutt, H., and M. Slack, eds., *Open Skies: Technical; Organizational; Operational: Legal and Political Aspects* (Toronto: York University Press, 1990).

Chestnutt, H., and M. Slack, eds., *Verifying Conventional Force Reductions in Europe: CFE I and Beyond* (Toronto: York University Press, 1991).

Citron, K., "Experiences of a Negotiator at the Stockholm Conference," in *Processes of International Negotiations*, ed. Mauter-Markof, F. (San Francisco: Westview Press, 1989).

Clark, J., "Don't Dismiss Open Skies," *New York Times*, July 5, 1989.

Clark, J., "Foreword," in *Open Skies: Technical; Organizational; Operational: Legal and Political Aspects*, ed. Chestnutt, H., and M. Slack (Toronto: York University Press, 1990).

Clark, M., "Opening the Skies," *Maclean's*, February 12, 1990.

Clark, Lt. Col. R. H., "Canadian Overflight and Landing Clearances," in *Open Skies: Technical; Organizational; Operational: Legal and Political Aspects*, ed. Chestnutt, H., and M. Slack (Toronto: York University Press, 1990).

Collina, T. Z., "CFE Treaty Talks Stall," *Arms Control Today* 41, (September 2011).

Conference on Security and Cooperation in Europe, "The CSCE Declaration on Open Skies," Helsinki, March 24, 1992.

Congressional Research Service, *Soviet Diplomacy and Negotiating Behavior—1989–1990: Gorbachev-Reagan-Bush Meetings at the Summit, Committee on Foreign Affairs, Special Studies Series on Foreign Affairs Issues, vol. III* (Washington, DC: U.S. Government Printing Office, 1991).

Cox, D., "Are Canada's Skies Open to Soviet Overflights?" *Toronto Star*, July 20, 1989.

*CSCE Declaration on Open Skies*, Helsinki, March 24, 1992.

Dean, J., "East-West Arms Control Negotiations: The Multilateral Dimension," in *A Game for High Stakes: Lessons Learned in Negotiating with the Soviets*, ed. Sloss, L., and M. Scott Davies (Cambridge: Harvard Press, 1986).

Dobrynin, A., *In Confidence: Moscow's Ambassador to America's Six Cold War Presidents, 1962–1986* (New York: Crown, 1995).

*Document of the Stockholm Conference on Confidence- and Security-Building Measures and Disarmament in Europe Convened in Accordance with the Relevant Provisions of the Concluding Document of the Madrid Meeting of the Conference on Security and Co-operation in Europe*, at http://www.state.gov/t/isn/4725.htm.

Dorn, A. W., "Blue Sensors: Technology and Cooperative Monitoring in UN Peacekeeping," Cooperative Monitoring Center Occasional Paper 36, SAND 2004–1380 (Albuquerque, NM: Sandia National Laboratories, April 2004).

Doughty, N., "NATO in New Push for Almost Forgotten Open Skies Treaty," *Reuters News Agency*, June 7, 1991.

Doughty, N., "Soviets Dampen NATO Hopes on Key Open Skies Treaty," *Reuters News Agency*, June 6, 1991.

Drell, S., and C. Stubbs, "Realizing the Full Potential of the Open Skies Treaty," *Arms Control Today* 41 (July/August 2011).

Duffy, T., in the December 14, 1990, issue of *Inside Defense Electronics*.

Dunay, P., and H. Spitzer, "The Open Skies Negotiations and the Open Skies Treaty," in *Open Skies: A Cooperative Approach to Military Transparency and Confidence-Building*, ed. Dunay, P., M. Krasznai, H. Spitzer, R Wiemker, and W. Wynne (Geneva: UN Institute for Disarmament Research, 2004).

Dunay, P., and H. Spitzer, "The Open Skies Treaty Post Signature," in *Open Skies: A Cooperative Approach to Military Transparency and Confidence-Building*, ed. Dunay, P., M. Krasznai, H. Spitzer, R. Wiemker, and W. Wynne (Geneva: UN Institute for Disarmament Research, 2004).

Dunn, L. A., and B. A. Henry, eds., "Open Skies and CFE Aerial Inspection," *Report of a Workshop Sponsored by the Arms Control Program of Los Alamos National Laboratory*, August 30, 1990.

Editorial, "Setback for Open Skies," *Winnipeg Free Press*, May 22, 1990.

Editorial, "In Verification, Trust," *New York Times*, August 6, 1990.

Eisenhower, D. D., *Mandate for Change: The White House Years, 1953–6* (New York: Doubleday and Company, 1963).

Evangelista, M., "Cooperation Theory and Disarmament Negotiations in the 1950s," *World Politics* 42, no. 4 (July 1990).

Evans, M., "Moscow Keeps up Pressure over Lance Row," *The Times*, May 9, 1989.

Evans, M., "West Sees Offer as a Ploy to Exploit Its Differences," *The Times*, January 20, 1989.

"Ex-Soviet States Join European Security Forum," *Washington Post*, January 31, 1992.

Fairhall, D., "NATO Gives up Hope on Open Skies Signing," *Guardian*, May 5, 1990.

Feinstein, L., "CFE Treaty Hits Potholes in Road to Ratification," *Arms Control Today* 21, no. 2 (1992).

Findlay, T., "Lessons of UNSCOM and UNMOVIC for WMD Non-Proliferation, Disarmament and Arms Control," in *Arms Control after Iraq: Normative and Operational Challenges*, ed. Sidhu, W. P. S., and R. Thakur (Tokyo: United Nations University, 2006).

Flight International, "CFE to Be Signed Despite Disagreement," *Flight International*, September 26–October 2, 1990.

Florini, A., "The Open Skies Negotiations," in *The Encyclopedia of Arms Control and Disarmament, vol. II*, ed. Burns, R. D. (New York: Charles Scribner's Sons, 1993).

Florini, A., "The United States and Open Skies," in *Open Skies: Technical; Organizational; Operational: Legal and Political Aspects*, ed. Chestnutt, H., and M. Slack (Toronto: York University Press, 1990).

Florini, A., and Y. Dehqanzada, *Secrets for Sale: How Commercial Satellite Imagery Will Change the World* (Washington, DC: Carnegie Endowment for International Peace, 2000).

"Forecast Improves for Open Skies Negotiations," *International Defense Review*, December 1991.

"Former Cold War Foes Sign Open Skies Treaty," *Reuters News Agency*, March 24, 1992.

Foxwell, D. (editorial), "CFE Should Re-open Open Skies," *International Defense Review*, November 1990.

Freedman, L., *US Intelligence and the Soviet Strategic Threat*, 2nd ed. (London: Macmillan, 1986).

Fursenko, A., and T. Naftali *Khrushchev's Cold War: The Inside Story of an American Adversary* (New York: W. W. Norton, 2006).

Gabriele, M. D., "The Treaty on Open Skies and Its Practical Applications and Implications for the United States," RAND Graduate School dissertation, 1997.

Gaddis, J. L., *Strategies of Containment: A Critical Appraisal Post-war American National Security Policy* (Oxford: Oxford University Press, 1982).

Gaddis, J. L., *We Now Know: Rethinking Cold War History* (Oxford: Oxford University press, 1997).

Garthoff, R., "Negotiating with the Russians: Some Lessons from SALT," *International Security* 1, no. 4 (1977): 3–24.

Gordon, M. R., "2 Suitors for Europe; Bush, Gorbachev Try to Impress NATO Allies with Offerings of Peace," *New York Times*, May 13, 1989.

Grier, P., "Treaty Precludes Military Surprises Worldwide," *Christian Science Monitor*, March 26, 1992.

Ground, J., "Open Skies Open and Reclose," *Trust and Verify*, no. 10 (May 1990).

Guk, S., "Does the USSR Advocate Open Skies with Exclusion Zones? The Soviet Position Has Been Distorted Says Deputy Minister of Foreign Affairs of the USSR Viktor Karpov," *Isvestia* (Translated in FBIS-SOV-90–043, March 5, 1990).

Guliver, P. H., *Disputes and Negotiations* (New York: Academic Press, 1979).

Handelman, S., "Shevardnadze Ready to Visit Canada to Discuss Open Skies, Kremlin Says," *Toronto Star*, November 18, 1989.

Hawes, J. H., "Open Skies: From Idea to Negotiation," *NATO Review* 38, no. 3 (1990).

Hawes, J., "Statement," Henry L. Stimson Center, Washington, March 31, 1990.

Hawes, J., "Testimony to the Committee on Foreign Relations," *U.S. Senate, Committee on Foreign Relations*, Washington, DC, January 30, 1990.

Hawes, J. H., "Transcript of a WorldNet Interview," *Wireless File 27*, February 9, 1990.

Hitchcock, W. I., "The Marshall Plan and the Creation of the West," in *The Cambridge History of the Cold War, vol.. I*, ed. Leffler, M. P., and O. A. Westad (Cambridge: Cambridge University Press, 2010).

Hoffman, D., "Bush Urges Soviets to Broaden Reforms; Arms Offers Sidestepped in Major Speech," *Washington Post*, May 13, 1989, A1.

Holsti, K. J., "Bargaining Theory and Diplomatic Reality: The CSCE Negotiations," *Review of International Studies* 8, no. 3 (1982): 159–79.

Howard, R., "Soviet Stance on Open Skies Linked to Struggles inside Kremlin," *Globe and Mail*, February 26, 1990.

Howard, R., "Talks on Open Skies Adjourn amid Impasses," *Globe and Mail*, February 28, 1990.

Hughes, D., "US, Soviet Differences Could Prevent Planned Signing of Open Skies Treaty," *Aviation Week and Space Technology*, April 2, 1990.

Hughes, D., "US, Soviet Impasse on Open Skies Reveals Key Differences on Overflights," *Aviation Week and Space Technology*, August 1990.

Huldt, B., "Neutrality and the Nordic Security Pattern: A Swedish Perspective," in *The European Neutrals in the 1990s: The Challenges and Opportunities*, ed. Neuhold, H. (Boulder, CO: Westview Press, 1992).

Jones, P. L., "CFE Aerial Inspections and Open Skies: A Comparison," in *Verifying Con-*

*ventional Force Reductions in Europe: CFE I and Beyond*, ed. Chestnutt, H., and M. Slack (Toronto: York University Press, 1991).

Jones, P. L., "The Determination of Overflight Quotas for an Open Skies Regime," in *Open Skies: Technical; Organizational; Operational: Legal and Political Aspects*, ed. Chestnutt, H., and M. Slack (Toronto: York University Press, 1990).

Jones, P. L., "Open Skies: A New Era of Transparency," *Arms Control Today* 22, no. 4 (1992).

Jones, P. L., "Open Skies: A Review of Events at Ottawa and Budapest," in *Verification Report 1991: Yearbook on Arms Control and Environmental Agreements*, ed. Poole, J. B. (London: Apex Press and VERTIC, 1991).

Jones, P. L., "Open Skies: Events in 1992," in *Verification 1993: Peacekeeping, Arms Control and the Environment*, ed. Poole, J. B., and R. Guthrie (London: Brassey's and VERTIC, 1993).

Jones, P.L, "Open Skies in Other Regional Contexts" in *Verification 1994: Arms Control, Peacekeeping and the Environment*, ed. Poole, J. B., and R. Guthrie (London: VERTIC and Brassey's, 1994).

Jones, P. L., "Open Skies: Opportunity for the 1990's," in *Open Skies: Technical; Organizational; Operational: Legal and Political Aspects*, ed. Chestnutt, H., and M. Slack (Toronto: York University Press, 1990).

Jones, P. L., and M. Krasznai, "Open Skies: Achievements and Prospects," in *Verification Report 1992: Yearbook on Arms Control and Environmental Agreements*, ed. Poole, J. B. (London: VERTIC, 1992).

Kalinowski, M. B., et al., "Conclusions on Plutonium Separation from Atmospheric Krypton-85 Measured at Various Distances from the Karlsruhe Reprocessing Plant," *Journal of Environmental Radioactivity* 73, no. 2 (2004).

Kalinowski, M. B., H. Daerr, and M. Kohler, "Measurements of Krypton-85 to Detect Clandestine Plutonium Production," *INESAP Bulletin*, no. 27 (December 2006).

Kemp, R. S., "Initial Analysis of the Detectability of UO2F2 Aerosols Produced by UF6 Released from Uranium Conversion Plants," *Science and Global Security* 16, no. 3 (2008).

Kimball, D. G., "US Suspends CFE Treaty Implementation," *Arms Control Today* 41, (December 2011).

Kissinger, H., *White House Years* (Boston: Little Brown and Company, 1979).

Kivinen, O., and G. Brock., "French Alarm NATO by Pressing for New Defence Alliance," *The Times*, March 25, 1992.

Koulik, S., and R. Kokoski, *Conventional Arms Control: Perspectives on Verification* (Oxford: SIPRI and the Oxford University Press, 1994).

Kramer A. E., and T. Shanker, "Russia Steps Back from Key Arms Treaty," *New York Times*, July 14, 2007.

Krass, A. S., *Verification: How Much Is Enough?* (London and Philadelphia: Taylor and Francis, 1985).

Krasznai, K., "Post Ratification Phase and Entry into Force," in *Open Skies: A Cooperative Approach to Military Transparency and Confidence-Building*, ed. Dunay, P., M. Krasznai, H. Spitzer, R. Wiemker, and W. Wynne (Geneva: UN Institute for Disarmament Research, 2004).

Kraznai, M., H. Spitzer, and W. Wynne, "Regional Applications of the Open Skies Approach," in *Open Skies: A Cooperative Approach to Military Transparency and Confidence-Building*, ed. Dunay, P., and H. Spitzer (Geneva: UN Institute for Disarmament Research, 2004).

Krey, P. W., and K. W. Nicholson, "Atmospheric Sampling and Analysis for the Detection of Nuclear Proliferation," *Journal of Radioanalytical and Nuclear Chemistry* 248, no. 3 (2001).

Krepon, M., "Bureaucrats Slow Open Skies," *Arms Control Today* 20 (December 1990).

Krepon, M., "Open Skies: Testimony to Committee on Foreign Relations," *U.S. Senate, Committee on Foreign Relations* (Washington, DC, March 29, 1990).

Krepon, M., and P. D. Constable, "Confidence-building, Peace-making and Aerial Inspections in the Middle East," Occasional Paper no. 6 (Washington, DC: Henry L. Stimson Center, 1992).

Krepon, M., and J. P. Tracey, "'Open Skies' and UN Peace-keeping," *Survival* 32, no. 3 (May/June 1990).

Krepon, M., and A. Smithson, eds., *Open Skies, Arms Control and Cooperative Security* (New York: St. Martin's Press, 1992).

Kriesberg, L., "Strategies of Negotiating Agreements: The Arab Israeli and American Soviet Cases," *Negotiation Journal* 4, no. 1 (1988): 9–29.

Ladygin, S., "Russia and Open Skies," *Military Parade, Armed Forces MIC and Politics*, November 2001.

Lawson, R., "Soviets Reviewing Proposal That May Close Loop on Open Skies Treaty," *Inside Defense Electronics Weekly Report* 5, no. 22 (May 31, 1991).

"Legitimizing Overflights by Spy Planes? An Interview with Major General Kuklev, First Deputy Chief of the General Staff," *Trud*, March 27, 1990.

Leopold, G., "NATO to Re-Open Negotiations on Open Skies," *Defense News* 6, no. 33 (August 19, 1991).

Leopold, G., "US Begins Effort to Revive Open Skies Talks with Soviet Union," *Defense News* 5, no. 50 (December 10, 1990).

"Letter from the Chairman of the Quantico Vulnerabilities Panel (Rostow) to the President's Special Assistant (Rockefeller). Summary of Recommendations: Quantico Vulnerabilities Panel," U.S. Department of State, *Foreign Relations of the United States, 1955–57, vol.. 5* (Washington, DC: U.S. Government Printing Office, 1988).

Lewis, P., "Dispute between US and Soviets Persists on Intelligence Overflights," *New York Times*, February 17, 1990.

Lewis, P., "Soviet Position at Open Skies Talks Puzzles West," *New York Times*, February 25, 1990.

Lindley, D., "Cooperative Airborne Monitoring: Opening the Skies to Promote Peace, Protect the Environment, and Cope with Natural Disasters," *Contemporary Security Policy* 27, no. 2 (November, 2006).

Lindley, D., *Promoting Peace with Information: Transparency as a Tool of Security Regimes* (Princeton: Princeton University Press, 2007).

Lysyshyn, R. J., "Open Skies Ahead," *NATO Review* 40, no. 1 (February 1992).

MacKenzie, C., "Bush Backs Gorbachev's Reform Bid," *Globe and Mail*, May 13, 1989.

MacKenzie, C., "Few Salute as Bush Unfurls His Foreign Policy," *Globe and Mail*, May 20, 1989.

Marquardt, J. J., "Open Skies and American Primacy," *Diplomacy and Statecraft* 18, no. 3 (September, 2007).

Marquardt, J. J., "Open Skies: Not a Moment Too Soon," *Bulletin of the Atomic Scientists*, January/February 2002.

Marquardt, J. J., *Transparency and American Primacy in World Politics* (Farnham, Surrey: Ashgate Publishing, 2011).

Marquardt, J. J., "Transparency and Security Competition: Open Skies and America's Cold War Statecraft, 1948–1960," *Journal of Cold War Studies* 9, no. 1 (Winter 2007).

Memorandum of Conversation (memcon), DDE and Zhukov, July 20, 1955, *Foreign Relations of the United States*, 1955–57, vol. 5, Austrian State Treaty: Summit and Foreign Ministers Meetings, 1955, ed. W.Z. Slaney (Washington DC: US Government Printing Office, 1987), 409.

Miles, E., "The Structure and Effects of the Decision Making Process in the Seabed Committee and the UNCLOS," *International Organization* 31, no. 2 (1977).

Ministry of Foreign Affairs of Georgia, "Statement of the Ministry of Foreign Affairs of Georgia on a Decision to Cease Performing Its Obligations vis-a-vis the Russian Federation under the Open Skies Treaty," April 5, 2012, on the website of the Georgian embassy to the UK at http://uk.mfa.gov.ge/index.php?lang_id=ENG&sec_id=193&info_id=14626.

Ministry of Foreign Affairs of the Russian Federation, "Statement by Russia's Ministry of Foreign Affairs Regarding Suspension by Russian Federation of Treaty on Conventional Armed Forces in Europe," December 12, 2007. Available at the website of the Russian Foreign Ministry at http://www.mid.ru/Brp_4.nsf/arh/10DA6DD509E4D164C32573AF004CC4BE?OpenDocument.

Molander, J., "Mandated Aerial Inspections: The Iraqi Case," in *Open Skies, Arms Control and Cooperative Security*, ed. Krepon, M., and A. E. Smithson (New York: St. Martin's Press, 1992).

Mooney, P., "Open Skies: Press Analysis," *Canadian Press Wire Service*, March 1, 1990.

Morrison, D. C., "Opening the Skies," *National Journal*, December 9, 1989.

"Moscow Agrees to Aerial Inspection Treaty," *New York Times*, November 6, 1991.

Mrazek, R., "Commentary: Open Skies Benefit All Countries," *Defense News*, May 28, 1990.

*National Security Directive 15: Open Skies*, Secret, June 22, 1989, available at http://bushlibrary.tamu.edu/research/pdfs/nsd/nsd15.pdf.

"NATO Members Agree on Draft Open Skies Pact," *Globe and Mail*, February 17, 1990.

"NATO Offers Soviets New Open Skies Plan," *Aviation Week and Space Technology*, June 10, 1991.

Newhouse, J., *Cold Dawn: The Inside Story of SALT* (London: Pergamon-Brassey's, 1989).

New York Times Editorial Board, "In Verification, Trust," *New York Times*, August 6, 1990.

New York Times Editorial Board, "Soviet Deeds, American Words," *New York Times*, May 14, 1989.

Noble, J., "The Open Skies Treaty Initiative: Prospects for an Agreement and Precedents," Paper given at a Canada-USSR conference entitled *Ending the Cold War: International Law and Global Co-operation in the Era of Perestroika and Disarmament*, Simon Fraser University, Vancouver, B.C., June 20–22, 1990.

North Atlantic Council, *Open Skies Basic Elements*, NATO Press Service, annex to M-2 (89), 46, December 15, 1989.

North Atlantic Treaty Organization, "Declaration of the Heads of State and Government Participating in the Meeting of the North Atlantic Council in Brussels." May 29–30, 1989.

North Atlantic Treaty Organization, Press Service (NATO-PS), "Council Discusses Open Skies and Lessons of the Gulf War," *Atlantic News*, no. 2317, April 26, 1991.

North Atlantic Treaty Organization, Press Service (NATO-PS), *Message from Turburry*, press communique M-1 (90) 29, June 8, 1990.

North Atlantic Treaty Organization, Press Service (NATO-PS), *Open Skies Basic Elements*, annex to M-2(89) 46, December 15, 1989.

North Atlantic Treaty Organization, Press Service (NATO—PS), "Reopening of Open Sky Conference—Baltic Countries as Observers," *Atlantic News*, no. 2349, September 11, 1991.

Olson, J., "Confidence-building Measures to Support the Sunshine Policy," SAND2001–2159P (Albuquerque, NM: Sandia National Laboratories, July 2001).

"Open Skies," Associated Press, November 5, 1991.

Open Skies Conference Secretariat (OSCS), *Amendments to the Open Skies Draft Treaty Text, ICO-CS-06* (Ottawa: Open Skies Conference Secretariat, February 27, 1990).

Open Skies Conference Secretariat (OSCS), *Open Skies Communique, ICO-CS-038* (Ottawa: Open Skies Conference Secretariat, February 13, 1990).

Open Skies Conference Secretariat (OSCS), *Open Skies Draft Treaty Text, ICO-CS-043* (Ottawa: Open Skies Conference Secretariat, February 16, 1990).

Open Skies Conference Secretariat (OSCS), *Record of Proceedings, ICO-CS-029* (Ottawa: Open Skies Conference Secretariat, February 26, 1990).

Open Skies Conference Secretariat (OSCS), *Record Warsaw Treaty Organization; Basic Elements Paper on Open Skies, ICO-CS-011* (Ottawa: Open Skies Conference Secretariat, February 12, 1990).

Open Skies Conference Secretariat (OSCS), *Report of Subsidiary Working Group A to the Open Skies Conference ICO-CS-068* (Ottawa: Open Skies Conference Secretariat, February 27, 1990).

Open Skies Conference Secretariat (OSCS), *Report of Subsidiary Working Group B to the Open Skies Conference, ICO-CS-069* (Ottawa: Open Skies Conference Secretariat, February 27, 1990).

Open Skies Conference Secretariat (OSCS), *Report of Subsidiary Working Group C to the Open Skies Conference, ICO-CS-066* (Ottawa: Open Skies Conference Secretariat, February 27, 1990).

Open Skies Conference Secretariat (OSCS), *Report of Subsidiary Working Group D to the Open Skies Conference, ICO-CS-070* (Ottawa: Open Skies Conference Secretariat, February 27, 1990).

Open Skies Conference Secretariat (OSCS), *Report of Working Group A to Plenary, ICO-CS-107* (Budapest: Open Skies Conference Secretariat, May 10, 1990).

Open Skies Conference Secretariat (OSCS), *Report of Working Group B to Plenary, ICO-CS-108* (Budapest: Open Skies Conference Secretariat, May 10, 1990).

Open Skies Conference Secretariat (OSCS), *Report of Working Group C to Plenary, ICO-CS-109* (Budapest: Open Skies Conference Secretariat, May 10, 1990).

Open Skies Conference Secretariat (OSCS), *Report of Working Group D to Plenary, ICO-CS-110* (Budapest: Open Skies Conference Secretariat, May 10, 1990).

Open Skies Conference Secretariat (OSCS), *Working Papers Distributed in Subsidiary Working Group A, Not Numbered* (Budapest: May 9, 1990).

Open Skies Consultative Commission, *Decisions*, at http://www.state.gov/t/avc/cca/os/c26158.htm.

"Open Skies Parties Drop Deadline for a Deal" [Reuters], *New York Times*, May 5, 1990.

Open Skies Review Conference, "Final Document of the Second Review Conference on the Implementation of the Treaty on Open Skies," OSRC (2) Journal, Agenda Item 4(b), Vienna, June 9, 2010.

Osgood, K., *Total Cold War: Eisenhower's Secret Proposal Battle at Home and Abroad* (Lawrence: University of Kansas Press, 2006).

Parkinson, F. W., "Open Skies: An Assessment of Its Impact and DND and the Canadian Forces," *Canadian Defense Quarterly* (October 1992).

Peel, D., "CFE and Open Skies," *Disarmament Bulletin*, Ottawa, Department of External Affairs, no. 15 (Winter 1990/91).

Petrie, G., and H. Spitzer, "Open Skies: Aerial Observation to Help Prevent Conflicts between Countries," *GEOInformatics*, July/August, 2007.

Pick, H., "Pact Legalises Aerial Spies." *Guardian*, March 24, 1992.

Pinchukov, Y., "Open Skies: A Source of Confidence or Suspicion?" Unpublished Paper, 1990.

Podwig, P., "History and the Current Status of the Russian Early Warning System," *Science and Global Security* 10 (2002).

Ponomarev, M., "Kuklev Elaborates on Military Openness, Security" (Interview with Major General V. Kuklev, Deputy Chief of the USSR General Staff, Armed Force Directorate) *Krasnaya Zvezda*, November 5, 1989 (Translation in FBIS-SOV-89–214, November 7, 1989).

Prados, J., "Open Skies and Closed Minds," in *Cold War Respite: The Geneva Summit of 1955*, ed. Bischof, G., and S. Dockrill (Baton Rouge: Louisiana State University Press, 2000).

Pravada Editorial Board, "Bush's Speech Repeats Offers from Past," *Pravada*, May 16, 1989 (Translation in FBIS, Soviet Union Daily Report, May 17, 1989).

Remnick, D., "Moscow Media Criticize Bush Policy Statement," *Washington Post*, May 17, 1989, A30.

"Re-opening of Open Skies Negotiations—USSR More Flexible," *Atlantic News*, November 8, 1991.

Richelson, J. T., *The US Intelligence Community* (Cambridge, MA: Ballinger, 1985).

Rostow, W. W., *Open Skies: Eisenhower's Proposal of July 21, 1955* (Austin: University of Texas Press, 1982).

Saey, P. R. J., "Ultra-Low-Level Measurements of Argon, Krypton and Radioxenon for Treaty Verification Purposes," *ESARDA Bulletin*, No. 36 (June, 2007).

Sarotte, M. E., *1989: The Struggle to Create Post-Cold War Europe* (Princeton: Princeton University Press, 2009).

Saunders, H., "We Need a Larger Theory of Negotiation: The Importance of Pre-Negotiation Phases," *Negotiation Journal* 1, no. 3 (1985): 249–62.

Schmemann, S., "Kremlin Move Adds to NATO Split," *New York Times*, May 13, 1989.

Sebestyen, V., *Revolution 1989: The Fall of the Soviet Empire* (New York: Vintage Books, 2009).

Shalnev, A., "Interview with Viktor Karpov," *Isvestia*, October 6, 1989.

Sharp, J., "Conventional Arms Control in Europe: Developments and Prospects in 1991," in *SIPRI Yearbook 1992: World Armaments and Disarmaments* (Oxford: SIPRI and the Oxford University Press, 1992).

Shelkov, V., "Interview with Soviet Deputy Foreign Minister V. P. Karpov at the Ottawa

Open Skies Conference," *Pravda*, March 4, 1990 (Translated in Foreign Broadcast Information Service, *Soviet Union Daily Report*, 90, 043, March 5, 1990).

Shultz, G. P., S. Drell, and C. Stubbs, "Modernize the Open Skies Treaty," *New York Times*, March 25, 2012.

Sloss, L., and M. Scott Davies, eds., *A Game for High Stakes: Lessons Learned in Negotiating with the Soviets* (Cambridge: Harvard Press, 1986).

Smith, H., *The Power Game* (New York: Random House, 1988).

Smith, R. J., "Bush Openness Plan a Bow of Symbolism," *Washington Post*, May 13, 1989.

Smith, R. J., and D. Oberdorfer, "Two Alliances Differ on Germany's Future: Open Skies Meeting Was Planned to Deal with Monitoring East-West Military Activities," *Washington Post*, February 12, 1990.

"Soviet Proposal Introduced in the Disarmament Subcommittee: Reduction of Armaments, the Prohibition of Atomic Weapons, and the Elimination of the Threat of New War, 10 May, 1955," in U.S. Arms Control and Disarmament Agency, *Documents on Disarmament, 1945–1959*, vol. 1 (Washington, DC: U.S. Government Printing Office, 1991), 456–67.

Spitzer, H., "The Improvement of Satellite Capabilities and Its Implications for the Open Skies Regime," in *Open Skies: A Cooperative Approach to Military Transparency and Confidence-Building*, ed. Dunay, P., M. Krasznai, H. Spitzer, R. Wiemker, and W. Wynne (Geneva: UN Institute for Disarmament Research, 2004).

Spitzer, H., "News from Open Skies: A Cooperative Treaty Maintaining Military Transparency," *VERTIC Brief, no. 8* (London: VERTIC, February 2009).

Spitzer, H., "Open Skies in Turbulence: A Well-Functioning Treaty Is Endangered by Outside Developments," *Security and Human Rights* 22, no. 4 (Winter 2011).

Spitzer, H., and R. Wiemker, "Technical Preparations for Treaty Implementation," in Dunay, P., and H. Spitzer, "The Open Skies Negotiations and the Open Skies Treaty," in *Open Skies: A Cooperative Approach to Military Transparency and Confidence-Building*, ed. Dunay, P., M. Krasznai, H. Spitzer, R. Wiemker, and W. Wynne (Geneva: UN Institute for Disarmament Research, 2004).

"Statement by President Eisenhower," *The Geneva Conference of Heads of Government, July 18–23, 1955* (Washington DC: Department of State Publication 6046, October 1955).

Stibrany, P., "Airborne and Space-Based Sensors: A Comparison," in *Open Skies: Technical; Organizational; Operational: Legal and Political Aspects*, ed. Chestnutt, H., and M. Slack (Toronto: York University Press, 1990).

Strobel, W., "Open Lands, Open Skies, Closed Issues," *Washington Times*, May 31, 1990.

Strobel, W., "White House Favors Not-Too-Wide Open Skies Proposal," *Washington Times*, July 18, 1989, A10.

"Summit in Washington: Key Sections from the Bush-Gorbachev News Conference," *New York Times*, June 4, 1990.

Swales, N., "Note to the Parliamentary Centre for Foreign Affairs and International Trade," undated (early December 1989).

Tal, D., "Eisenhower's Disarmament Dilemma: From Chance for Peace to Open Skies Proposal," *Diplomacy and Statecraft* 12, no. 2 (June, 2001).

Tal, D., "From the Open Skies Proposal of 1955 to the Norstad Plan of 1960: A Plan Too Far," *Journal of Cold War Studies* 10, no. 4 (Fall 2008).

Talbott, S., *Deadly Gambits* (London: Pan Books, 1984).

TASS, July 19, 1990 (translated in FBIS-SOV, July 20, 1990).

Thomas, E., *Ike's Bluff: President Eisenhower's Secret Battle to Save the World* (New York: Little Brown and Company, 2012).

Tomlin, B. W., "The Stages of Prenegotiation: The Decision to Negotiate North American Free Trade," in *Getting to the Table: The Processes of International Prenegotiation*, ed. Stein, J. G. (Baltimore, MD: Johns Hopkins University Press, 1989).

Toronto Star, "Canadians Fly over Hungary in First Test of Open Skies," *Toronto Star*, January 7, 1990.

Tucker, J., "Back to the Future: The Open Skies Talks," *Arms Control Today* 20, no. 8 (1990).

Tucker, J., "Negotiating Open Skies: A Diplomatic History," in *Open Skies, Open Control and Cooperative Security*, ed. Krepon, M., and A. Smithson (New York: St. Martin's Press, 1992).

Tyler, P., "Agreement Will Open Skies to Reconnaissance Flights," *New York Times*, March 21, 1992.

U.S. Air Force Deputy Chief of Staff for Operations, Atomic Energy Office, Section 1, "U.S. Weather Bureau Report on Alert Number 112 of the Atomic Detection System," September 29, 1949, Top Secret, Source: Harry S. Truman Library, President's Secretary's Files, box 199, NSC-Atomic. Declassified version available at http://www.gwu.edu/~nsarchiv/nukevault/ebb286/doc08.PDF.

U.S. Air Force Instruction 16–604, Implementation of, and Compliance with, the Treaty on Open Skies, March, 28, 2012, at http://www.fas.org/irp/doddir/usaf/afi16–604.pdf.

U.S. Congress, Office of Technology Assessment, *Cooperative Aerial Surveillance in International Agreements, OTA-ISC-480* (Washington, DC: U.S. Government Printing Office, July 1991).

U.S. Department of State, *Change and the Soviet Union, Current Policy, no. 1175* (Washington, DC: U.S. Department of State, Bureau of Public Affairs, 1989).

U.S. Department of State, *Dispatch*, March 30, 1992.

Visuri, P., "Neutral Military Security in a Changing Europe: The Finnish Value," in *The European Neutrals in the 1990s: New Challenges and Opportunities*, ed. Neuhold, H. (Boulder, CO: Westview Press, 1992).

Warnke, P., "Lessons Learned in Bilateral Negotiations," in *A Game for High Stakes: Les-*

*sons Learned in Negotiating with the Soviets*, ed. Sloss, L., and M. Scott Davis (Cambridge: Harvard Press, 1986).

White, S., "Old Enemies Agree to Surveillance Flights," *Financial Times*, March 21, 1992.

Wise, M., "Moscow Moves to Open Skies," *Independent*, November 6, 1991.

Wise, M., "Soviets Back Open Skies Pact," *Washington Post*, November 6, 1991.

Wise, "24 Countries Agree on Open Skies Pact," *Washington Post*, March 21, 1992.

Yost, D. S., "France," in *The Allies and Arms Control*, ed. Hampson, F., H. von Reikhoff, and J. Roper (Baltimore, MD: Johns Hopkins Press, 1992).

Zelikow, P., and C. Rice, *Germany Unified and Europe Transformed: A Study in Statecraft* (Cambridge: Harvard University Press, 1997).

Zhukov, Y., "Open Skies: New Confidence-Building Factors," *Pravda*, November 1, 1989 (Translated in FBIS-SOV089–212, November 3, 1989).

Zubok, V. M., "Soviet Policy Aims at the Geneva Conference, 1955," in *Cold War Respite: The Geneva Summit of 1955*, ed. Bischof, G., and S. Dockrill (Baton Rouge: Louisiana State University Press, 2000).

## INTERVIEWS

Mr. Alex Garroch, various email and telephone interviews, summer of 2012 and February 2013.

Mr. Ross Francis, June 12, 1992, Ottawa.

Mr. Ralph Lysyshyn, various interviews, 1991–92, 2012 Brussels and Ottawa.

Ms. Diana Marvin, various conversations and email, 2012 and 2013, Palo Alto and Washington.

Mr. John Noble, various interviews, 1993, 2012, Ottawa.

Cmdr. F. W. Parkinson, various interviews, Vienna 1991–92 and Ottawa 2012.

Mr. Jason Reiskind, October 13, 1992, Stockholm.

Professor Hartwig Spitzer, interviewed by various emails, 2012–13.

The anonymous interviewees are officials of the Canadian and other governments. All of them took part in the Open Skies negotiation at some stage.

# Index

Abkhazia, 156
Accession formulas, *see* Open Skies membership
ACDA, *see* Arms Control and Disarmament Agency
Adapted CFE Treaty of 1999, 157, 212n23
Aerial monitoring: compared to satellites, 28; of nuclear activity, 161–62; by private companies, 161; Stockholm Document, 16–17. *See also* Cooperative aerial monitoring; Reconnaissance flights
Aircraft: certification, 151, 154–55, 210n10, 211n18; Hercules series, 97, 154–55; hidden sensors, 74; Russian, 133, 155; U2, 15, 178–79n26, 215n47
Aircraft inspections: for illegal sensors, 74, 80; mock certification exercises, 151; operational details, 138, 139, 140, 150; U.S. positions, 30, 71
Aircraft ownership: in CFE aerial inspections, 94; host-country, 14, 29, 88, 120, 128, 152, 155; NATO positions, 37–38; negotiations, 74–75, 102; neutral countries, 16; pool proposal, 34, 37–38, 48–49, 60, 74, 105; requesting country, 30, 36, 37–38, 74, 80, 102, 155; Soviet positions, 34, 48, 60, 74, 79, 88, 95, 105, 128, 155; Stockholm Conference debates, 16; U.S. positions, 30, 105; Western European Union members, 121–22
Air traffic control, 39, 52, 53, 185n13
*Amendments to the Open Skies Draft Treaty Text*, 70
Arms control: Bush-Gorbachev discussions, 93; cooperative aerial monitoring for verification, 22, 44, 161–63, 170, 171–72, 173; nuclear disarmament, 9–10, 11, 12, 162–63, 173; Russian policies, 152; Soviet policies, 12, 99; Strategic Arms Limitation Treaty, 31–32, 56; Strategic Arms Reduction Talks, 44, 93, 167, 198n5; U.S. policies, 19, 162–63, 173. *See also* Conventional Forces in Europe Treaty; Weapons of Mass Destruction
Arms Control and Disarmament Agency (ACDA), U.S., 27, 165
Austria, Open Skies negotiations and, 118. *See also* Neutral countries; Vienna Conference

Baker, James: Irkutsk Formula, 96, 97, 98, 99, 100; meetings with Canadians, 21–22; Ottawa Conference speech, 59; Shevardnadze meetings, 6, 33, 81, 82–83, 95–96, 99, 100, 167
Baltic countries: invitation to Vienna Conference, 108, 202n77; Open Skies

implementation and, 153; Open Skies membership, 107–8, 155
Basic Elements Paper (BEP), NATO: development, 36–37, 53, 166; draft treaty and, 53–55, 166; Mission Operations, 40; Ottawa Conference negotiations, 64; political aspects, 47–48, 145; technical aspects, 47, 48, 56, 138
Basic Elements Paper, Warsaw Treaty Organization, 61, 63
Belarus: Open Skies negotiations and, 129–30; Open Skies Treaty ratification, 149; passive quotas, 136; quotas combined with Russia, 136, 154, 210–11n12
Belgium, shared sensor pod, 211n17
BEP, *see* Basic Elements Paper
Blackwill, Robert, 19, 165
Bryson, John, 102–3
Budapest, preparatory meeting for Ottawa Conference, 51, 53
Budapest Conference: absence of prenegotiation, 89; informal negotiations, 87–88, 91; issues, 83–88; meeting schedule, 87; obstacles, 4–5; opening, 83; results, 88–90; sensor exhibit proposed, 82, 196n125; treaty signing target date, 81, 88–89; working groups, 83–87, 114–15, 116
Bulganin, Nikolai, 13
Bulgaria: aircraft and sensor certification, 155; Ottawa Conference delegation, 71. *See also* Non–Soviet Warsaw Pact countries
Bureaucracies: constraints on negotiations, 31–32, 76, 95; political leadership and, 3, 25, 165–66; Soviet, 4, 33, 95, 99, 103; of United States, 4, 31–32, 35, 92–93, 94, 95, 96, 98, 165–66. *See also* Intelligence community
Bureaucratic politics, 25–27, 31
Bush, George H. W.: meetings with Canadians, 21–22, 23; motives for Open Skies, xvi, 22; Open Skies proposal (Texas A&M speech), 22, 23–24, 35, 57, 165–66; summit meeting with Gorbachev (1990), 6, 93, 167; view of U.S.-Soviet relations, 18, 19, 23
Bush administration: arms control policies, 19; interagency politics, 25–26; leaks, 29; lobbying of NATO members, 24–25; National Security Directive 15, 27; national security team, 18–20, 27, 165–66; Open Skies discussions, 19–30, 32, 35; opponents of Open Skies, 4, 24, 57; strategic review, 18–19, 23. *See also* Bureaucracies; Open Skies negotiations

Cameras, *see* Sensor technology
Canada: ambassador to Soviet Union, 31; Budapest Conference delegation, 85, 86; Chief of Defence Staff, 126; Department of External Affairs, 20, 21, 23; as depository state, 151; draft Open Skies treaty, 53–55, 70; External Affairs minister, 21, 22, 30, 34, 65–66; interest in Open Skies, 20–22; links to Hungary during negotiations, 32, 33, 48; lobbying for Open Skies, 21–22, 23, 24–25, 30–31, 57–58, 165–66, 167–68; negotiating approach, 55; Open Skies proposal (1955) and, 14; Ottawa Conference delegation, 76–77, 78; papers and nonpapers in negotiations, 93–94, 98, 124–25, 139, 206n57; quotas, 45, 151, 208n35; refueling facilities, 33; shared sensor pod, 211n17; support of Grand Compromise, 93–94; trial overflight of, 126, 206n65; Verification Research Unit, 23; Vienna Conference delegation, 114, 116, 124–25, 128, 129, 135, 139. *See also* Ottawa Conference
Canadian Armed Forces, trial overflight of Hungary, 52–53, 125–26
CBMs, *see* Confidence-building Measures
Central and Eastern Europe: NATO expansion, 152, 153, 155; overflight

quotas, 124, 136, 137; overflights of former Warsaw Pact allies, 47, 73, 124, 136, 137, 153; regional crises, 148. *See also* Non–Soviet Warsaw Pact countries; Political change in Europe; Small states; Warsaw Treaty Organization; *and individual countries*

CFE Treaty, *see* Conventional Forces in Europe Treaty

Clark, Joe, 21, 22, 30, 34

COCOM, *see* Coordinating Committee on Export Controls

Cold War: bloc-to-bloc negotiations, 46, 116, 169–70; end of, 148, 160; U.S.-Soviet relations in 1950s, 9–10, 11. *See also* Political change in Europe

Comprehensive Test Ban Treaty, 152, 163

Conference on Security and Cooperation in Europe (CSCE): Confidence-building Measures, 41–42, 143; Conflict Prevention Centre, 124, 125, 143, 144, 206n57, 206n61; former Soviet republics as members, 129, 207n13; Helsinki ministerial meeting (March 1992), 110, 112, 132, 145, 147; ministerial meeting (Jan. 1992), 129; Paris Summit, 98; rules of procedure, 50–51; U.S. view of, 41–42. *See also* Conventional Forces in Europe Treaty; Neutral countries; Organization for Security and Cooperation in Europe

Conference on Security and Cooperation in Europe (CSCE), Open Skies link: Conflict Prevention Centre, 143, 144, 206n61; Cyprus issue and, 142–46; French position, 5, 43, 44, 60, 65, 129, 142–44, 145; future membership, 126, 142, 143–44, 146, 154; "joker" quotas and, 124–25, 131; members represented at Open Skies negotiations, 42–43, 107, 115; Ministerial Declaration on Open Skies, 146; NATO discussions, 40–43, 145; OSCC participation, 146; secretariat services, 107; Turkish position, 60, 143; U.S. positions, 5, 41–42, 126, 143. *See also* Neutral countries and Open Skies

Confidence-building Measures (CBMs): of CSCE, 41–42, 143; in future, 1; Open Skies as, xvi, 44, 45, 47, 72–73, 169, 173; Stockholm Document, 16–17. *See also* Cooperative aerial monitoring

Conflict Prevention Centre (CPC), 124, 125, 143, 144, 206n57, 206n61

Conventional Forces in Europe (CFE) Treaty: Adapted, 157, 212n23; Aerial Inspection Protocol talks, 94–95, 96, 97–98; implementation dispute, 98–100, 103–4; NATO positions, 94; negotiations, 5, 6, 27, 50, 88, 90; Open Skies data used in monitoring, 6, 41, 149; relationship to Open Skies, 6, 42, 43–44, 94–95, 96, 99–100, 168, 171–72; Russian ratification, 152; Russian suspension, 148, 156–57; signing, 97–98; Soviet positions, 94

Cooperative aerial monitoring: advantages over satellites, xvi, xvii, 1–2; within alliances, 46–47, 73, 82; border area overspill, 118–19, 205n30; cooperative aspect, 2; costs, 1–2, 28, 123–24, 135, 152, 153, 172; crews, 39, 138, 139–40, 150; demonstration flight over Hungary and Romania, 104; discussions in 1950s, 10; entry and exit points, 40; flight plans, 39–40, 119–20, 138, 140, 208n38; flight safety, 39–40, 52; future use of, xvi–xvii, 1, 158–63, 170–73; goals, 170–71; "Golden Rules," 170; host-country observers, 37, 40, 120; mission plans, 54, 208n38; notice periods and timelines, 30, 36, 38–40, 46, 138–41, 185n13; operational issues, 138–41, 150–51, 154–55, 157, 171; refueling and maintenance facilities, 33, 40; regional applications, 158–59, 160, 170, 213–14n37; shared flights, 137, 208n35, 208n37; transited countries, 121; trial flights, 52–53, 125–26,

206n65; triggers, 46. *See also* Aircraft inspections; Aircraft ownership; Data-sharing issue; Open Skies; Quotas; Sensor technology; Territorial scope issue
Coordinating Committee on Export Controls (COCOM), 82, 85
CPC, *see* Conflict Prevention Centre
Crisis management, use of overflights, 124, 156
CSCE, *see* Conference on Security and Cooperation in Europe
Cuba, Soviet bases, 49. *See also* Third-country bases
Cyprus: Open Skies membership request, 155, 156, 157–58; Ottawa Conference observers, 67
Cyprus issue: compromises, 143–46; future Open Skies membership, 65, 142; as obstacle, 5, 7, 42–43, 55, 67, 126, 142, 145, 157–58; at Open Skies Review Conferences, 156, 157–58; in provisional application period, 154; representation in negotiations, 42–43, 60, 107, 108, 115, 130, 157
Czechoslovakia: breakup, 153; Budapest Conference delegation, 84; Grand Compromise, 79–80, 93–94; Ottawa Conference delegation, 78, 79–80, 93–94. *See also* Non–Soviet Warsaw Pact countries
Czech Republic, 153, 211n18

Data processing: equipment, 78; joint, 77, 86; Soviet proposals, 48–49, 60, 64, 67, 77; tests, 151; by United States, 86
Data-sharing issue: within alliances, 15–16, 77; at Budapest Conference, 86; in CFE context, 94, 95; in future, xvii; in Hungarian-Romanian Treaty, 104; implementation, xv; NATO positions, 38, 77, 103; at Ottawa Conference, 77–79, 80; of raw data, 78, 80, 86, 103; Soviet proposals, 64, 77, 86; U.S. positions, 37, 41, 77–78
Department of Defense (DOD), U.S., 29, 86, 158
Department of External Affairs, Canada, 20, 21, 23
DOD, *see* Department of Defense
Drell, Sidney D., 162
Dulles, John Foster, 10–11, 177n9

Eastern Europe, *see* Central and Eastern Europe; Political change in Europe; *and individual countries*
East Germany, political change, 41. *See also* Non–Soviet Warsaw Pact countries
Eisenhower, Dwight D.: Four Power Summit (1955), 9, 11–14; nuclear weapons policies, 9–10; Paris Summit, 15; U2 aircraft shot down by Soviets, 15. *See also* Open Skies proposal (1955)
Environmental monitoring, xvii, 156, 160–61
Estonia, *see* Baltic countries
Europe: flood damage, 161; importance of Open Skies, 6, 99–100, 101–2, 168, 172. *See also* Central and Eastern Europe; Conference on Security and Cooperation in Europe; Conventional Forces in Europe Treaty; *and individual countries*
European Union, 145–46
Export controls, 82, 85

Finland: active quotas, 136; constitution, 119; Helsinki ministerial meeting (March 1992), 110, 112, 132, 145, 147; mistrust of Russia, 120–21; Open Skies implementation and, 146, 153; Open Skies membership request, 154, 155; Open Skies negotiations and, 118–21, 129–30, 146
Foreign ministers: NATO meetings, 47–48, 81, 93; at Ottawa Conference, 59–62, 65–68. *See also* Helsinki ministerial meeting; Soviet Foreign Ministry; *and individual countries*

Four Power Summit (1955), 9, 11–14. *See also* Open Skies proposal
France: foreign minister at Ottawa Conference, 60; Four Power Summit (1955), 9, 11–14; interest in Open Skies, 145, 167–68; objections to bloc-to-bloc approach, 42, 46, 60, 73; Paris Summit, 15; pro-CSCE agenda, 5, 42, 129, 145; shared sensor pod, 211n17; Vienna Conference delegation, 113, 116, 124–25, 129, 131, 135, 136, 137, 142–45, 146; Western European Union and, 121, 137
France, Open Skies positions: compromises, 143–45; on CSCE as framework, 5, 42, 129, 142–43, 145; on CSCE role in regime operation, 125, 131, 142–43; inflexibility, 47; in NATO Basic Elements Paper, 47–48; on neutral country inclusion in negotiations, 5, 43, 60, 107; on neutral country membership, 4, 65; objections to bloc-to-bloc approach, 4, 5, 42; at Ottawa Conference, 56–57, 60, 65; on quotas, 46, 82, 124–25, 131, 144; reaction to 1955 proposal, 13, 14; relationship to CFE Treaty, 43–44
Francis, Ross, 50–51

Garthoff, Raymond, 31–32
Genscher, Hans-Dietrich, 105
Georgia: Open Skies membership, 155; war with Russia, 156, 157
Germany: aircraft, 161, 210n10, 211n18; foreign minister, 105; interest in Open Skies, 145, 167–68; Open Skies proposal (1955) and, 14; Open Skies Review Conference, 155–56; reunification, 59, 66; Vienna Conference delegation, 113, 116, 132, 135, 137, 139, 143; Western European Union and, 121, 122, 135, 137. *See also* East Germany
Global Positioning System (GPS) devices, 120
Golovko, Yevgeni, 109, 112, 113, 128, 203n80
Gorbachev, Mikhail: coup attempt and, 6, 106; foreign policy, 18, 62, 89, 104; *glasnost*, 20, 21, 22, 27; interest in Open Skies, 98; political change in satellite states and, 41; relations with West, 22; response to Open Skies proposal, xvi, 33–34, 37; Stockholm Conference and, 16; summit meeting with Bush (1990), 93, 167
GPS, *see* Global Positioning System
Grand Compromise, 5, 6, 79–80, 93–94, 95
Greece: foreign minister at Ottawa Conference, 67; mistrust of Turkey, 142; Open Skies regime expansion issue and, 142, 143–44; Ottawa Conference delegation, 65; shared sensor pod, 211n17; Vienna Conference delegation, 131, 142, 143–44, 145–46. *See also* Cyprus issue
Greek-Cypriot government, *see* Cyprus

Hawes, John H., 38, 41, 44–45, 95–96
Helsinki ministerial meeting (March 1992), 110, 112, 132, 145, 147
Host-country observers, 37, 40, 120
Hungary: aircraft and sensor certification, 154; bilateral Open Skies Treaty, 104, 155; borders opened (1989), 41; Budapest Conference delegation, 84, 88; as depository state, 151; foreign minister at Ottawa Conference, 61; interest in Open Skies, 32–33, 48, 167–68; links to Canada during negotiations, 32, 33, 48; NATO membership, 155; preparatory meeting for Ottawa Conference, 51, 53; Soviet bases, 53; trial overflight by Canada, 52–53, 125–26; trial overflight of Canada, 126, 206n65; Vienna Conference delegation, 124–25. *See also* Budapest Conference; Non–Soviet Warsaw Pact countries
Hurricanes, 160–61

India, potential for cooperative overflights, 158, 159, 213–14n37

Information sharing, *see* Data-sharing issue
INF Treaty, *see* Intermediate Nuclear Forces Treaty
Inspection systems: in Conventional Forces in Europe Treaty, 27; Eisenhower's proposal, 11–13; in Intermediate Nuclear Forces Treaty, 16, 18; in Stockholm Document, 16–17, 18. *See also* Aircraft inspections
Intelligence, *see* National Technical Means; Reconnaissance flights; Signals Intelligence
Intelligence community, UK, 76
Intelligence community, U.S.: agencies, 28; CFE negotiations and, 95; collectors, 27–28, 71, 75, 76, 77–78, 86, 100, 105; as constraint on negotiating flexibility, 31, 32; influence on negotiating positions, 76, 77, 86, 90, 96; internal divisions, 27–29, 30, 71; National Technical Means, xvi, 2, 31, 172; opponents of Open Skies, 20, 57, 92–93, 165–66, 169; protectors, 28–29, 30, 39–40, 71, 73–74
Intermediate Nuclear Forces (INF) Treaty (1987), 16, 18, 25–26
Iraq, aerial monitoring, 159, 162, 215n47
Ireland, Open Skies negotiations and, 118
Irkutsk Formula, 96, 97, 98, 99, 100, 167
Italy: Open Skies negotiations, 42, 72, 139; shared sensor pod, 211n17

Japan, U.S. bases, 34, 49. *See also* Third-country bases
Joint Chiefs of Staff (JCS), policy office, 29
"Joker" quotas, 82, 124–25, 131, 144

Karpov, Viktor: at Budapest Conference, 88; Canadians and, 31, 103; Hawes meeting, 95–96; on hidden sensors, 74; at Ottawa Conference, 66, 67, 68, 76, 79, 80; on treaty deadline, 51
KGB, 106
Khrushchev, Nikita, 13, 14, 15, 178–79n26
Korea, potential for cooperative overflights, 158
Krepon, Michael, 83
Kyrgyzstan, Open Skies membership application, 155

Lake Balaton, Hungary, 88, 89
Latvia, *see* Baltic countries
Legal issues, 68, 71, 116, 123
Lithuania, *see* Baltic countries
Lockheed Corporation, Hercules series aircraft, 97, 154–55
Lysyshyn, Ralph, 20–21, 23, 51, 54, 102–3

Marquardt, J. J., 159–60
MBFR, *see* Mutual and Balanced Force Reduction
"Measurement and signatures intelligence" (MASINT) devices, 75
Media: Canadian lobbying in, 30; interest in Open Skies, 14, 53, 89, 97; reaction to Bush proposal, 24
Meech Lake, 79
Middle East, potential for cooperative overflights, 158, 159. *See also* Iraq
Millikan, Max, 10
Mulroney, Brian, xvi, 3–4, 21–22, 23, 31, 34
Mutual and Balanced Force Reduction (MBFR), 42, 115, 204n17

National Security Agency (NSA), U.S., 28
National Security Council (NSC), U.S., 19–20
National Security Directive (NSD) 15, 27
National Technical Means (NTM), xvi, 2, 15–16, 31, 172
NATO, *see* North Atlantic Treaty Organization
Negotiations: bloc-to-bloc, 5, 42, 116, 169–70; centrifugal pressures, 69; deadlines, 132; deferred issues, 134; inefficiency, 69–70, 80–81, 114, 122–23; informal, 96–97, 115; as ongoing, 145;

working groups, 114. *See also* Open Skies negotiations
Netherlands: shared sensor pod, 211n17; Vienna Conference delegation, 124–25
Neutral and Non-aligned (NNA) observers, at Vienna Conference, 118–21, 122
Neutral countries, in CFE process, 43–44. *See also* Conference on Security and Cooperation in Europe
Neutral countries and Open Skies: active observer status, 107–8, 146; exclusion from Open Skies negotiations, 41; French positions, 4, 5, 43, 60, 65, 107; future membership, 4, 43, 65, 142; inclusion in Open Skies negotiations, 5, 7, 42–43, 60, 107–9, 115, 129–30, 131; inclusion in Open Skies regime, 108; increasing roles in negotiations, 5, 107–9; membership procedures, 143–44, 153–54; observers at Ottawa Conference, 43, 56, 67; observers at Vienna Conference, 107–8, 118–21, 122, 146; OSCC participation, 146; quotas for, 82; U.S. positions, 41, 43, 126. *See also* Cyprus; Cyprus issue
Newhouse, J., 26, 56
News media, *see* Media
*New York Times*, 30
NNA, *see* Neutral and Non-aligned observers
Noble, John, 20–21, 49–50, 54, 61, 63–64, 65–66
Non-aligned countries, *see* Neutral countries
Non–Soviet Warsaw Pact (NSWP) countries: bilateral treaties, 104, 124, 155; cooperation during Open Skies negotiations, 117; differences from Soviet positions, 5, 49, 60–63, 64, 66, 90; Ottawa Conference delegations, 60–63, 64, 66, 70, 73, 75, 76–77, 78, 79; sensor technology available to, 76–77, 81–82, 83, 84–86. *See also* Central and Eastern Europe; Warsaw Treaty Organization; *and individual countries*
North Atlantic Assembly, *see* Senior Political Committee
North Atlantic Treaty Organization (NATO): all members included in Open Skies regime, 21; Budapest Conference delegations, 88; Conventional Forces in Europe Treaty and, 94; data sharing within, 77; disagreements within, 4, 5, 47–48, 70–71, 81, 85; draft Open Skies treaty, 53–55, 70, 166; expansion, 152, 153, 155; foreign ministers at Ottawa Conference, 59–60, 65–67; French view of, 42; German reunification, 59, 66; members lobbied on Open Skies proposal, 24–25; ministerial meetings, 47–48, 81, 93; missile defense system, 157; Open Skies negotiation strategy, 101; Open Skies positions, 32, 35, 93–94, 98, 102–3, 105; Ottawa Conference delegations, 5, 69, 76; Short-range Nuclear Forces, 19, 20, 21, 25; Summit (1989), 19, 21, 25; Vienna Conference caucuses, 117–18, 135
NPT, *see* Nuclear Non-proliferation Treaty
NSA, *see* National Security Agency
NSC, *see* National Security Council
NSWP, *see* Non–Soviet Warsaw Pact countries
NTM, *see* National Technical Means
Nuclear fuel, xvii
Nuclear Non-proliferation Treaty (NPT), 162
Nuclear power stations, 126
Nuclear weapons: detection of activity, xvi–xvii, 161–62; disarmament talks in 1950s, 9–10, 11, 12; Obama's disarmament proposal, 162–63, 173; Short-range Nuclear Forces, 19, 20, 21, 25; test bans, 163. *See also* Weapons of Mass Destruction

Obama, Barack, 162–63, 173
Obama administration, 212n23
Open Skies Consultative Commission (OSCC): CSCE Conflict Prevention Centre and, 144; Cyprus issue and, 155, 156, 157–58; decisions, 149–50, 211n19; emergency overflight procedures, 144; environmental monitoring seminars, 160; first session procedures, 146, 147, 209n60; functions, 149; informal groups, 146, 147, 149, 210n9; issues referred to, 134, 135–36, 146, 147, 149–50; neutral participants, 146, 153; new member applications, 143–44, 149, 153–54, 155, 156, 157–58; quota revisions, 153; "Sensor Guidance Document," 149–50; Turkish delegation, 209n60; working groups, 154, 157
Open Skies membership: applications, 149, 153–54, 155, 156; debates on future accession procedures, 65, 128–31, 142, 143–44; of former Soviet republics, 107–8, 144, 154, 155; future expansion, xvii, 41, 67; NATO positions, 40–43, 70; neutral countries, 4, 43, 65, 142, 143–44, 153–54; restricted to alliance members, 37, 41; U.S. positions, 37, 41; veto power, 65, 142, 157. *See also* Cyprus issue
Open Skies negotiations: absence of agreed goals, 26, 57, 58, 75, 90–91, 166; beginning, 33–34; Bush administration proposal, 19–30; challenges, 62–63, 113, 140–41, 165–67; compromises and trade-offs, 91, 96–97, 101, 102–3, 105–6, 110–11, 132, 141–42, 143; conclusion, 146–47; deadlines, 51–52, 110, 112–13, 132; end-game phase, 113, 118, 120–21, 125, 131–46; factors in success, 167–70; Grand Compromise, 5, 6, 79–80; hiatus after Budapest Conference, 6, 89–90, 92, 95–98, 110; informal consultations (1990–91), 95–97, 99, 100, 102–3, 104–5; interrelationships of details, 123, 127, 132; Irkutsk Formula, 96, 97, 98, 99, 100, 167; legal issues, 68, 71, 116, 123, 195n108; NATO members' support, 25; objectives, 26; obstacles, 4–5, 80–81, 90–91; participating countries, 41–43; political change and, 110, 128–31, 141, 142, 160, 168–70; superpower tactics, 90–91, 92–93. *See also* Budapest Conference; Cyprus issue; Ottawa Conference; Vienna Conference; *and individual countries*
Open Skies proposal (1955): allied reactions, 13, 14; Bush on, 24; Canadian interest, 14; Eisenhower's statements, 11–13; motives, 2, 9, 159–60, 175–76n1; origins, 10–11; political leadership, 9; Soviet reaction, 13–14, 15, 34, 178–79n26; talks, 14
Open Skies regime: advantages for small states, 20–21, 25, 30; bilateral treaties, 104, 124, 155; Bush proposal, 22, 23–24, 57, 165–66; expansion, 109, 142–44, 153–54, 155; flexibility, 125; future applications, xvi–xvii, 44, 156, 158–63, 170–73; implementation, 149–54, 156, 163; malaise, 163, 172; number of flights, xv; as stand-alone regime, 37, 41. *See also* Cooperative aerial monitoring; Open Skies membership; Open Skies Treaty
Open Skies Review Conferences: of 2005, 155–56; of 2010, 157–58
Open Skies Treaty: completion, 146–47; depository states, 151; entry into force, xvi, 148, 149, 154–55; lessons, 160, 170–73; as model, xvii, 160; Preamble, 116, 119, 205n27; ratification, xvi, 149, 151–53; signing, 7, 147. *See also* Open Skies regime
Organization for Security and Cooperation in Europe (OSCE), 5, 153, 154. *See also* Conference on Security and Cooperation in Europe
Organization of American States, 158
OSCC, *see* Open Skies Consultative Commission

OSCE, *see* Organization for Security and Cooperation in Europe
Ottawa Conference: absence of prenegotiations between blocs, 4, 35, 50, 51, 56, 57, 166–67, 168; Canadian goals, 51–52; communique negotiations, 63–68; compromises and trade-offs, 69, 70, 76–77, 78–80; differences among NATO allies, 56–57; draft treaty, 53–55, 70–71, 79, 81, 166; foreign ministers, 59–62, 65–68; German reunification negotiations, 59, 66; Grand Compromise, 5, 6, 79–80, 93–94, 95; heads of delegation meetings, 69, 79–80; inefficiency, 69–70, 80–81; informal negotiations, 69, 70, 79–80, 91; intersessional period, 81–83; issues, 68, 71, 72–79; meeting schedule, 69, 192n58; NATO caucuses, 69; obstacles, 4–5, 80–81; participating countries, 43, 56; plenary sessions, 69, 71; prenegotiations within NATO, 35, 36–48, 50, 54–55, 56; preparatory meeting, 51, 53; proposal, 34; rules of procedure, 50–51, 56; timing, 34, 50, 52, 55–56, 57, 168; translators, 81; working groups, 68–79, 114–15, 116; WTO Basic Elements Paper, 61, 63
Overflights, *see* Cooperative aerial monitoring; Reconnaissance flights

Pakistan, potential for cooperative overflights, 158, 159, 213–14n37
Paris Summit, 15
Peel, David, 98
Philippines, U.S. bases, 34, 49. *See also* Third-country bases
Poland: foreign minister at Ottawa Conference, 68; Ottawa Conference delegation, 195n108; quota negotiations, 137. *See also* Non–Soviet Warsaw Pact countries
Political change in Europe: breakup of Czechoslovakia, 153; in East Germany, 41; effects on Turkey, 130, 145; effects on Warsaw Treaty Organization, 5, 42, 46, 47, 48, 49, 61–62, 118; end of Cold War, 148, 160; German reunification, 59, 66; Hungarian view, 33; Open Skies negotiations and, 40–41, 110, 128–31, 141, 142, 160, 168–70; Soviet breakup, 118, 128–29, 145
Political leadership of Open Skies: bureaucracies and, 3, 25, 165–66; by Bush, 18, 23, 25, 35, 93; by Gorbachev, 93; importance, 111, 167–68; by Mulroney, 21–22, 23, 31; in 1955, 9; in period following Budapest Conference, 6, 93, 111; shared goals, 6
Powers, Francis Gary, 15
*Pravda*, 24, 76
Psychological warfare, 13–14, 176n2
Putin, Vladimir, 153

Quantico panel, 10, 15, 176n3
Quotas: active, 45–46, 87, 135–37; allocation, 135–37, 208n35; in CFE Treaty, 42, 94; compromises, 80, 103; de-confliction exercise, 136–37; flexibility, 103; French proposal, 82, 124–25; "jokers," 82, 124–25, 131, 144; NATO positions, 37, 45–46, 103; negotiations on, 44–47, 55, 72–73, 87, 122, 135–37; for neutral countries, 82; passive, 45–47, 72, 82, 87, 112, 124, 136, 151; requests, 143; revisions, 153; Soviet proposals, 87, 112; U.S. proposal, 44–46

Radar, *see* Sensor technology; Synthetic aperture radar
Reagan administration, relations with Soviet Union, 18
Reconnaissance flights, by United States, 14–15, 178–79n26, 215n47. *See also* Cooperative aerial monitoring; Sensor technology
Reconnaissance satellites, 153. *See also* National Technical Means; Satellite imagery

*Resumption of the Open Skies Conference*, 102–3
Rockefeller, Nelson, 10–11, 176n2
Romania: aircraft, 211n18; bilateral Open Skies Treaty, 104, 155; NATO membership, 155; Ottawa Conference delegation, 64; overflights by, 156
Romanov, Colonel, 109, 203n80
Russia: aircraft, 133, 154, 155; arms control treaties, 152; benefits of Open Skies, 153; Conventional Forces in Europe Treaty and, 148, 152, 156–57; Duma, xvi, 152, 153; mistrust of, 119–21; Open Skies implementation and, 151, 155; Open Skies Treaty ratification, xvi, 149, 152–53; overflights of, 155, 156; passive quotas, 136, 137, 152, 153, 208n35; reconnaissance satellites, 153; sensor technology, 132–33, 154, 155; trial overflights, 152; Vienna Conference delegation, 123, 128–29, 132–34; war in Georgia, 156, 157. *See also* Soviet Union
Russian military: aircraft, 133; in Georgia, 156, 157; Open Skies implementation and, 121, 122, 152, 153, 155; Open Skies negotiations and, 123, 128, 132–34; sensor calibration, 123, 133. *See also* Soviet military

SALT, *see* Strategic Arms Limitation Treaty
Samson Pod, 97
SAR, *see* Synthetic aperture radar
Satellite imagery: aerial monitoring compared to, xvi, xvii, 1–2, 28; costs, 1–2; development, 15. *See also* National Technical Means
Scowcroft, Brent, 20
Senior Political Committee (SPC): American "straw man" paper, 36–37, 44–45; Canadian paper on compromises (1990), 93–94; Open Skies deliberations, 32, 35, 36–47, 93–94, 99, 100–102; Ottawa Conference follow-up, 81–82
Sensor technology: Budapest exhibit proposed, 82, 196n125; calibration procedures, 97, 120–21, 122, 123, 133, 134, 149–50; certification, 149–51, 154–55; in CFE aerial inspections, 94, 95; covers, 121; equal availability, 5, 64–65, 76–77, 78, 80, 81–82, 84–85, 102–3, 109–10, 133; experts, 76, 85, 115–16, 133, 150–51; export regulations, 82, 85; in future, xvi–xvii, 102, 172; Grand Compromise, 5, 6, 79–80, 93–94, 95; hidden, 74, 80; host-country monitors and, 40; in Hungarian-Romanian Treaty, 104; NATO positions, 38, 102–3; negotiations on, 67, 74–77, 83–86, 123, 133–34; pods, 97, 121, 154–55, 199–200n23, 211n17; Russian, 132–33, 154, 155; shared by WEU members, 121–22; Soviet and Russian proposals, 64, 75–76, 79, 82–84, 85–86, 100, 123, 132–33; technical issues, xvi, 65, 97, 133–34; test targets, 77, 120–21, 122, 134, 151; of United Kingdom, 86, 155; of United States, 77–78, 86, 96, 97, 154, 158, 172; U.S. positions, 5, 36, 109–10; Western, on Soviet aircraft, 96, 97, 105
Sensor technology capabilities: all-weather, day/night, 64–65, 67, 75, 80, 82, 93–94, 95, 102; comparable, 81, 83, 84–85, 132–33; for environmental monitoring, 161; quality, 64; SIGINT, 29–30, 36, 74; technical characteristics, xv, 77, 84, 85, 102, 109, 119, 150; upgrading, 157, 163, 172; verification, 77, 120
Sensor types: digital, 126, 155, 211n19; electro-optical, 75, 102, 150, 151; negotiations on, 75, 76, 102; thermal, 150–51; video cameras, 104, 151. *See also* Synthetic aperture radar
Shevardnadze, Eduard: Baker meetings, 6, 33, 81, 82–83, 95–96, 99, 100, 167; at Bush-Gorbachev summit, 93; Clark meeting, 34; at Ottawa Conference, 60, 61, 63, 66, 67–68; resignation, 99

Short-range Nuclear Forces (SNF), 19, 20, 21, 25
Signals Intelligence (SIGINT): electronic, 28; sensors banned from overflights, 29–30, 36, 38; sensor technology, 29–30, 36, 74
Slovakia, 153
Small states: benefits of Open Skies, 20–21, 25, 30; inclusion in Open Skies regime, 21, 25; influence, 113–14; interest in Open Skies, 168; Ottawa Conference delegations, 69, 116; overflight quotas, 45, 124–25; at Vienna Conference, 113–14, 116–17, 129–30, 141–42. *See also* Neutral countries
Smith, Hedrick, 145
SNF, *see* Short-range Nuclear Forces
Soviet Army, 98. *See also* Soviet military
Soviet Defense Ministry, 103, 109. *See also* Soviet military
Soviet Foreign Ministry, 65, 68, 90, 103, 109. *See also* Karpov, Viktor; Shevardnadze, Eduard
Soviet military: in Baltic countries, 107; bases in third countries, 49, 53, 61; capabilities, 10, 14, 62; CFE Treaty implementation dispute, 98–100, 103–4; coup attempt, 6, 106; opposition to Open Skies, 49, 68, 80, 99, 101, 104, 169; Ottawa Conference delegation, 65, 74, 76; Vienna Conference delegation, 109. *See also* Russian military
Soviet Union: agreement on Open Skies negotiations, 33–34; arms control policies, 12, 99; Budapest Conference delegation, 83–84, 85–86, 87–88; bureaucracy, 4, 33, 95, 99, 103; Conventional Forces in Europe Treaty and, 94; coup attempt, 6, 106; dissolution, 118, 128–29, 145; former republics, 107–8, 128–31, 144, 145, 154, 155, 157, 207n13; Four Power Summit (1955), 9, 11–14; *glasnost*, 20, 21, 22, 27; nuclear disarmament proposals, 12; nuclear weapons, 162; Ottawa Conference delegation, 63–65, 66, 67–68, 70, 72–76, 79, 80, 81; passive quotas, 45, 72–73, 87; political change, 89; Reagan administration and, 18; secrecy, 9, 10, 14, 15; Stockholm Conference and, 16–17; U.S. reconnaissance flights over, 14–15, 178–79n26; Vienna Conference delegation, 106, 109, 110, 112, 113, 203n80. *See also* Cold War; Gorbachev, Mikhail; Russia; Warsaw Treaty Organization
Soviet Union, Open Skies positions: on aircraft ownership, 34, 48, 60, 74, 79, 88, 95, 105, 128, 155; caution, 4; compromises, 112; on data processing, 48–49, 60, 64, 67, 77; on data-sharing, 64, 77, 86; internal debates, 101, 103; Irkutsk Formula, 96, 97, 98, 99, 100, 167; negotiation tactics, 90–91; Open Seas and Open Space proposals, 42, 60, 67; before Ottawa Conference, 48–50, 51, 56, 166–67; at Ottawa Conference, 57, 60, 62, 63–64, 66, 67–68, 70, 72–76; on quotas, 72–73, 87, 112; reactions to Bush proposal, xvi, 24, 33–34, 35; reaction to Eisenhower's Open Skies proposal, 13–14, 15, 34, 178–79n26; on sensor technology, 64, 79, 82–84, 85–86, 100; on territorial scope, 60, 73–74, 87, 112. *See also* Third-country bases
Spain: Open Skies negotiations, 42, 72; shared sensor pod, 211n17
SPC, *see* Senior Political Committee
Spy satellites, 153. *See also* National Technical Means; Satellite imagery
START, *see* Strategic Arms Reduction Talks
Stassen, Harold, 11
State Department, U.S.: arms control negotiations, 19, 44; Open Skies negotiations, 30, 98, 100, 165; Open Skies options paper, 27. *See also* Baker, James

Stockholm Document, 16–17, 18, 38, 46–47
Strategic Arms Limitation Treaty (SALT) talks, 26, 31–32, 56
Strategic Arms Reduction Talks (START), 44, 93, 167, 198n5
Stubbs, Christopher, 162
Surveillance flights, *see* Cooperative aerial monitoring; Reconnaissance flights
Sweden: active quotas, 136; aircraft, 211n18; mistrust of Russia, 119–21; Open Skies implementation and, 146, 153; Open Skies membership request, 154, 155; Open Skies negotiations and, 114, 118, 119–21, 129–30, 146. *See also* Stockholm Document
Switzerland: Four Power Summit (1955), 9, 11–14; Open Skies negotiations and, 118
Synthetic aperture radar (SAR): digital, 126; Russian, 133, 155; Soviet positions, 82–84, 85–86, 100; technical characteristics, 82–83, 85–86, 119, 133; use of, xv, 75, 76, 102

Talbott, Strobe, 25–26
"Technical Characteristics for a Selection of Sensors," 84
Technology, *see* Data processing; Sensor technology
Technology transfer: concerns, 126; export regulations, 82, 85
Territorial scope issue: border areas, 118–19, 156; exclusion areas, 29–30, 31, 40, 73–74; in Grand Compromise, 80; NATO position, 103; Soviet and Russian proposals, 60, 73–74, 87, 112, 133; U.S. positions, 29–30, 36. *See also* Third-country bases
Texas A&M University, 22, 23–24, 35, 57, 165–66
Third-country bases: compromises on, 80, 96; NATO position, 103; negotiations with host countries proposed, 61; Soviet position on overflights, 14, 34, 49, 60, 64, 74, 87, 95–96; of Soviets, 49, 53, 61; U.S.-Soviet negotiations, 95–96
Transparency: confidence building and, xvi, 100, 159, 172; differences among NATO allies, 56–57; neutral countries and, 41, 42; as U.S. goal, 25, 27, 159–60
Turkey: foreign minister at Ottawa Conference, 60, 67; former Soviet republics and, 130, 145; interest in Open Skies, 145; Open Skies regime expansion issue and, 142, 143–44, 154; Open Skies Review Conferences and, 156, 157–58; OSCC delegation, 209n60; Ottawa Conference delegation, 65; relations with Greece, 142; Syrian border, 40; Vienna Conference delegation, 130, 131, 135, 142, 143–45. *See also* Cyprus issue
Turkish-Cypriot government, *see* Cyprus
Turnberry communique, 93, 94

U2 aircraft, 15, 178–79n26, 215n47
UK, *see* United Kingdom
Ukraine: aircraft and sensor certification, 154; Open Skies negotiations and, 129–30; Open Skies Treaty ratification, 149, 152; passive quotas, 136, 208n37
United Kingdom: aircraft, 155, 211n18; Budapest Conference delegation, 84–85, 86; Four Power Summit (1955), 9, 11–14; intelligence community, 76; interest in Open Skies, 145, 167–68; Open Skies proposal (1955) and, 13; Ottawa Conference delegation, 76; sensor technology, 86, 155; Vienna Conference delegation, 113, 115–16, 135, 139, 143
United Nations peacekeeping operations, 158–59
United States: aircraft, 154, 158, 160–61; arms control policies, 19, 162–63, 173; bases in third countries, 61, 64, 74, 80, 87, 95–96, 103; benefits

of Open Skies, 2, 22, 27, 28, 29; Budapest Conference delegation, 83, 86; budget cuts, 158; bureaucratic constraints on negotiations, 31–32, 95; bureaucratic divisions, 4, 94, 98, 165–66; CFE negotiations, 95; foreign policy, 159–60; military opposition to Open Skies, 20; military strength, 10, 13; national interest, 172; nuclear weapons, 9–10, 162–63; Ottawa Conference delegation, 57, 71, 75, 76–78, 80, 81, 166; overflights by, 155, 156; passive quotas, 44–45, 208n35; public reaction to Open Skies proposal, 24; reconnaissance flights over Soviet Union, 14–15, 178–79n26; sensor technology, 77–78, 86, 96, 97, 154, 158, 172; trial overflights of, 153; Vienna Conference delegation, 109–10, 113, 116, 124–25, 126, 132, 135, 136, 139–40. *See also* Bush administration; Cold War; Eisenhower, Dwight D.; Intelligence community, U.S.

United States, Open Skies positions: after Budapest Conference, 92–93; on aircraft inspections, 30, 71; on aircraft ownership, 30, 105; CFE negotiations and, 95; compromises, 105–6, 109–10; on CSCE linkage, 5, 41–42, 126, 143; on data-sharing, 37, 41, 77–78; draft treaty, 54–55, 70–71; goals, 25, 27, 32, 44, 100; intelligence community's influence, 31, 32, 76, 77, 86, 90, 96; interagency process, 27–30, 31–32, 35, 47, 55, 56, 57–58, 98, 100; Irkutsk Formula, 96, 97, 98, 99, 100, 167; on membership, 37, 41; negotiation tactics, 90–91, 92–93; on neutral country participation, 41, 43, 126; on operational procedures, 30; options, 27, 28, 29; at Ottawa Conference, 166; on quotas, 44–46; on sensor technology, 5, 36, 109–10; on territorial scope, 36; on third-country base overflights, 95–96

U.S. Senate Foreign Relations Committee, 83

USSR, *see* Soviet Union

Vienna Conference (1991–92): accomplishments, 113, 126; active observers, 107–8, 146; announcement, 106; beginning, 106, 109, 112; coalitions, 117–22, 127; custody of texts, 116–17, 146; deadline, 112–13, 132; deferred issues, 134–36; differences from previous conferences, 114, 116, 117–18; draft treaty, 113–14; informal contact groups, 114–16, 122–25, 130–31, 132, 141; issues, 6–7, 109–11, 115–16, 123–25, 126–27, 128–29, 131–41, 142–46; leading countries, 113–14, 116–17, 123, 127, 131–32, 133–34, 141–42, 146; NATO caucuses, 117–18, 135; participants, 107–8; plenary sessions, 114, 115, 129, 130; political agreements, 113, 126, 127; political change and, 128–31, 141, 142, 144; proposals, 98, 103; schedule, 114; structure, 107, 108; technical issues, 116–17, 118, 122–23, 127, 133–34, 144, 171

Vietnam, Soviet bases, 49. *See also* Third-country bases

Warsaw Treaty Organization (WTO): Basic Elements Paper, 61, 63; demise, 61–62, 117, 118; foreign ministers at Ottawa Conference, 60–62, 68; inclusion in Open Skies regime, 21; Open Skies negotiations positions, 48, 60–63, 64, 66; Ottawa Conference delegations, 69, 70; political change and, 42, 46, 47, 48, 49; Soviet power in, 61–62. *See also* Non–Soviet Warsaw Pact countries; *and individual countries*

Weapons of Mass Destruction (WMD), verification of reductions, xvi–xvii, 161–63, 170, 172, 173. *See also* Nuclear weapons

Western European Union (WEU): cooperation among members, 121–22, 205n44; demise, 205n44; Open Skies negotiations and, 105, 127, 135, 137; overflight quota allocation in, 137
West Germany, *see* Germany
WEU, *see* Western European Union
WMD, *see* Weapons of Mass Destruction
Workshop on Open Skies, 52–53, 185n13, 188n73
WTO, *see* Warsaw Treaty Organization

Yeltsin, Boris, 152
Yugoslavia, former, 154

Zelikow, Philip, 19, 165
Zhukov, Y., 12
Zubok, Vladislav M., 13–14

Kolibri 360 GmbH
Ferdinand-Jühlke-Straße 7
99095 Erfurt, Deutschland
produktsicherheit@kolibri360.de